A PASSION FOR FREEDOM
THE LIFE OF

Sharlot Mabridth Hall, 1909

For Roger Bowen,
good friend and
former UIU colleague
Margaret F. Maxwell

A PASSION FOR FREEDOM

THE LIFE OF Sharlot Hall

Margaret F. Maxwell

THE UNIVERSITY OF ARIZONA PRESS
TUCSON & LONDON

About the Author...

Margaret F. Maxwell, whose research and writing has focused on history and library cataloging, was a collaborating editor of *Voices From the Southwest* and author of *Shaping a Library: William L. Clements and the Clements Library of Americana.* She was a librarian at the Library of Congress from 1950 to 1956 and received her Ph.D. from the University of Michigan in 1971. In 1971 she became professor of library science at the University of Arizona, where she has taught courses in the history of children's literature, the history of the book, and cataloging.

THE UNIVERSITY OF ARIZONA PRESS

Copyright © 1982
The Arizona Board of Regents
All Rights Reserved

This book was set in 11/13 V-I-P Fairfield Medium.
Manufactured in the U.S.A.
⊗ This book is printed on acid-free, archival-
quality paper.

Library of Congress Cataloging in Publication Data

Maxwell, Margaret F., 1927-
    A passion for freedom.

    Bibliography: p.
    Includes index
    1. Hall, Sharlot Mabridth, 1870–1943.
2. Historians—Arizona—Biography.   3. Arizona—
Biography.   1. Title.
F811.H175M39   979.1'052'0924[B]   82-4866
                                          AACR2
ISBN 0-8165-0776-7
ISBN 0-8165-1506-9 (pbk.)

*Reprinted in paperback, 1994, with the generous
assistance of the Sharlot Hall Museum of Arizona
History, Prescott, Arizona.*

To

Lawrence Clark Powell

—Librarian, Educator, Humanist—

Who kindled my interest in the Southwest

Contents

ILLUSTRATIONS

PHOTO CREDITS: Arizona Historical Society, pages 28, 29, and 34; University of Arizona Library, Special Collections, pages 70 and 108; *Arizona: The New State Magazine*, December 1910 (photo by Robert A. Turnbull), page 113; all others, Sharlot Hall Museum.

Foreword

WITH PUBLICATION of *Cactus and Pine,* a resplendent little volume of
desert visions and Arizona lore, Sharlot Hall emerged as the first
indigenous voice of Arizona literature. Her writings in *Out West*
stirred national interest in Arizona during the campaign for statehood. As Territorial Historian, she ransacked the four corners of
Arizona, collecting documents, recording oral history and speaking
out for historical preservation, efforts of fresh relevance in a state
reawakening to its cultural heritage.

The true importance of this biography by Professor Maxwell
is that it brings alive in three dimensions the sensitive, talented,
ambitious, tormented woman behind the achievements. In a time of
heightened concern about the role of women in society, it is instruc-
tive to look back and inquire how it was that a young woman with
sporadic schooling and no college training, raised on a remote homestead in Lonesome Valley presided over by a domineering, anti-
intellectual father, could blossom forth like a cactus flower in such a
parched cultural environment.

As Sharlot Hall grew to womanhood and literary skill, she
also confronted a nineteenth-century society that mirrored the pre-
judices of her father. A woman seeking intellectual freedom and
achievement threatened a social order which expected women to be
subservient and submissive. For many women the high price of freedom was forsaking marriage, children and polite society, and assum-
ing instead the less threatening role of eccentric outcast. Sharlot Hall

followed that pattern and sublimated her womanhood in an unhappy life of unattainable romantic fantasy, psychosomatic illness and slavish attachment to her father.

Sharlot Hall's achievements are the more remarkable for the personal sacrifice that enabled them. On one hand, her story reminds us how much we have reshaped our attitudes toward women: in 1981 another Arizona ranch woman, Sandra O'Connor, took her place on the United States Supreme Court, the same Court that once told Illinois women they were constitutionally unfit to practice law. On the other hand, the life of Sharlot Hall ought equally to remind us that women in America are still subjected to myriad forms of economic and social discrimination. The struggle for equality is by no means finished.

BRUCE BABBITT

A PASSION FOR FREEDOM
THE LIFE OF

The only possible course toward the
greatest ideals of human development
is by the road of absolute freedom —
and unswerving personal responsibility —
for both men and women, in every phase
of life in home and outside world alike.

I believe that woman's first duty is to
herself. . . and that she must be free to
find her own way toward the greatest good
and most harmonious development without
any purely arbitrary man-made restriction.

SHARLOT HALL

Sharlot Hall

Individualist
and
Historian

SHARLOT HALL was born in the late nineteenth century, a period of active feminism during which many women were attacking masculine bastions of privilege. But, except for her sensitive, intelligent mother, who seems to have been alive to the feminist ideas of her day, Sharlot was cut off during her formative years from the stimulation of contact with intellectual women. Sharlot's mother's silent, repressed outrage against her surly, uneducated husband and against the matrimonial bondage that made her by fiat his inferior had an enormous impact on Sharlot, who resolved even as a young girl to make the contribution to humankind that had been denied her mother. To do so she must avoid the trap that had been instrumental to this denial: marriage. And so Sharlot sought freedom.

Sharlot's free spirit found wings at first, however, in ways traditionally acceptable for women: she wrote poetry. Her early efforts were praised, sometimes overly extravagantly, by her contemporaries. Her poetry, especially that of her mature years, still reads well, particularly her evocations of heat and the parched land of southwestern ranches.

Sharlot did not regard herself solely as a poet, or even as the journalist which she later became. She had a deep affection for the Southwest, an affection which led her not only to describe its natural features in vivid detail, but to want to preserve what she clearly perceived by the turn of the century to be its vanishing heritage. A pioneer in recognizing the need to record the ways of earlier generations, she collected Arizona artifacts, early documents, and oral histories. She tracked down pioneer Arizona miners, cattlemen, sheepherders, and prospectors, no matter how many miles she had to drive, alone or with a guide, over roads that were often only dim trails in the desert. Narrow-minded neighbors regarded this activity with scandalized horror.

When the Territory of Arizona made the business of collecting Arizona history official, Sharlot saw no reason why sex should make a difference in the choice of the appointee. And after a sharp battle, with help from influential friends of both sexes, Sharlot became Territorial Historian, the first woman to hold office in Arizona. The trail she broke in gaining this official appointment made it easier for other women, some of them her friends, to follow even into elective offices after Arizona became a state in 1912.

Philosophically, Sharlot also sought independence. As a young woman she enthusiastically embraced Freethought, with its tenets of the equality of men and women, human dignity, atheism, and responsible parenthood. Later she turned to Christian Science and theosophical mysticism for guidance; these helped her emerge from a long period of self-imposed physical and spiritual isolation which began after her mother's death. Alone at her ranch with her aging and virulent father, Sharlot—ironically, despite her passionate belief in equality—entered into the same bondage of incessant chores and submission to her father's will that her mother had endured. With the help of philosophical reading, a steadfast friend, and a curious turn of events, Sharlot reclaimed her freedom and again became an active writer, speaker, and traveler.

Once back in public life Sharlot went on to make her most lasting contribution: the awakening of a sense of the importance of Arizona's past in the people of Arizona through her restoration of the Governor's Mansion and her collection of Arizona artifacts. Poet, journalist, ranchwoman, historian, conservator: Sharlot Hall was all of these. She was also a warmly charismatic human being who particularly in her later years lived her philosophy of caring and sharing. Devoid of personal family, she made all who came to the Mansion a part of her family. And to the last, Sharlot kept her passion for freedom.

1

Frontier
Heritage

SHARLOT HALL CHARACTERIZED her father's family as "wanderers." Some of the Halls fought in the American Revolution and afterward moved, in stages, from Virginia through Tennessee and finally to Missouri. Here one John Wesley Hall settled long enough to take a wife, Mary Bradley, and here, on what was at the time the edge of the American frontier, Sharlot's father, James Knox Polk Hall, was born on December 2, 1844. His mother seems to have died shortly after the birth; then, according to Sharlot's account, the motherless baby was left with a neighbor in the care of Mary Hall's slave while father John Hall disappeared from his small son's life. As Sharlot put it with considerable bitterness, "The men of my family were the sort that for a thousand years probably had walked away from all their problems and responsibilities—they have been called Crusaders, explorers, adventurers, pathfinders—in reality they were just human beings who wanted to do as they pleased and not be bothered with the care of anything, home or country—so when the novelty of things was over they always went on where there was no one to enforce responsibility."[1]

News of the formation of the Territory of Kansas on May 30, 1854, and the ensuing turmoil between "Free Staters" and the Missouri Border Ruffians, those favoring the admission of Kansas as a slave state, may have drawn John Hall back to the midwest. Despite his earlier residence in slave-holding Missouri, family tradition states that he allied himself with the Kansas Free Staters. The

Hall family Bible records that John Hall died in 1859 near Olathe, Kansas, from the effects of smoke inhalation suffered while fighting a fire set by the Missouri Border Ruffians.

As for young James Knox Polk Hall, who had been precipitously abandoned by his peripatetic father fifteen years earlier, he seems to have grown up hand-to-mouth in the little backwoods settlement of his birth, described later by his daughter as a miserable place "with its half dozen cabins in a little clearing along the creek — its fireplaces of sticks and mud with a split puncheon for a 'mantel board' on every one of which stood an earthen jug of home still corn whiskey and a gourd dipper."[2] No Abraham Lincoln was James K. Hall. Growing up a generation later than that model for ambitious, nineteenth-century farm boys, although in equally primitive surroundings, the young Jim Hall encountered many of the same conditions that had shaped Lincoln's character. Unhappily, he reacted differently to them. Schools were poor, but Jim Hall does not seem to have felt the lack of them. On the contrary, he, like the other men of the crude frontier settlement of his boyhood, gloried in the innate superiority of the man who had no formal schooling. In another of Sharlot's fragments she said that he, like the other men of his acquaintance, had

> the feeling that unless the uneducated, untrained man was recognized as the equal or superior of the educated man he was being treated unjustly and deprived of some inherent right. Especially he held the once general idea that the ignorant man was inherently more moral, more honest, and more humane than the educated or well-born man.... That was what the Declaration of Independence had always meant to him and his neighbors — "all men are born free and equal."

James Hall suffered a further disability as a result of severely burning both his feet when he was very small. The accident stunted his growth and crippled him slightly for life. However, he seems to have been a good horseman; in later years he delighted to tell of his youth as a buffalo hunter on the plains of Kansas, where he shot the great lumbering beasts from horseback and left them to rot where they fell.

The young James Hall may have joined his father in Kansas. Gold was discovered near Pikes Peak in what is now Colorado in early 1858. Perhaps John Hall joined the adventurers in their search for gold that year and took his son, now thirteen years old, with him. After the older Hall's death, James worked for the ox caravans going to the gold strike, crossing the plains a number of times with different parties. The boy's free and easy nomadic existence as buffalo hunter, guide, and freighter ranging the plains of Kansas was interrupted by the start of the Civil War in April 1861. James was sixteen years old, hardly old enough to enlist, and his small size (as an adult he stood five feet eight inches in height and weighed 140 pounds) was against him. The recruiting officer looked at him and laughed, "Abe Lincoln wants men, not scrawns!" But according to the story Hall told his children, he somehow managed to enlist in a Kansas regiment of sharpshooters. He claimed to have served with the Union forces until he was mustered out at the end of the war, when he again took up his rootless wanderings on the Kansas frontier.[3]

As for her mother's people, the Bobletts, Sharlot characterized them as "typical dark-eyed Latins (Hungarians) with gifts of song and hands of natural artistry that astonished their backwoods neighbors, and feet light in the dance and tongues of ready oratory— they were of those moved by great hopes and dreaming mysticism."[4] Like the Halls, a Boblett ancestor served with distinction in the American Revolution. As a reward for his services, he was given a tract of land in Bedford County, Virginia, at the close of the war. He had two sons, Peter, born in 1791, and John, born in 1798, the latter being Sharlot Hall's grandfather. Of Grandfather Boblett, Sharlot said with romantic enthusiasm, "He could not rest in the new republic which permitted the slavery of people, even though those people were black." So, said Sharlot, John Boblett left the farm in Bedford County to his brother and struck out for the western wilderness of frontier Ohio. By 1834 he was married and had four sons, Jacob, John Charles, Isaac, and Samuel Morgan. Sharlot's mother, Adeline Susannah, was born on December 23, 1844, in the little town of Dayton, Ohio.

According to family tradition, the Bobletts moved to Indiana not long after Adeline's birth. Here, in the fall of 1849, little Addie, not quite five years old, watched her mother waste away with the dreaded "milk sickness." Among the few memories that Adeline carried into adulthood of her mother was the loneliness and hatred she had for the dark forests of the Indiana wilderness, and how she begged as she was dying that her husband not bury her in the forest surrounding their cabin on the river bank. So she was buried under a crabapple tree on the edge of a natural meadow. On September 30, 1854, John remarried and settled down to raise a second family in Iowa. Adeline learned a great deal from either her father or her stepmother about the medical uses of wild plants and herbs; later she was much sought after by her country neighbors because of her knowledge and skill as a healer.

At about this time the abolitionist John Brown left Kansas and began his series of underground "war colleges" to support the anti-slavery movement in Kansas, Iowa, and elsewhere. Sharlot remembered her mother telling of Father John Boblett's sympathy for Brown's cause; one of Adeline Boblett's recollections was of "seeing a man with a face like one of the old prophets come and go through the home, conferring with her father."[5] By 1860 John Brown had been hanged for treason following the Harper's Ferry raid, and the three eldest Boblett brothers had disappeared from the Iowa census records. Sharlot states that they had been so inspired by John Brown's tales as he related his own part in the struggle to make Kansas a "Free State," that they took covered wagons and went to "plant a human barrier against the westward move of slavery."[6] Since Adeline Boblett is not listed in that same census as a member of John Boblett's family, it lends support to Sharlot's claim that the intrepid young woman went with her brothers "to make part of that barrier."

During the Civil War Adeline, according to Sharlot, served as a nurse in the siege of Vicksburg in 1863 under the direction of the famed "Mother" Mary Bickerdyke.[7] Mother Bickerdyke, a woman who at the start of hostilities decided that her mission was to care for the sick and wounded private soldiers of the Union Army, became a living legend by the end of the war. She seems to have taken a liking to the earnest young Adeline Boblett with her soothing hands and her carpetbag full of salves and healing herbs. After the last screaming shell had flown over the battlefields and Adeline had returned to her home, the two women kept in touch. Sharlot stated that one of her own earliest memories was of "that fat, uncouth, heroic woman who was Florence Nightingale and Clara Barton in one" coming to visit her mother in Kansas.[8]

In 1867 the twenty-two-year-old Adeline joined her brother John and his family to teach in the little school at Minneapolis, Kansas, in the Solomon River Valley. In August came the first Sioux Indian raid on the Solomon Valley. All the settlers in the outlying region rushed to the little log settlement of Minneapolis for safety. Afterwards many of them found their dugouts or cabins destroyed and animals run off by the Indians. A second raid came later in the summer. This one Adeline Boblett, living in a small cabin on the side of a hill near the settlement, witnessed, watching in horrified helplessness as Indians shot and wounded one of her neighbors, carrying his wife off tied to one of the horses.[9]

And what of James Hall during this period? Sharlot said that "after the Civil War he was a scout and guide and a buffalo hunter on the Kansas plains." He met and wandered with hunters like "Old Billy Shinn," and "Dutch Henry," an old trapper who saved grease from poisoned wolf carcasses to use in frying his buffalo steaks. On one occasion he got careless, and Jim Hall, a short, wiry man in his early twenties at the time, almost died from a dose of strychnine from the wolf fat. He seems to have been freighting through the area during the worst of the Solomon Valley Indian troubles. Sharlot claimed that he and the young schoolteacher, Addie Boblett, met at Minneapolis in 1868 during one of the raids. As Sharlot's friend Alice Hewins recalled hearing the episode,

> The plains Indians were on the war path and Mr. Hall drove into the village with the Indians in pursuit. He found no one in the village but the old men and boys as the rest were away on a buffalo hunt. The ammunition in town was scant and the powderhouse up the river with the Indians in between. They knew any man going to the powderhouse would never reach it but there was a chance the Indians would not molest a woman riding away from the town. So little Miss Boblett...offered to try to get the keg of powder. They lifted her on a big white horse. She got safely to the powderhouse. She said she never knew how she got on the horse again with the keg of powder but she did and then swam the horse down the river between the high banks of the stream, coming up when she reached the village....[10]

It is difficult to fathom what attracted this sensitive and intelligent young woman to the opinionated backwoodsman James Hall. To all

appearances he and Adeline had nothing in common either intellectually or emotionally. But in an age when a girl often married almost
as soon as she reached puberty and had her first baby by the time she
was sixteen, Adeline at twenty-two was far gone on the way to that
most dreaded of fates: old maidhood. Hall may have looked pretty good
to her in contrast to the other grizzled trappers and weatherbeaten
homesteaders who frequented the crude settlement that had been her
home for three years. Presumably she had lived all this time in close
quarters in a log cabin with her brother's family. She may have
decided it was time she had a home and children of her own.

The Kansas territory was open for homesteading; a bona fide
settler could lay claim to 80 acres of land after the Civil War. As Hall
roamed the unsettled Kansas frontier scouting Indians, trapping, and
freighting, he probably kept an eye out for a choice spot to stake a
claim. By the fall of 1868 when he met Adeline Boblett, he had found
the land he was looking for. It was not in the Solomon Valley area.
The Solomon Valley, while hardly a hotbed of civilization, proved
increasingly attractive to settlers after the Indians were subdued in
1868. Between 1865 and 1870 the population of the county jumped
from 178 to 2,310.[11] It was obvious even in 1868 that the Solomon
Valley was no place to settle for a man who wanted room to turn
around and spit. But in year-old Lincoln County, just west of Ottawa
County, there were so few inhabitants that it is likely that fraud was
used in its original organization; there were fewer than the 600 voters
required by law for organization even in 1870, when the census listed
a total of 516.[12] Here, in the northeast corner of the new county,
Jim Hall staked his claim, on Prosser Creek, a tributary of the
Solomon River.

As Sharlot remembered it, this first homestead was "on a
small stream thickly lined with oak, elm, walnut and hackberry trees,
and with thickets of tall wild alum bushes all along in which the poles
forming the framework of the Indian tepees were still standing when
I was old enough to play in the abandoned teepee shelters. The giant
oak trees in the yard had been peeled of their bark as high as a man
could reach, where the Indians had peeled it off to feed their starving
ponies during deep snow." Jim Hall had staked his claim in the
middle of one of the favorite campgrounds of the Arapahoe Indians;
the Indians' understandable antagonism was to put fear into the Hall
family on more than one occasion.

James Knox Polk Hall and Adeline Susannah Boblett were married on January 31, 1869. They lived out the winter on Hall's claim in a fairly large dugout excavated above the banks of Prosser Creek. During the same year Adeline's brother, Sam Boblett, stopped on his way east from the California goldfields where he had been prospecting. They made him welcome, and when Jim suggested that he might like to stay with them a while, he moved in. Ten years older than Jim Hall and still single, he seems to have shared Jim's quarrelsome disposition. It could not have been a happy arrangement for any member of the family, but he remained with the Halls for the next decade, until his own marriage.

During these early days Adeline must have wept many secret tears as she realized that far from being a rough diamond that she could smooth and polish, her husband was more like the traditional sow's ear. Sharlot said later of her mother that she "had never let her through out to its full stride since the first weeks of her married life—those weeks when she was learning with startled wonder that [Jim] did not like to think fast and strong like the sweep of a flying hawk—that his mind liked to loiter along or stop and doze in the sun, and that he expected her mind to keep always just a little behind him." Adeline soon realized, as Sharlot put it, that

> A gifted woman was a tragedy for there was no place for her in this period. Inevitably the time demanded of women two things—her physical labor and child bearing.... Praise for a woman was only on the basis of the work she could do—"a powerful hard worker" excused all else. No mental gifts were equal to it. I never heard a man speak of his wife with praise or pride for anything but hard physical labor—and a young man who had picked out a "Dam' fine worker" for a wife was as much congratulated as the man who owned the best pulling team of oxen....

Adeline, although she was a hard worker, was criticized in those early days for her "high falutin' idys" which were too "dam' high toned" not only for her husband but for the neighbors and travelers who occasionally stopped at the cabin to visit and to take a meal. Most of the Halls' Prosser Creek neighbors were uneasy with niceties such as a tablecloth or the use of serving dishes for the food. Things tasted just as good straight out of a frying pan or a blackened kettle. What was wrong with setting these utensils right on the table?

Even harder to bear was Jim Hall's constant profanity:

> To have taken [his] swear words away from him would have been to
> rob him of all the shades and variations of meaning which men have
> invented adjectives and verbs to express. He did not use profanity or
> blasphemy—he would not have known what those words meant. He
> used his cuss words to voice his likes or dislikes in a way which meant
> everything and did not demand any thought. [Adeline] watched him
> one day as he was trying to describe a neighbor whom he liked. His
> face grew red, his eyes had a strained and set expression like one
> lifting a heavy load. His lips moved but no words came until he shot
> out "He's a Hell of a good man!" So great a look of relief swept over his
> face that [she] herself felt suddenly released from a strain. . . ."

It was James Hall's tobacco-chewing habit that seems to have
bothered poor Adeline Hall more than anything else:

> He was always chewing—if [she] needed to talk to him [she] had to do
> it while his jaws rolled doggedly over a wad. If he answered, he had
> first to squirt enough spit to relieve his mouth and probably to slobber
> the wad round till it got out of the way in the back of his jaw where it
> made his cheek stick out like mumps. . . . If anything came up suddenly
> that called for alertness or decision an almost agonized look swept over
> his face—he would reach for his chunk of tobacco in almost frantic
> haste—tear and worry off a chew as fast as his teeth could bite, roll it
> around in his mouth till the saliva flowed freely and then his face and
> whole body would relax so visibly that it was often funny to look at it.
> A sort of veil, a mask of dullness came over his face, like that of a man
> half nodding to a nap and it was impossible to penetrate this to really
> reach his mind with any question.

Behind this mask he was slow, surly, sullen. "He was always angry
with [Adeline] and resentful if she spoke of any new way of doing the
work or of any opportunity to improve their circumstances; showing
his irritation as naturally as the slower horse in a team bites at his
mate who strikes up a faster gait or responds to slap of rein or cluck
from the driver more readily." He refused to "plan for even the
simplest comforts for the home—a place to do the washing, a tank to
catch soft water. He belonged to the time when women went to some
pond or creek to wash, built a fire (on the edge of the creek) and
boiled water in a kettle, and hung the clothes on bushes," and he felt
that what had been good enough for the women of his Missouri
frontier boyhood ought to be good enough for his wife.

Adeline soon discovered that it was of no use to make suggestions or to plan for their lives in any way that involved her husband's participation. James almost invariably reversed her decision. And so, gradually, taught by many bitter experiences, she learned to hold her tongue, no matter what happened. She withdrew into herself as within a fortress from which she looked out upon the world warily, without visible emotion, went about her necessary duties silently, speaking only when some response was demanded of her—and then choosing her words carefully so as not to give offense.

As a kind of defense against the crudity of the world in which she spent her days, Adeline turned to reading almost as a drug. She borrowed from her neighbors and read the old issues of the weekly *Waverly Magazine* and *Literary Repository* that came her way until they fell into tatters; then from some magazines that were given to her, she clipped her favorite articles, household hints, and jokes and pasted them over the pages of some of the books from her father's old library of medicine and esoteric religion that she had brought with her from Iowa.[13] She fed her mind on pining love lyrics and guaranteed cures for cancer and skunk bite indiscriminately.

When Adeline found herself pregnant the real horror that she felt for her surroundings rose up about her until it threatened to overwhelm her. Not that she gave in to her weakness and constant nausea; as she told Sharlot later, "a woman who laid down to rest in the daytime, even when carrying a child, felt herself almost committing a sin." When the first cramp gripped her, Jim Hall set out on his horse through a wind-whipped rainstorm over the prairie to fetch the nearest neighbor woman to help. The October day, with the wind whistling through the cracks in the cabin wall and icy trickles of rain dripping through the leaking roof, became blurred into an eternity of agonizing spasms, not helped by the concern of the kindly neighbor woman who mopped her face with a wet cloth and told her to pull hard on a towel knotted around the bedpost when the pains came. But by sunset the ordeal was over. Adeline cradled a healthy, squalling, newborn daughter in her arms. October 27, 1870, was the date. It would seem that not even in the naming of her infant daughter did Adeline have a say. Sharlot said that her uncle, Adeline's brother Sam, gave her her name with its peculiar spelling: Sharlot, an Indian name, he claimed.

2

A Kansas Childhood

LITTLE SHARLOT IDOLIZED HER MOTHER, who was almost literally the only woman she had ever seen. She trotted happily after her as her mother fed the chickens, weeded the garden, washed the clothes, and baked bread in a dutch oven set in the coals of the big fireplace in the cabin. She loved to sing and to play with words, for when she began to talk she delighted in the sound of language and, according to her own statement, almost at once began to make up little rhymes. Adeline looked at her dark-haired daughter with wondering pride and determination that this gifted child would grow up to be a lady. So it pleased her when Sharlot patterned her speech on her mother's careful English. But Sharlot, who early in life discovered that her father was a brute force to be reckoned with, and who stayed out of his way when she could, was bewildered and dismayed when she asked him innocently, pointing to some unfamiliar implements, "What are those things?" to have him turn to her, snarling, "Say 'What is them things,'" he told her. "'Someone might hear ye and think ye was trying to talk high-toned.'"

Soon Sharlot, like her mother, learned to hold her peace when her father and uncle were at home. As for Adeline, Sharlot realized many years later that

My mother could not give me the answers to any of my questions because every bit of her strength and time were given to meeting the needs and desires of my father's body—the body in which, so far as she was concerned, he lived his entire life. She was busy all day long cooking the food he liked and just as he liked it—making much of the little provided—keeping clothes clean and whole and bearing the children that came because he had to be satisfied whether he could give a child any chance in life or not.

That was what life meant to him—men chewed and spit and swore and told stories and gossiped and voted and quarreled over political parties and spent what money there was but women worked at home and bore children who soon helped them support the family.

My mother could not tell me that she, too, had asked why—and that she had thought that life was one long, fine search for the highest answer. To tell me that she had thought my father would join with her in making life a finer thing would have been disloyalty to him.

But life was far from grim for a little girl growing up on the Kansas prairie. In a charming essay published in the *Atlantic Monthly* in January 1903 Sharlot told of the "roly-poly old gentleman" who used to toss her up in a swing in a big oak tree until she could look into the nest out of which a baby blue jay had fallen the week before, and of the

> gray-bearded scouts and hunters, with great caps of fur and long rifles that seemed to tower above my head as far as the oaks. Children were rare novelties to those men of the plains, and I was passed from shoulder to shoulder, delighted with the tales of bear and buffalo, and fingering with awed hands the beaded shot-pouches and belts of embroidered buckskins, but feeling all the while almost as far above earth as when I swung over the blue jay's nest. . . . [1]

The Halls' second child, a son, was born September 14, 1872, less than two years after Sharlot's birth. It is doubtful if Sharlot had any recollections of John Wesley Hall, as they named the sickly infant. He lived only six weeks; on November 1, 1872, they laid the tiny body in a grave dug on the banks of the creek. Sharlot memorialized him many years later with a fragmentary poem.

The Brother Who Died

Six weeks of life—and then my mother sewed
A little shroud out of her wedding smock—
For stores and muslins fine were far away
From that log cabin on the lone Frontier.
Ten miles a neighbor drove and brought a board,
Long, clean and smooth—left when his own child died
And through a blizzard he drove fifty miles
To fetch the coffin wood. With saw and knife
He helped my father shape the tiny box—
As if his hands had more experienced skill.
My mother cut her wedding dress to fit
And with her own hands lined the little nest
And made a pillow for the nestling head.

A year and a half later, on March 11, 1874, Sharlot's brother Edward
V. Hall was born. Sharlot was three-and-a-half years old, too young to
know of her mother's fear of losing this weak, spindly baby as she had
the one before. She was too young to sense her mother's growing
revulsion toward her too-frequent pregnancies and her loathing of the
masculine assumption that another young-un would arrive each season "reg'lar as the crop's laid by," no matter what the cost. Perhaps
illness and infection made further pregnancies impossible or Adeline
turned on her uncouth husband and refused him further intimacies.
At any rate, after three children had been born in three and a half
years, there were no more.

      Sharlot, who was a robust, sturdy child, adored her frail
younger brother. As soon as he was old enough to leave his mother, he
and Sharlot slept together in a trundle bed. One of her earliest recollections in which he figured was that of a threatened Indian raid
which probably happened about 1875. Because the Halls' cabin was
stout enough to withstand an attack, all the neighbors came to stay
with them for protection. The children were put to bed upstairs,
while the adults remained below. Recalled Sharlot, "We were all
frightened and listening to sounds from below in the yard and house.
Once when we were especially afraid I heard my Forty-niner uncle
swearing and saying that he had not lost any Indians [so he] was going
up to bed and stop looking for them. Then I felt that we were per-
fectly safe and we children all went to sleep."

The ever-present possibility of an Indian raid was one thing to worry about, but natural disasters were even more certain each year. Although grasshoppers were chronic pests to Kansas farmers, the summer of 1874 is still remembered more than a century later as the year of the great grasshopper plague. All sections of Kansas were affected; the skies were darkened with grasshoppers; they fell on roofs, gardens, and fields with a noise like hailstones, according to one account.[2] They devoured everything before them, even clothing on the line, and when they passed they left a wasteland in their wake.

Sharlot also remembered prairie fires that threatened their home nearly every autumn when the grass was dry. Such fires, started by lightning or a careless traveler's campfire and driven by the interminable winds of the Kansas plains, were terrifying experiences. Crackling, roaring flames lit the sky all night long. Whole towns were sometimes destroyed in great fires that could last for weeks. For the isolated settler such a fire was an ever-present threat. Sharlot remembered her mother battling prairie fires more than once; one time her mother's shoes were burned off her feet as she beat at the blazing grass. Small as she was, Sharlot recalled that she "was big enough to drag a bucket of water to her to wet the blanket with which she beat out the fire and also to pour cold water over her feet when she crawled back into the house after the fire turned away."[3]

The summers were blisteringly hot with winds that blew incessantly, day after day. Winters were equally severe; icy gales drove the snow in fine particles through cracks and chinks in the log house. Stock froze to death in drifts higher than a man's head, and the howling of wolves seeking to bring down the weakened cattle frightened the young Sharlot. One of her earliest memories was of a couple of brown, knobby buffalo calves that her father brought home with him from a hunting trip. The calves, penned with the Halls' cow, grew quite tame, and Sharlot, a sturdy three-year-old, loved to run after them. But that winter they disappeared, and Sharlot wept bitterly when her father told her that the wolves had carried them off and killed them.

When Sharlot was "a little past four," she started school, riding four miles on horseback behind a young boy who did chores around the Halls' place for his keep. Her mother had already taught her to read from some of Grandfather John Boblett's books, such unlikely primers as Doctor Dodd's *Library of Mesmerism* and the *Phrenological Journal.* The school was held in the sod house of the teacher, a man with little education but with a family of eight children, enough in itself to constitute a school.

Sharlot did not remember learning anything in the few weeks that the school term lasted. A short time later the Halls moved further up Prosser Creek to an area of limestone bluffs. As Sharlot afterward observed, "It was not very favorably located, but I think that father was led to it by instinct because the limestone hills made it impossible that many people would ever settle near."

Sharlot never forgot the lime pits with their burning fires where the grey limestone was turned into plaster. The first Christmas she remembered, she spent at the pits, according to a probably romanticized account which she wrote many years later:

> The wet flakes whirling against my face and the snow crunching under my feet recalled the first Christmas I could remember. . . . Then I had crunched the snow under copper-toed boots and my head had brushed the flakes from the low bushes. The trees, interlaced and bending with snow, had made a roof over the little creek where we walked on the ice. Far at the end of this low white tunnel a light streamed out from the arched openings of the lime-pits full of burning logs. . . .
>
> Black figures ran in and out in front of the pits, poking the fires with long poles and sliding fresh logs into the yawning, red mouths. Beside one fire they were cooking supper—boiling coffee in an iron pot and toasting strips of buffalo-meat on sharp sticks held over the coals.
>
> On a ledge above the pit-mouth was a red apple and a little china box with blue bands, and two hands clasped on the lid. That was my Christmas; and, curled in a buffalo-robe behind a pile of logs, I watched the leaping flames and marveled at my wealth. The apple was eaten, reluctantly, weeks after when it had begun to wither; but I have the box yet, and in every Christmas fire I see the red coals of the lime-pits and the dark figures of the men—and the snow and a little, wondering child. . . . [4]

Of this period, Sharlot said that her father "pecked around all summer at a crop that didn't always feed the stock. . . . We had enough to eat," she concluded, "because [mother] was a wonderful cook and 'rustled.'" Sharlot's recollection, however, hardly agrees with the description of the Halls' property given in the census of Salt Creek Township, Lincoln County, in March 1875. Of 150 acres which James Hall had claimed, he had fenced fifty acres and had sown them to rye, corn, and sorghum. Ten acres of millet and hungarian grass provided fodder for the livestock, which numbered five horses, thirty milk cows, and ninety beef cattle. A pig and two dogs made up the rest of the animal family. Hall's personal property was valued at $1270, farm implements at $40, and the land at $800. [5]

Sharlot's schooling in this new area seems to have been as informal as before. She met a strange misanthrope of a man, generally feared by the neighboring settlers, who shut himself up for days at a time with his books or wandered alone in the hills. The odd old man and the equally unconventional little girl found a bond in books, recalled Sharlot: "He lent me quaint old histories and philosophies, full of big words that sounded very fine as he rolled them off in a sonorous voice. I learned to know Swedenborg from Kant and Kant from Comte." [6] The old gentleman, Mr. Cushion, also presented her with an almost startlingly unsuitable gift for an impressionable child, Daniel Defoe's *The History of the Devil,* which she cherished for years until "some book thief of abnormal tastes robbed me." [7] Along with Defoe she acquired "a little book of Bret Harte's poems. These I loved and soon I could shout them from every hilltop," she recalled. [8]

The summer of 1879 was hot and dry; the stunted corn rustled and turned brown in the parched fields, and passing wagons churned up clouds of choking dust from the powdery dry dirt trail near the Hall land. There were too many people in Lincoln County, thought Jim Hall to himself—close to three thousand already. He and Adeline's brother Sam made a trip south across Kansas to the Cimarron River to get salt at the salt beds. On their way they passed through newly formed Barbour County, Kansas, at that time a region of cattle ranches and few homesteaders because of its proximity to Indian Territory. Its location had made it a sort of no-man's-land, a refuge for gangs of outlaws who terrorized Kansas towns and train passengers during this period. In Barbour County, reasoned James Hall, a man could turn around without stepping on his neighbor.

So that fall the Halls moved again, with teams and covered wagons, down into the wild, beautiful hilly country just north of

Indian Territory, on Little Mule Creek some ten miles southwest of Medicine Lodge, where Jim Hall decided to try his hand at cattle-ranching. The ranch was right on the edge of one of the old cattle trails to Fort Dodge, the well-known Western Trail. Sharlot remembered climbing the fence in front of their log house to watch the endless herds of bony, dun-colored Texas steers as they clacked and rattled their way north along the wide, bare, dirt trail. She also recalled how those dusty old trail-drivers would edge over to the fence and ask her mother "if maybe she didn't have a drink of butter-milk because it was mighty dusty ridin' drag behind 2,000 steers. And most always she did—and likely a baking of salt rising bread and some fresh butter—and it wasn't any wonder—after their daily soda biscuits and flapjacks—that mother knew most of the outfits that drove on the early trails."[9]

One of those drovers gave Sharlot's mother the little Texas pony Fanny that Sharlot later rode across the plains to Arizona.[10] On Fanny, or on a big black race mare that Uncle Sam Boblett had gotten in a trade, Sharlot and her brother Ted rode to a little dugout school.[11] At this time Sharlot's beloved Billy Goat joined the family circle. The pride of her life and her favorite companion, Billy usually followed Sharlot to school and waited for her outside until the end of the day. What happened to Billy one day made the first great tragedy in Sharlot's young life. Sharlot told the story in a letter to a friend more than thirty years later.

> Billy was big and jet black and wire-haired and all fight and I loved him like a brother—in fact I always did the fighting for my brother, he being a sickly child and always beset by the new school children— until they met his sister and got sense—and the bond between Billy and myself was deeper than blood.
>
> We then had a small cattle ranch on Little Mule Creek south of Medicine Lodge and near the Indian Territory Line. I was a regular little squaw and rode after the cattle on a little bay Texas pony—or more often on a big black Printer race mare of famous record, who had gone mad on the track, flung her rider and trampled him to death, and broken her right fore leg at the knee.
>
> Some breeder doctored her up for the sake of the colts she might bring and my wild horseman uncle got her in some trade. The stiff knee kept her from running too hard but the way she and I covered ground made

all the neighbor mothers promise their children a whipping if they ever dared ride behind me—as they all wanted to do.

Billy always tagged along, no matter how far in the rear, and when the cattle were quiet he and I planned bull fights such as Mexico never touched. Billy fought on his hind legs, walking toward his enemy like a black whirlwind, till he picked out the best place to land his vicious short horns. The range champions one by one went down before him—not because he was so big but because a goat on his hind legs seems to hit all the soft places in the biggest bull and miss all the knocks himself.

The cattlemen had long tolerated a big old muley bull because he could whip every other animal on the range and when Billy laid him out and scared him till he was meek as a milk cow I swelled up to the bursting point. I guess it was the "pride that goes before a fall" but neither Billy nor I believed there was anything on earth he couldn't whip.

Like Mary's lamb he followed us to school but stopped at a grassy flat about half way between and there on our evening trip I saw a black heap on the grass. I thought Billy was asleep and I called and called, then climbed off to see what was the matter. There was a pool of blood on the ground and a bullet hole in his breast. I gathered him up in my arms and cried till my brother got cold and begged me to go on home.

Next day we learned that an army of strange cowboys was hunting the owner of that black Billy goat with the intent to make things lively for him—they had been driving six hundred big stags up the trail from Texas to turn them into canned beef in Kansas City. They were crossing Billy's grass patch when he got up on his hind legs in fine fighting trim and sailed into the leader.

How many he whipped I never knew but he stampeded the herd and as long as we lived on that range trail-branded stags were turning up with our cattle every few days—and I suppose canned beef was short on the market.

The boss of the herd shot Billy while he was making a noble charge and I have always considered it not only cowardly but an insult to every drop of sporting blood above grass. [12]

Sharlot was a girl of eleven by this time. Uncle Sam Boblett had gotten married at last; Sharlot went with him and her new Aunt Mary to Medicine Lodge where the three of them had their pictures taken, first together, and then Sharlot alone. Symbolic of Sharlot's interest, perhaps, is the fact that she holds a book in her hand.

Sharlot Hall at age eleven

Sharlot was a voracious reader. Not only did she devour Doctor Dodd's *Library of Mesmerism,* Swedenborg, Kant, and the *History of the Devil,* but she sandwiched in every other scrap of printed material that she could lay her hands on. One day she found a tattered magazine by the side of the road with something in it that set the course of her dreams for many years. It was an article about the Elizabethan poet Sir Philip Sidney: "The writer dwelt much upon his kindness, courtesy, and intelligence—three qualities which I had long since ceased to associate with any male human being. I kept the magazine many years. . . . Some of his sonnets, quoted in it probably suggested some of my own verse making, which had already begun."[13] Sharlot put the magazine away carefully. It was hard after reading about Sir Philip Sidney to go back to the stories in *Farm and Ranch* magazine, in which the noble farmhand was the hero and the city clerk or doctor the villain. Lest Sharlot get ideas above herself, her father often read from these stories to her. She seems to have tried once to share some of her ideas and ideals with her father; she never forgot his jeering rebuff. Many years later she relived the scene as "Anne," in an episode meant for the autobiographical novel which she never completed.

> Before a "teen" had appeared in her calendar Anne had learned to a finish that no one cared what she thought or felt so the chores were done. There was, indeed, a brief time when she tried to put her sense of the wonder and possibilities of life into words; a time when she ran a gauntlet of loud laughs and delighted jeers, such as met the efforts of a young horse to buck the saddle off his back or rub off the bridle bit against the snubbing post in the corral.
>
> Anne, like the "pinto bronco," learned almost in a flash that it was easier not to "pitch" against the saddle, or fight the customs that reined and controlled her every step as surely as the big Spanish bit with its cruel spade in the mouth controlled every step of the pinto. Like the wise pinto she sensed that to accept the work of life as it came and do it so well that it forestalled all action on the part of these tormentors was to escape into a certain freedom. So those strong young hands of hers took on a swift skill as her lips set into quiet lines that never broke into a word of useless speech.
>
> Like the pinto she did not sulk—she accepted the fact that nobody cared what she felt or thought, but that what she did certainly made things easier all around. She had the sense to see that thoughts and feelings got nowhere, but that saddles hung up and gates wired shut with a length of baling wire against roving calves, and meals cooked even if she did have to cut the stove wood, made the home atmosphere more peaceful than the harping of angels or the charm of queens of the tournament.[14]

Even at best, life was difficult on the isolated ranch in southern Kansas to which the Halls had come in 1879. But the year 1880 was one of real disaster for Kansas farmers and ranchers. Summer came on, hot and dry. Day after day the searing winds blew and the sun burned the parched soil. Adeline and Sharlot carried water from the creek to save the kitchen garden, but the corn shriveled in the field. The rains came in the fall, too late to save the crop. All autumn long, weary groups of discouraged homesteaders from farther west passed on the trail near the Hall cabin with their meager possessions piled in farm wagons pulled by teams of horses or oxen, headed for the east, driven out by two consecutive years of drought and crop failures. Adeline often had extra people to cook for, and beds were sometimes made up on the floor at night for travelers.

With the coming of autumn the exodus ended, and the Hall family dug in to prepare for the cold months ahead. The first blizzard came in October. This was followed by a thawing wind, and rain that turned to sleet and froze on the ground, making an icy coating over the entire earth that kept the cattle from feeding on the range. Another blizzard the week before Christmas sent temperatures plummeting to 22 degrees below zero. Sharlot was always cold. No matter how much clothing she put on when she went out to do the chores or feed the animals her fingers and toes were frostbitten before she got back to the house. She never forgot the distress of the hungry, freezing cattle as they sniffed the air, lifted their heads to the wind, and ran, wheeling and bellowing, with tails and heads up as another sleet storm began. The sight of those cattle driving south before the sleet, only to pile up against a line fence in Indian Territory, where they died in the drifting snow and icy gales, was one that she never forgot.

That spring a letter arrived from Adeline's brother John Boblett. John had not stayed long in Minneapolis after Adeline's marriage. Some time after 1873 he had left his family in Kansas and had started west to Arizona to hunt gold.[15] He had located a mining claim in the Lynx Creek area near Prescott in 1875, and in November 1876 had returned to Kansas and brought his wife and three children to Arizona. The Bobletts enjoyed their new life; the weather in mountainous, northern Arizona was clemently warm in the summer and cool in the winter, a real paradise in contrast to the harsh winters and searing summers of Kansas. There was plenty of unclaimed grazing land with lush grass growing belly-high to a horse for anyone who had a notion to try his hand at ranching, and there was gold practically for the picking up in the streams that ran down from the mountains. By 1881 the Apache Indians had ceased to be a problem since they had been moved onto the San Carlos reservation, leaving the territory open to white settlement.

Arizona sounded good to Jim Hall, and it sounded good to Sam Boblett. The two men sold the rest of their cattle. Hall had decided to try his luck at horse-ranching, so he bought a small herd of twenty blooded horses. The family packed what they could get into two wagons pulled by four horses each; with Sam and Mary Boblett in the lead wagon and Sharlot bringing up the rear to ride herd on the twenty horses, they were ready to go. On November 3, 1881, the Halls and the Bobletts left Barbour County and turned their faces west toward the old Santa Fe Trail.

3

First Years in Arizona

This way walked Fate — and as she went flung
    far the line of destiny
That bound an untracked continent to brother-
    hood from sea to sea;
That long gray trail of dream and hope, marked
    mile by mile with graves that keep
On every barren hill and slope some stout heart
    lost in dreamless sleep.
Patience and faith and fortitude were willed to it
    and justified —
Strong-armed to wrest from Mystery their birth-
    as the sky, and wide.
Nor ever sea-king dared the sea in braver mood
    than those who went
Strong-armed to wrest from Mystery their birth-
    right, half a continent.

        Sharlot Hall, "The Santa Fe Trail"[1]

SHARLOT SEEMS TO HAVE ENJOYED much of the difficult trip to Arizona, at least in retrospect. As she wrote many years later, she

counted the graves half lost in the grass and more than once on many days climbed off my pony to set some rotting head board straight or pile a little mound of stones over some grave more nearly lost. I watched from the very start for all the old forts and regular camps, most of which my father knew of course, and used to fill the day with imagining that Fremont or Kit Carson, or some troop of those first old trappers was just around the hills ahead and I was bringing them some message. . . . [2]

Early in the journey, however, as she rode behind the wagons, her horse shied and threw her. She had been seated on a new sidesaddle, although on the ranch she had always ridden bareback. She landed flat on her back, injuring her spine so severely that she never fully recovered. Sharlot claimed that she was so afraid of her Uncle Sam Boblett, the wagon boss, who she felt would not stand for any weakness on her part, that despite what must have been excruciating pain she climbed back into the saddle and jolted the rest of the day on her cracked spine before she told anyone of her injury.

In Albuquerque, Sharlot remembered, "the alkali water made the horses sick, and two of them died. But it was a pleasant town—shady—and the people were kindly. I remember one white woman who called to me as I went by. She was lovely, with a sweet voice. She was taking her bread out of one of those Mexican outdoor ovens, and she gave me a loaf for my mother, who wasn't well."[3] As Sharlot said many years later, "It must have been a time of great discomfort and anxiety for my mother, but she was wonderfully brave and patient." She had to be; camping out in freezing winter temperatures every night and living in the cramped quarters of the family wagon piled with furniture, farm implements, and supplies for three long winter months must have tried her soul. In addition, a smallpox epidemic was raging along the trail, adding the danger that some of their party might contract this illness. "Building a campfire and cooking in iron kettles and Dutch ovens and then settling down for the night with the crunch of grazing horses all around"[4] may have had nostalgic charm in retrospect, but at the time it must have been hard.

From Albuquerque the family struck out on the old east-west military trail, Camino del Obispo, that was followed by most settlers heading for northern Arizona. Traveling through the snow-covered sand hills, barren except for sagebrush and greasewood, they crossed the Río Puerco and sighted the Indian pueblo of Laguna. The Río Laguna was poisonous with alkali, and wood was scarce, but the young Sharlot was charmed by her first sight of Indians, who eyed her curiously as she rode the trail on her pony.

The next day, Christmas 1881, the little party topped the continental divide just beyond old Fort Wingate and made a snowy camp on the trail. Sharlot remembered that their wagons stood

> in a cluster of piñons, half buried in snow and the one green thing in a world of white.... The first [Navajo] Indians we had seen helped us to eat up our rabbit stew and wanted to buy me (probably because I was plump enough to make another stew). My brother and I had our stockings pinned outside the wagon cover, in firm faith that Santa Claus would find us, as he did with my first book of poems, and second book of any sort that was really my own. [5]

Soon the travelers arrived at the great, pine-clad Mogollon range. Wood and water were now plentiful, but the snow was so deep that it made travel difficult. In fact, as Sharlot remembered, their party could not have gotten through "that great solemn Mogollon forest with the pines standing four to six feet deep in snow" except that a government party from Fort Wingate had been through the area a few days before and had broken the trail. To add peril to their discomfort, Sharlot remembered, "We were lost about half the time for my uncle, who drove in the lead, had a genius for taking sheep trails and wood roads." In addition, although the warlike Apache Indians were by this time living on government reservations, the little party could not help remembering that only six years before the Apaches had ambushed the United States cavalry at this very pass. [6]

It was February 1882 when the Halls and the Bobletts reached the Agua Fria Valley and turned off into the Lynx Creek area that was to be their new home. Thirty years later, in a letter to a friend, Sharlot described the land as she had first seen it.

> The creek was hidden in undergrowth and the hills were lost in pines, all snow-covered. As we journeyed along with our two covered wagons... we passed the hydraulic mine....
>
> I was... full of stories of California which my Forty-niner uncle [Sam Boblett] had told, and I watched the road, all ready to fall off my pony the minute I saw a nugget under foot....

Our journey ended at three log cabins under a cluster of huge pines where my uncle [John Boblett] and his family lived. In a day or two every miner on the creek had been in to see the new family—and I like to think how they all appreciated my mother. I was shown nuggets and given enough to start me hunting in earnest—and that spring I began...placer mining....[7]

While James Hall took time to find a suitable location for the horse ranch he had decided to start, the Halls camped in their two wagons and a tent on John Boblett's land. Sharlot recalled that, shortly after they arrived, they all went in to see the "big city" of Prescott, about ten miles away.

In 1882 Prescott boasted five churches, two school buildings, a theater, a concert building, a new brick city hall, three newspapers, two banks, four livery and feed stables, five blacksmith shops, two assay offices, fifteen or twenty miscellaneous stores, and eighteen saloons.[8] The city was connected with the railroads, both north and south, by regular stagecoach service. The northbound stage ran three times a week to connect with the Atlantic and Pacific Railroad. "Good coaches and careful drivers are the mottoes of this company. NO INDIANS ON THIS ROUTE!" proclaimed the regular advertisement in the *Weekly Arizona Miner.*[9] There might not have been any Indians, but stage robberies were extremely common. Bandits stripped passengers of their valuables and vanished again into the mountain wilderness around the little frontier community. But when caught, these desperadoes were dealt with in a summary fashion. The *Miner* on Mondays almost routinely reported the previous Saturday's public hanging in great detail, complimenting the sheriff for having made the event a pleasant one for all.

With only 1,836 inhabitants, Prescott was still the second largest city in the territory, being exceeded only by Tucson's 6,994.[10] As the county seat of Yavapai County as well as the territorial capital, it was, according to the proud editor of the *Miner*, "The City of Arizona, and has the handsomest ladies on the Pacific Coast."[11] As Sharlot remembered it,

The mountains around were white with snow; the little trees on the plaza were almost bushes—newly set around the new red brick courthouse that was the only striking building in the little frontier town.

Prescott in about 1880

In the outskirts the houses were all fenced with "worm fences" of pine rails or straight fences of big pine logs laid one on top of another and "stake and ridered" at every long end. A few homes had picket fences of sawed timber from the little saw-mills up in the hills—the homes of the frontier aristocrats.

As I followed down the trail that is now east Gurley Street I looked over across Granite Creek to a sprawling log building in a cluster of tall pine trees—and I was told that it was the first governor's house—a governor's mansion of hewed pine logs with a "shake" roof—but grand enough to me who remembered the sod houses and "dug outs" of the Great American Desert which we had just crossed. [12]

James Hall soon found a small ranch in a valley about fifteen miles southeast of Prescott. Lonesome Valley, as the area was called, was

as bare and brown and lonesome as its name implies—and as beautiful as only the southwestern plains can be—dappled with little hills and marked by long sweeping lines of color as rich and bright as if some titan painter had just drawn his wet brush down the rolling slopes. Vegetation is not needed to produce beauty in the land for the earth herself is many-hued, streaked with strange bright sands and clays and walled with mountains of rich-hued rock.... [13]

For the rest of the year the Halls camped on their new acreage in the same wagons and tent which they had used on the trip from Kansas. Sharlot described her life at that time:

> ...our lives were like those of all families on the small ranches—lots· of work and little schooling or other opportunities. No Indian troubles as all the Indians of the region had been removed to San Carlos [Reservation] just before we came in. . . .

> I studied mostly at home, between whiles of watering or herding the cattle. We watered from a well in long troughs and the water was pumped by a clumsy wheel which rolled in a circle on the ground and was drawn by a horse. It was my job to drive the horse and open and shut the gates so only our own stock got water. . . .

This protracted season of camping in wagon boxes and a tent on the barren expanse of Lonesome Valley must have been difficult for Adeline. Sharlot hinted at trouble:

> I remember the amazed and resentful astonishment on the face of one old man who had dragged his family clear across the western half of

Gurley Street, Prescott, in about 1880

the United States... into a spot without schools or companionship for
his half grown children or any of the comforts or pleasures of life for
his weary wife. There had not been the least reason for the last move,
beyond his own desire to get into a place more like his boyhood home
in the remote corner of a then new state. He was fascinated with
a place where life had no conventionalities to hinder his doing as
he pleased.

When his wife told him that she was going back to a little town they
knew and never come back he said, "Why mother, what's the matter
with this place? I thought you always liked to go anywhere I wanted
to." It never entered his poor old head that he had robbed his children
of a fair chance by selecting their home in a region remote from all the
influences of civilisation. . . .

Although Lonesome Valley was isolated, it was not utterly deserted.
It would seem that Adeline, like her daughter after her, had a horror
of liquor and of those who made their living from the sale of "demon
rum." Years later, Sharlot recalled this side of country living.

It was then a cattle country and thinly settled, but a wagon road
between two military posts [Fort Whipple and Camp Verde] crossed it
and near this road two old-time road houses with saloons had been
started for the soldier and other trade. Almost every man who travelled
on the road stopped for water or horse feed or meals, and drank more
or less in the saloons. . . . The two saloons were the social gathering
places for the men of the whole region. . . .

The first time I ever met the settlers all together after we had located
on our own ranch was at a cowboy dance given at one of the ranches
after the spring round-up was over and the cattlemen about to go home
with the cattle they had been gathering. By midnight many of the
cowboys were drinking too much to be sure what they were doing and
by morning several were dead drunk. I saw their friends sober them up
by pouring sour and salty pickle juice down their throats till they
vomited enough to wake them up so they could get into a wagon and
I never forgot, though I was only a child, that all the men joked about
it and no one seemed shocked or sorry but a few of the women. . . . [14]

Adeline had high ideals for her two children; she decried the influence of such associations, particularly for her son Ted, who was
nine years old the year the Halls arrived in Arizona. However, from
Sharlot's description of the Kansas cowboys of her childhood, it is
doubtful that the miners and ranchers who lived in the Agua Fria

area were less civilized than the men with whom she and Ted had grown up.

Adeline became ill on the trip over the Santa Fe Trail; the rigors of settling into yet another wilderness homestead were probably almost more than she could bear. She was apparently extremely ill by fall; a Mrs. Hall, identified in the hospital records only as a native of Ohio, was admitted to Mercy Hospital in Prescott in October that year, suffering from morphine addiction. She was discharged as cured in a month.[15] Sharlot stated that after this time

> my mother wore a look of repression that never changed except to grow deeper—More and more her lips were pressed together in a straight line—her eyebrows lifted and bent like those of Lincoln in his latest portraits.
>
> She always spoke kindly, gently, in a flat even voice, seldom expressed an opinion. I know that my father was much happier after she reached this state.

It seems obvious from Sharlot's later reminiscences that Adeline from this time on turned more and more to her daughter, who was just developing into maturity when the family moved to Arizona. Sharlot hinted that James Hall may have "carried on" in a casual fashion with hired girls and other women of the area; witnessing these encounters and loathing her father with all the pitiless scorn of which the young adolescent is capable, she concluded, "No man was ever true to any woman.... Taught from childhood by the experience of the woman I loved best, I have never trusted any man."[16] Even more painful to the young girl's sensitivity were the trips she made with her mother when Adeline was called, as she was many times, to help with the birth of a neighboring woman's baby. Sharlot learned young that in her social milieu

> the mother is forced to bear children without the slightest regard for the welfare of herself or her offspring—babe after babe being hurried out of her arms that the ever-weakening succession of new-comers may have a few months hurried care. Nine tenths of our social problems begin right here—in the birth of children whom selfish indulgence robs of the forethought which should insure mental and physical health and harmony of temperament.... I have gone with many and many a mother down into the Valley of the Shadow and

helped her bring back a pitiful babe maimed and marred by the father's selfishness and predestined to pain and failure by his dull, stolid, witless attitude toward wife and family.

Indeed, these tragedies, witnessed in such naked agony in poor frontier homes, made me deliberately decide when still a young girl never to marry. [17]

In the spring of 1883 Sharlot and her brother Ted attended their first three-month term at the little country school about four miles from their ranch. The two children, one nine years old, the other twelve, rode their horses or walked to the rough lumber schoolhouse; childlike, they must have loitered sometimes on their way, as Sharlot remembered forty years later:

> Once in a wind-swept, sunburned land
> Where long, rough hills come crawling down,
> Crowding the little valley hard
> With buttes like paws, rock-clawed and brown,
> One great split boulder in the sand
> Made spots of shade where wild vines grew,
> All hung with swinging bells of bloom—
> In sunset colors pink and blue.
> Small morning glory vines that clung
> Back in the rock rifts dim and cool—
> And two ranch children all through May
> Were tardy every day at school. [18]

In "the little log and slab and stone and adobe schoolhouse" they "sat on wooden benches, without desks enough to go around, and wrote lessons on the red felt edged slates that were counted a riotous luxury—for plain wooden framed slates were the usual thing."[19] That fall, Sharlot recalled,

I wrote my first book of verse in one of the little yellow paper backed notebooks called "The Farmer's and Mechanic's Note book" and sent out yearly by some patent medicine company....

This "first edition" showed my early historical bent for it contained verses about the discovery of Florida, about Columbus, and all sorts of ballads about Indian fights and frontier life. It was largely written when I was supposed to be laboring with my geography lesson—but that study was such fun for me that one reading "got" a lesson and I generally could reel off all the reading matter in the book "by heart."[20]

Teachers never stayed at the little country school outside Prescott for more than a term or two at the most; the next year, 1885, school was taught by Miss "Neenah" Johnson. Although Sharlot in later years was to characterize her father as being almost belligerently opposed to any kind of cultural or educational activity, this seems not to have been the case during the school term under Miss Johnson's direction. James Hall was one of the three school trustees.[21] His duties probably included listening to the children recite each Friday afternoon; he seems to have taken an active part in school affairs. At the end of the term he provided his military uniform and gun for a school skit.[22]

By the end of the term, it was evident that Sharlot had learned as much as the young teacher at the little Agua Fria school could teach her. Evidently Miss Johnson persuaded Jim Hall that his daughter should have a chance to go on to school in Prescott. So, despite James Hall's fears that she would "Git high toned and think she's above us," October 1886 saw the young and rather frightened Sharlot in Prescott, away from her family for the first time.

Sharlot worked for her board and room that first semester at the home of Judge Sumner Howard. She stayed in town during the week and went home each weekend to help out on the ranch, for although her mother's health was better this year than it had been since they had been in Arizona, Adeline was never strong.

Classes must have been a mixture of terror and delight to the shy sunburned girl from Agua Fria; for the first time she tried her hand at public speaking. Her classmate and lifelong friend Ida Williams never forgot the fiery poetry recitations Sharlot practiced for elocution class. "The old pieces in Appleton's Fifth Reader were certainly made to yield every shade of meaning," Ida recalled.[23]

While still in Prescott that year, Sharlot ventured across Granite Creek to West Gurley Street and the old log Governor's Mansion under the towering pines on the hill west of town. Here she met Henry W. Fleury, an elderly man who lived in the mansion. Fleury had come to Prescott as private secretary to Arizona's first territorial governor, John N. Goodwin, in 1864, and had stayed on in Prescott after the other men of that first administration had died or

The Governor's Mansion in about 1880

left. He lived in the mansion for the rest of his life. Sharlot seems to have been fascinated by the gruff, grey-bearded Fleury, and he warmed to her interest. He told her of his trip across the plains with Governor Goodwin's party in a covered wagon and of other personal recollections which he had of the first years of the territory.

> The sweetest and saddest story he told was of a lovely young bride who had lived in the old house only a brief year or two and who had been buried with her tiny babe in her arms under one of the big pine trees. Her husband had been our second governor and a delegate to congress, and a writer of brilliance—and that was good to put in school compositions, but in my school books I pressed little red roses from a bush under the window—a bush which the young bride had carried all the way from her eastern home and planted beside the pine logs.
>
> Even then I had a dream—that someday I might live in the big log house that seemed full of memory of the lovely Lady of the Red Rose Bush. As I passed by and the gray old man said good morning to me or handed me a tiny bouquet of clover pinks or ragged sailors I seemed to see a lovely young face behind the window of the room where she had died....[24]

At the end of the school term in June 1887 Sharlot went home to the little cattle ranch on Lynx Creek, never to return to school again.

There was trouble at home. Her mother was increasingly unwell and unable to take care of the chores that were every ranchwoman's lot. In addition, hard times had fallen on the entire area. The first summer that the Halls were in Arizona was one blessed with abundant rain. Cattle prices were high, fodder was plentiful and cheap, and on the ranges the tall grasses stood green and fragrant and belly-deep to a horse. But James Hall did not realize when he optimistically bought a herd of Oregon cattle that the ranges were already overstocked. As Sharlot recalled the tragedy of the next four dry years,

> ...every cow seemed to bring two calves a year, but he didn't worry—not until the Lord forgot to send any rain for a year or two and the overworked grass dried up and blew away. It is good to be young enough to forget the tragedy of those dry years—but I happen to be old enough to remember the dry water holes out of which we snaked the bogged cows at the end of a riata—the pitiful lines of cattle that before sun-up weaved along the trail to what springs and wells were left— and drank and often fell beside the water boxes too weak to carry back the weight of the water they had drunk.... Our own ranch contributed all but a few heads to the toll of death and for several years thereafter the wagons of the bone hunters were familiar sights on our range....[25]

Then, one month after Sharlot had returned from Prescott came such heavy rainfall that the whole area was flooded. James Hall figured there was nothing to be done but to leave the ranch and try something else.

It would have been surprising indeed had he not thought of mining. Both of his brothers-in-law had staked and sold and staked again numerous mining claims in the Lynx Creek area in the years that the Halls had been in Yavapai County. James himself in 1886 had claimed twenty acres in the Walker mining district near the mouth of Flume Gulch and adjoining the famous "Old Hydraulics" placer mine.[26] Late in the summer of 1887 the Halls moved to a shack on the claim. Here they were to live for the next three years.

Life at the hydraulic mine must have been difficult for all of them. Certainly the mining operation which was to engage much of James Hall's time in the next few years was hard, dirty, cold, wet business. As explained in an article in the Prescott *Journal-Miner* of December 3, 1890, "The key to the entire system is a dam on Lynx Creek." A tunnel was built in the base of the dam, with a gate which could be closed to back the water up in the reservoir behind the dam when needed. Water flowed through the tunnel down the creek bed and into a flume, or channel, which delivered it to a pressure box at the top of the bluff. From the pressure box the water went to canvas hoses, which were some fifty to sixty feet long, ending in big nozzles which could shoot the water at high pressure against the side of the bluff. The force of the water washed the gold-bearing earth out of the side of the bluff into the bed of the creek, where it was channeled into sluice boxes and the gold separated from the sand and gravel.

James Hall's hydraulic mine on Lynx Creek, 1890

Such mining operations could only be carried on during the winter, when Lynx Creek was full—and the water was ice cold—generally from December until about March or April. The rest of the year the miners repaired the dam and the equipment; some of them probably farmed or ranched, and others prospected or worked in underground mines in the area.

As for Sharlot, she later summarized her role as being that of "chief cook, timekeeper, and guardian of the bullion." The last task must have been frightening in those lawless days. Sharlot remembered that "we were always on the lookout for a raid, especially after each 'clean-up'.... Not a door in the ram-shackle old house would lock and I slept with a big revolver under my pillow and one eye open...."[27]

James Hall worked with some success as a hydraulic miner on Lynx Creek until 1890. On August 6, 1890, the *Journal-Miner* announced; "J. K. Hall is building a good, commodious residence in the lower end of the Lynx Creek valley. When completed it will be one of the finest and most substantial in that section of the country." Mining days were over for the Halls. That summer they moved to Orchard Ranch, which was to be the family home until it was sold in 1927.

4

Orchard Ranch
and
Freethought

THE HOUSE AT ORCHARD RANCH rose stark and raw, an affront to the desert solitude of Lonesome Valley. It was a well-built house, a large one for the area and the time, built in the shape of a T with a crossbar running east and west, fronting the highway to Camp Verde from Prescott. Two porches were built against the north-south stem of the T; the front door of the house was on the west side of the stem, looking toward Prescott.

James Hall's brother-in-law, John C. Boblett, who was an agent for mail-order fruit trees, may have talked Hall into diversifying the ranch by growing fruit as early as the fall of 1890, when the Halls first moved into their new home. At any rate, some time between 1890 and 1895, the first fruit trees—apples, pears, and peach—were planted. Evidently these efforts at horticulture met with considerable derision from some of the old-timers; Sharlot recalled:

> Farmers from the Verde driving to town watched us setting out the trees. At that time no one believed trees could be grown in the higher altitudes and drier parts of Yavapai. An old man leaned off his wagon seat and called to us: "You all will shore raise hell with fruit on that dry land." We replied that we expected to raise apples instead of the commodity he mentioned.... There were times when the old man's crop seemed more likely to be abundant than apples—we weathered a long series of dry years in which the trees just hung to life and no more.... [1]

[38]

Orchard Ranch

James Hall certainly must have been aware of the uncertain water supply in the Lynx Creek area after his years of working the hydraulic mine; one of his first tasks was the digging of a well and tank at the end of the orchard. While he was digging the tank, he turned up a well-preserved Indian jar, mute evidence of the ancient people who had inhabited Lonesome Valley long before the white man came. This find was enough to prick Sharlot's interest in investigating the prehistoric Indian ruins which dotted the area. Her cousin Ed Boblett, who like the other men of the family spent a good deal of time prospecting, riding the range, and generally wandering about the countryside, had discovered a ruin south of Camp Verde near Squaw Peak. He invited Sharlot and her brother Ted to pack in on horseback and explore the area with him. Sharlot took her notebook with her, and as she rode she put down what she saw. It had occurred to her that this rugged, almost inaccessible area would be of as much interest to easterners as it was to her, and that she might be able to turn her trip into ready cash by selling an article describing it.

Sharlot had by this time discovered that her literary talents could be translated into income. About a year after the Halls moved to Orchard Ranch, Sharlot sold a short article entitled "The Genesis of the Earth and the Moon, a Moqui Folk Tale," to a well-established children's periodical, *Wide Awake*.[2] This undistinguished offering, which tells how Wabano, the Great Goddess, made the earth with the help of her husband the Fire God, netted the young author a check for four dollars.[3] It is easy to imagine how this concrete recognition of her talents must have fired Sharlot's ambition. Times were always hard; nearly everyone in the Lynx Creek area lived on the edge of chronic financial disaster, none more so than the Halls. Here was a way that Sharlot could help out, as well as a way that she could show her father that her "high-toned" reading and writing was worth something after all. Easterners were interested in Indians; Sharlot would give them Indians.

"Of the cliff dwellings," wrote Sharlot,

the village most easy of access is situated on a high bluff, about seven miles below Camp Verde. The road leading to it, winds in and out among the farms of the valley, through thickets of feathery-leaved mesquite trees, and past great fields of alfalfa. Signs of the prehistoric settlements are on every hand; but the first important one is a reservoir, perhaps two hundred yards long and one hundred and fifty wide. Its banks are sharply defined, and its greatest depth at present about ten feet. Mesquite trees of considerable size cover the bottom and testify to the great age of the ruin.

Mounds of earth and stone dotted here and there mark the site of ancient dwellings; and continuing the drive down the river, we come upon a series of cultivated fields. . . .

On the opposite bank, the eastern bank of the river, rises a great ragged bluff of gray sandstone, with a deep ravine cutting sharply into it. . . . The distant view shows only dark spots on the face of the gray cliffs, but on coming nearer the openings become distinct, and a few show the entrance surrounded by a wall of masonry.[4]

The three explorers picketed their horses and scrambled almost straight up the side of the cliff where they found the rubble-filled entrance to the first row of houses. Stooping, they crawled into the ruin. They marveled at the extent of the cliff city:

> The rooms had been excavated out of softer layers in the rock—rooms shaped like the half of an egg shell and varying in size from cubby holes to council chambers. Hundreds and hundreds of these strange rooms could be reached from one entrance—for we could crawl through the low hallways between them for hours and still find unexplored rooms far back under the mountains of soft stone which jutted out to the Verde River which had furnished water to these long-vacant cities. . . . [5]

The notes which Sharlot took were turned into an article, but it was not written immediately. The struggle to get the new ranch started must have used all of the family's energy those first months. Sharlot described the ranch some years later, when the fruit trees were well established; things could not have been easier in the early days.

> The little ranch lies pinched in a foothill canon in the most drouth-bitten region of the Southwest. The trees in the orchard are dwarfed like a Japanese toy garden—because they never had a full drink in their lives—yet they bear loads of little sweet fruit marketable in the mountain mining camps. The rough coated ranch cattle browse sun-dried brush and weeds all summer and during the winter keep the skin taut over their outstanding ribs by the scant coarse hay yield—or lie down and die patiently among the close eaten brush, but what live are marketable, too, as beef for the camps.
>
> The pigs literally "root hog or die" for weed roots on the hills—and make sweet "gamey" bacon at last—also marketable in the mines— and the chickens and drouth-stunted vegetables fill up the chinks in the ever lean income.

In March 1891, just after the Halls had weathered their first bitterly cold, snowy winter on the new spread, James Hall fell seriously ill. [6] It was three months before he was even able to be out of bed. Adeline Hall rose to the challenge and joyfully took charge. Sharlot recalled,

> This was mother's happiest time I know—her mind was free to work—to play. . . . Father made fun of it all when he got up—he was surly and grudging about everything that had turned out well. He tore

down the trellis over which she and [Ted] had trained squashes as they
do in Italy and he would never admit the quality of the seventy perfect
squashes they had ripened on such a small space.

He would never let [them] plan anything again, and his face always
hardened into the resentful look when they even spoke of what might
be done. He wanted them to listen to what he said as an oracle and to
work as he planned as if they were machines moving by his will. . . . As
soon as another year came [Ted] got a job away from home.

The years on the ranch must have been trying for Ted as well as for
Sharlot. A bright boy, whose interest in mining engineering is evident
from some of his books which are among those in Sharlot's personal
library, he evidently received a formal education of only a few short
terms at the little Agua Fria school which he attended with his
sister.[7] James Hall viewed his son, as he did Sharlot, as simply another hand to help with the work around the ranch. Sharlot recalled,

I never heard my father express a wish or make a plan for my own or
my brother's education or for our future. He did not make any more
attempt to give either of us any sort of training for our grown up lives
than if we had not been his children. When my brother showed his gift
for machinery and engineering my father never showed the least interest nor even made a suggestion as to his training—we could have sent
him to a good technical school by a little denial and effort but father
apparently never dreamed of such a thing but instead spent every
dollar the boy earned till mother rebelled and obliged him to bank part
of it in Ted's name. . . .

He made fun of any neighbor boy who tried to fit himself for anything
but farm or cowboy life—always said they were "Hunting a soft job"—
or "Trying to live without work."

When Adeline ventured to suggest that some plan should be made for
Ted's education past the Agua Fria country school, James simply
growled, "Aw there's plenty of time an' [he'll] have as much as I ever
had."

The year 1892 was marked in Sharlot's memory as one of
physical agony. The damage she had done to her spine in the fall from
her horse on the Santa Fe Trail trip of 1881 had apparently not
surfaced up to this point, but ten years of hard work on the ranch as
well as at the placer mine must have taken their toll. For months that

Adeline, Edward, Sharlot, and James Hall in 1895

year she could neither sit nor stand without pain; the only comfort she could find was in lying flat on her stomach on the floor. For want of anything better to do with her time, and probably to take her mind off her discomfort, she began to write, using the floor for a desk.

The writing she did during those months of enforced inactivity reaped a harvest of publication the following year and set her firmly on the path of professional authorship at the age of twenty-two. Her output was diversified; her description of the trip to the Verde Valley cliff dwellings appeared in *The Archaeologist* in April 1893. The Denver-based publication *The Great Divide* took a poem, "A Border Tale," which appeared in March 1893, and a short story, "Tailings, a Tramp," which was published in May 1893.

Sharlot must have recovered from her back trouble by the summer of 1893, for the month of July found her on the first leg of an extended camping trip through northern Arizona with some Verde Valley friends, John and Lizzie Davis. It is evident that Sharlot fully realized that such a trip could be turned into grist for her literary mill, for she kept a detailed diary of her experience.[8] As with her description of her visit to the Verde Valley Indian ruins in 1891, Sharlot later exploited her trip to the Canyon in two articles, one appearing in *Travel Magazine* ("How I Saw the Grand Canon of the Colorado at Midnight,") in September 1897, and the other ten years later in *Out West* ("A Christmas at the Grand Canon") in January 1907.

How keenly Sharlot felt her isolation from the world of learning and literature on the remote ranch on lower Lynx Creek we can only guess. She seems to have gone only occasionally to Prescott for shopping, visiting, and cultural events. A brief notice in the *Journal-Miner* on January 2, 1895, may have caught her attention. It read:

> If you fail to attend Putnam's lectures you will always regret it. Such treats of reasoning, of eloquence, of Encyclopedic knowledge don't come our way every day. Watch the papers for date and place. Remember that the lectures are free to all, and criticism is invited.

Samuel Porter Putnam, the lecturer to whom the notice referred, was to change the direction of Sharlot's life and alter her thinking in a dramatic fashion.

Samuel Putnam

Samuel Putnam was a minor American novelist, an essayist, and an itinerant lecturer. Putnam was also a man with a cause, and that cause was the conversion of the ignorant and gullible Christian world to the true gospel of secular Freethought and skepticism. To this end he devoted most of his adult life; his novels and poems are thinly disguised tracts; his essays are curious mixtures of contemptuous gibes at Christians and Jews who believe in Biblical revelation and miracles combined with self-righteous assurances to the followers of Freethought that "we are the people; all truth is in us."

Putnam was born on July 23, 1838, in Chichester, New Hampshire, the son of a Congregational minister. He attended Dartmouth College, leaving without graduating to fight on the Union side in the Civil War. After the war, he studied theology and became, like his father, a Congregational minister. He preached for several years in the Midwest until, disillusioned with the tenets of Christian doctrine, he met Robert G. Ingersoll, fiery advocate of the principles of Freethought.

The Freethinkers of the late nineteenth century believed in the efficacy of human reason as opposed to the blind acceptance of divine revelation. Charles Watts, a British Freethought leader of the day, summarized the principles which governed the movement: "The Free Thought Philosophy is based on three fundamental principles. The first is that supreme attention should be paid to this life. The second is that reason, aided by experience, is the best guide. The third is that the eclectic principles should be applied to all thought and movement."[9] These principles appealed to Putnam as they did to intellectual liberals all over the United States who had come into contact with the persuasive logic of Robert Ingersoll's oratory. Putnam left the Christian ministry to become one of Ingersoll's trusted lieutenants and friends. In 1887 he was elected secretary of the American Secular Union and Free Thought Federation and in 1892 succeeded Ingersoll as president. He devoted the rest of his life to traveling, lecturing, and writing on Freethought, both in the United States and abroad.

The Freethought movement already had a strong base in Arizona when Putnam came to Prescott in January 1895. Charles T. Hayden, father of Carl Hayden, later long-time senator from Arizona, headed the Tempe group; there were also active organizations in Tucson, Phoenix, and Prescott.[10] Putnam came to Arizona that year at the invitation of Dr. J. Miller, one of Prescott's most prominent Freethinkers, as part of his lecture tour of the United States. He spent the better part of two months, with one short interruption, in Prescott and seems to have won many converts to his cause.

As for Sharlot, it would seem that she and her family were already attuned to Freethought philosophy when Putnam came to Arizona. It is likely that Sharlot's grandfather, John Boblett, who was interested in the New Harmony community of Freethinker Robert Owen, was himself a Freethinker; he could well have passed his secular skepticism on to his daughter Adeline. At any rate, Putnam, in a report made at the close of his Arizona campaign to the *Truth Seeker,* official organ of the Freethought movement, singled out the entire Hall family, "Mr. and Mrs. J. K. Hall and daughter and son," as "indomitable Freethinkers . . . [who] represent the growing element of this country."[11]

Putnam was fifty-six when he came to Arizona, five years older than Sharlot's father. A close friend described him as "short, red-faced and chubby, and spry as a cat."[12] But he seems to have been a spellbinding orator capable of captivating his audiences with the same sort of dry humor and razor-sharp logic that had already made Ingersoll famous. And as later events in Putnam's life were to prove, he was possessed of the kind of charm that was irresistibly appealing to more than one intellectually ambitious young woman.

Sharlot carefully marked and annotated a small calendar for 1895, noting Putnam's activities and other Freethought events that year.* On Saturday, January 5, she went to Prescott to hear the gentleman from the East who was giving his first lecture the next day. Sharlot attended each of Putnam's lectures during the next two weeks. Whether she stayed in Prescott the entire time is not known, but she certainly did not leave town during the second week of the Freethought campaign. It began to rain the night of January 15; the downpour continued the whole of the following week. Despite sandbagging efforts by the Prescott chain gang, Granite Creek burst its banks, flooding north Prescott. No word was received from Orchard Creek until a neighbor of the Halls came in from Lonesome Valley late in the week and related that the Agua Fria River was "running like the Mississippi" and that the entire Lonesome Valley was one big lake. The wild weather was a special aggravation to Sharlot, for it kept her from taking Putnam to visit the Hall ranch as she had planned.

---

*This calendar was discovered by the Sharlot Hall Museum staff in an obscure corner of the attic in the Governor's Mansion in 1978 where it had evidently been lying since Sharlot's death in 1943. No diaries, letters, or other personal material relevant to Samuel Putnam or Sharlot's interest in Freethought, aside from this calendar, are to be found with her personal papers at the Museum. It is possible that material of this type was removed from the archives shortly after her death. Grace Sparkes, who organized the monumental task of sorting through Sharlot's effects, directed an assistant to use discretion in saving personal papers: "If in handling Sharlot's personal affairs, her letters and notes you come across matters that were solely her own *personal* life may I ask that you either hold them for me or do not permit others to see them?...There were so many complicated periods in her life and I am sure collector as she was, there may be strictly personal letters or other effects which she would not have wanted others to see...[Grace's punctuation] or perhaps even know" [Grace Sparkes Collection, Arizona Historical Society, Tucson]. Museum staff members suspect that personal letters and at least one of Sharlot's diaries were destroyed.

It is clear that by this time Sharlot and Putnam had established a close friendship. Evidence of Putnam's growing admiration for the exceptional young woman is found in the elaborate inscription on the flyleaf of his monumental history of Freethought, *Four Hundred Years of Freethought,* which he presented to his new disciple on January 15. The inscription reads:

To Sharlot M. Hall, with best wishes of the Author

> Weave then the golden future of the race,
> With heart hand hope and all your action's grace;
> In sorrow labor, for the joy will burst;
> Still bare the burden, and endure the worst,
> For evil passes, while the good remains;
> The seed we plant will laugh along the plains;
> The Golden Age is more than poet's fire;
> 'Tis more than happy thought or bright desire;
> It is within the humblest deeds we do;
> In faithful work the golden strands we view;
> Day after day we make the beauty vast;
> In farm, in shop where'er our lot is cast:
> The iron rail, as well as roses' light:
> The sturdy blow as well as music's flight
> Make beautiful the life of coming years;
> Give glory to the dawning day that cheers;
> Our whole humanity from least to great,
> With every varied talent and estate,
> Each hope, each thought, each living heart and brain
> Unfold the grandeur of the one vast strain.

Always yours,
Samuel P. Putnam
Prescott Arizona   January 15, 1895[13]

Rain did not dampen the enthusiasm of the Freethought cadre in Prescott; as Putnam put it in his next weekly report to the *Truth Seeker,* "Through rain and shine... we hav proceeded with the campaign here. The Prescott Freethought Federation has completed its organization and on Friday night last [January 18] elected its officers...."[14] Among the officers listed in Putnam's report were Dr. J. Miller as president and Sharlot Hall as one of the five vice presidents. The Prescott Federation, according to Putnam, numbered one hundred members.

Putnam gave three final lectures, "Bible Cruelties and Contradictions," "Agnosticism, Christianity, and Heathenism," and "Evolution and Creation," before he wound up the series, as the *Journal-Miner* put it, with a "big Freethought blowout," on January 29, honoring one of the "saints" of the Freethought movement, Thomas Paine. By this time, Putnam seems to have been thoroughly smitten by Sharlot's charms. In his January 28 report to the *Truth Seeker* he said of her:

> She was born into Freethought with every fibre of her being and has never had to fight any ghosts to get rid of them. They do not haunt any portion of her intellectual horizon. She is a healthful representativ of the abounding life of this great western land. She is entering upon a literary career of bright promis; is a contributor to many journals east and west on various subjects, especially the pre-historic relics of Arizona, of which she is a thorough student.... we can be proud of this fearless and gifted exponent of Freethought who has such a brilliant future in the ranks of our Western authors. [15]

The Prescott campaign closed, as Putnam put it, "in a blaze of glory" with the Paine celebration, featuring music by the Prescott Orchestra, readings, recitations, an address by Dr. Miller on the work of Thomas Paine in the American Revolution, and an address by Sharlot Hall on the career of Thomas Paine in England and France. Said Putnam, "This was her first appearance befor an audience, and she was applauded to the echo. I am sure that our young friend will be one of our most brilliant representatives upon the Freethought platform, and will carry our flag to victory when we older heads hav made our pillow in the dust.... [16] After a brief trip to Phoenix, Putnam was back in Prescott again on February 8, ready to start a second series of Freethought lectures and visit Orchard Ranch.

The avowed support of the American Secular Union and Freethought Federation for equality for women and men and the easing of marriage laws which discriminated against women also embraced another idea: free love. The Kansas of Sharlot's childhood seems to have been a real hotbed of radical Freethinkers, including the Kansas Liberal League which sponsored the National Liberal League Camp meeting, September 5–10, 1879, in Bismarck Grove, near Lawrence. The belief of these Kansas Liberals that birth control, sex, and sexual relations were matters for open discussion had led them to support the cause of D. M. Bennett, then editor of the *Truth Seeker,* who had recently been convicted and jailed on charges of sending obscene literature (a birth-control pamphlet entitled *Cupid's Yokes*) through the mail.[17] There is no evidence that Sharlot or her parents attended the Bismarck Grove meeting, but certainly Sharlot's mother, with her firm convictions of the necessity of responsible parenthood and family planning, must have known about the matter and would have agreed with the Liberal League's stance. Some of these early League members were open advocates of free love; it was Robert Ingersoll's distaste for this "plank" in the Liberal League's platform that led him to withdraw his support for the League until 1884, when some of the membership split off to form the American Secular Union and Samuel Putnam began to assert himself as a leader.[18]

Were Freethinkers free lovers? As late as 1891, the *Topeka State Journal* denounced the annual meeting of the Kansas Liberal League at Ottawa as a "Free Love Fest."[19] However, as one historian has pointed out, "the press commonly mistook toleration of free-love viewpoints for advocacy of them."[20] And what of Samuel Putnam's ideas on the subject? The best evidence of his views on marriage and love is to be found in his own works, a number of which he gave to his ardent disciple Sharlot on February 11, the day he left Orchard Ranch to continue his lecture tour. One of these, later characterized by Sharlot as "the best Freethought novel ever written... whose every page... contains some great maxim, some fine aphorism, or some beautiful exposition of the most vital truths of Freethought,"[21] was entitled *The Golden Throne.* These passages were marked in Sharlot's personal copy:

> It is a curse to bear children in hatred. Forced motherhood is iniquitous; and a system is either wrong in itself, or has much in itself to reform, which makes it necessary or possible for children to be born except in love.... We have found that marriage has no object nor value, and should therefore have no claims in itself, except those of love. Now, when love ceases to such a degree as to make marriage

odious... it can have no further claims nor justification in itself for continuance.... The functions of motherhood shall be forever guarded by her love, and so made absolutely free. Woman is most deeply concerned in this question, and it is she who should speak for herself. If, therefore, motherhood should be free, consistent with this position, must not marriage be free?...

When I speak of love, I do not mean mere appetite nor desire, but the total expression of a man's nature, wherein his reason and conscience are exerted as well as passion and affection....

... Until a man infringes upon the rights of others, he should be held subject to his own reason and authority, and not the reason or authority of others.... With what should law concern itself? It should certainly not attempt to legislate in matters of love, for love will brook no laws but its own. Love enforces itself, is its own law, and needs no other so long as it endures.... If love is worth anything,... it must be free; for love cannot be love, unless it is free. Then why should state or society interpose their authority, when the love which alone makes a marriage sacred or tolerable has departed.

If two human beings most deeply interested and most thoroughly acquainted cannot be supposed to know or decide what is best for themselves, how can any other body or organization decide for them? Some marriages are so discordant that they are simply degrading. The highest and finest feelings are daily insulted, and perhaps truth itself is sacrificed. This must not be.

I only ask that marriage remain, as everything else should be, an open question—open to more light and truth. No arbitrary fiat should be placed upon it; but, with love and science, it may be committed to the ever living manhood and womanhood of our race....[22]

It is not known if Sharlot and Putnam carried Putnam's credo to its logical conclusion, but it is clear from Sharlot's later writing, that whether or not a physical union had taken place, a mystical, spiritual union of tremendous import, at least to Sharlot, had occurred.

Putnam left Orchard Ranch on Monday morning, February 11, for a final lecture in Prescott before he caught the train for Ash Fork and from there San Francisco and the rest of his campaign. The topic of his last lecture was "Christianity and Woman," which, as he said in his report to the *Truth Seeker,*

I found to be a very interesting and ghastly subject. The treatment of woman by christianity is one of the most terrific pages of human history. It makes the blood boil to think of the indignities that hav been poured upon the "daughters of Eve" simply because woman was the first to begin the upward path of learning and progress; while Adam was a sneak and a coward. Ever since the theologian has tried to wreak his vengeance on woman, denying her an immortal soul, declaring her to be the child of the devil and the way of hell. Kings and priests have united to outrage, disgrace, dishonour, and deny her every right and privilege. Her personality has been absolutely annihilated by the holy authority of the Christian religion, and I do not understand how woman can any longer bend her neck to the yoke.

I had a good audience, and after a campaigne where so much has been accomplished, it was a pleasure to gather our ranks once more, shake hands all round, and look forward to the broadening future. . . . I have no doubt the winter's work in Arizona will hav its summer's harvest. . . . [23]

As for Sharlot, she was left with a stack of Putnam's books inscribed to her by the author on the day of his departure, and her memories, which were to grow more poignant as time passed.

> Little room that twice from dusk till dawning held me —
> Fold close your peace around me like still wings —
> Take this shadow of the soul that rested in you —
> And will keep you long with memory's sweetest things.

> "Because I love you" — and its own excuse
> Love was and is and ever still shall be —
> Till time grow weary of the numbered years,
> Forgets their measure in eternity:
> Yet even there some dreams of you I think
> Will follow like sweet music after me. [24]

5

The Death
of
Samuel Putnam

AS LATER EVENTS WOULD DEMONSTRATE, Sharlot loved Samuel Putnam deeply and without reservation. Perhaps she hoped for a future as a partner with the great man himself, a second Annie Besant to Putnam's Charles Bradlaugh. From various passages underlined in the books Putnam gave Sharlot, it would seem that some such thought may have crossed her mind.

Life must go on, even though the master has departed, and on March 20, 1895, the *Journal-Miner* announced:

> The Prescott Free Thought Federation has secured Miss Charlotte [*sic*] M. Hall for a lecture on Sunday evening, March 24th. This talented young Arizonan should have a hearty welcome and a full house. Music—instrumental and vocal. Admission 25¢...Howey's Opera House, 7:30 P.M.

This Sunday evening lecture was Sharlot's first independent Freethought lecture; what subject she covered is not known, but it is clear from the passages she marked and underlined in Putnam's and Ingersoll's books which topics were of most concern to her. For example, Sharlot heavily underlined Ingersoll's statement: "I find in that book [the Bible] that it was a crime to eat of the tree of knowledge...as for me, give me the storm and tempest of thought and action rather than the dead calm of ignorance and faith. Punish me when and how you will, but first let me eat of the fruit of the tree of knowledge."[1] She probably thought of the contrasting situation in her own home as she read Ingersoll's ringing credo:

> I believe in the republicanism of home, in the equality of man and woman, in the equality of husband and wife, and for this I am denounced by the sentinels upon the walls of Zion. They say there must be a head to the family. I say no—equal rights for man and wife, and where there is really love there is liberty, and where the idea of authority comes in you will find that love has spread its pinions and flown forever.[2]

Sharlot may well have chosen these themes for her Sunday evening discourse. She must have been successful, for she gave two more lectures, on April 14 and April 28, 1895.[3]

Meanwhile, her mentor Samuel Putnam concluded his lecture tour of the United States. On April 24, 1895, he sailed for England where he was to spend the summer as guest of the British Secular Society in lecturing for the cause. He and Sharlot must have corresponded regularly; it is evident that she wrote to him about Mrs. Mattie A. Freeman's series of Freethought lectures which brought her to Prescott in May.[4] In a letter from Glasgow, Scotland, dated June 8, Putnam responded,

> My dear friend,
>
> Recd yours. It was a good long letter, and went to the spot like a drink of whiskey. I am glad to hear that Mrs. Freeman is with you and I hope the campaign will progress. I am delighted that you are taking hold of things, and I hope that you will never give up.... [5]

Mrs. Freeman remained in Prescott until May 28.[6] On June 6 the *Journal-Miner* announced that "Miss Sharlot Hall left for California this morning for a visit." There is a strong possibility that she had been asked to join the lecture circuit for the Freethought Federation. At any rate, while she was in southern California she visited George and Ida Richardson of Santa Paula and their children, who became her lifelong friends.[7] On June 8 the Richardsons took their guest to Ventura, where she had her first glimpse of the ocean.[8] For the prairie-born Sharlot, it was an unforgettable experience. As she recalled it later: "The day was very calm, the beach smooth, and I

Barnes & Noble, Inc.

invoice

SOLD TO:

ROGER BOWEN
528 OLIPHANT
W BRANCH, IA 52358
UNITED STATES

SHIP TO:

DR. MARGARET MAXWELL
3771 EAST EDISON STREET
TUCSON, AZ 85716
UNITED STATES

CUSTOMER SERVICE:
1451 CORAL RIDGE AVE
CORALVILLE, IA 52241

CUST NO: 9839667	ORDER NO: 14625270	Loc: 11 53 79		
QTY	DESCRIPTION	ITEM #	LIST PRICE	OUR PRICE	TOTAL
1	A Passion for Freedom: The Life of Sharlot Hall	9780816515066			

THANK YOU
FOR YOUR
ORDER

PLEASE EXCHANGE OR RETURN AT ANY BARNES & NOBLE, INC. OR B. DALTON RETAIL LOCATION OR CALL
(310)337-3337 FOR MORE INFORMATION

PLEASE NOTE: Shipping charges reflect only the portion of your order that has been shipped.

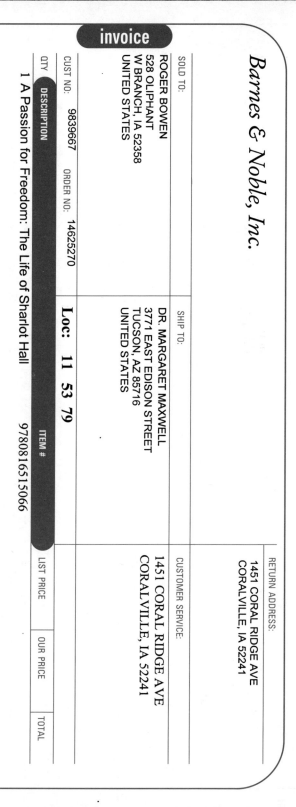

return instructions

32-15 R

PLEASE CHECK THE APPROPRIATE BOX:

○ Replace   ○ Refund   ○ Other (explain under comments)

REASON FOR RETURN (PLEASE CHECK ONE):

○ Damaged in Transit   ○ Defective   ○ Wrong Quantity

○ Wrong Merchandise Received   ○ Dissatisfied   ○ Other
                        (explain below)   (explain below)

COMMENTS: _____

easy returns

We are committed to bringing you not only the best values, but also the best service.

If for any reason you are not satisfied with your order and would like to return or exchange an item, please use the following form below.

QTY	DESCRIPTION	ITEM #	UNIT PRICE	AMOUNT
			TOTAL	

PLEASE ADD APPLICABLE POSTAGE

for your own protection we suggest you return items UPS or insured parcel post. Should the items be lost or damaged in transit, carriers require that you file the tracer or claim.

FOR RETURNS: PLEASE USE THE LABEL PROVIDED TO ADHERE TO CARTON BEING RETURNED

RETURNS

Credit My Charge:

VISA   MC   DISC
AMEX   DINERS

CC #:
Exp. Date

From:
DR. MARGARET MAXWELL
3771 EAST EDISON STREET
TUCSON, AZ 85716
UNITED STATES

020300146252700101

To:
BARNES & NOBLE 2917
1451 CORAL RIDGE AVE
CORALVILLE, IA 52241

12/2/1999   8:15:25PM

mistook the water for a wide stretch of sand like the 'dry lakes' which I had seen in New Mexico and Arizona. Not until I saw it again at Santa Barbara, with a big storm on, did I realize the ocean of the poems, songs and pictures that had formed my ideas of it as an inland child."[9]

Sharlot returned to Orchard Ranch on July 27.[10] For the rest of the year she seems to have settled into a routine of ranch work and writing. In December, however, a friend sent her a copy of a new, Los Angeles-based periodical called *Land of Sunshine,* edited by Charles F. Lummis. Lummis described the magazine in his regular column, "The Lion's Den":

> This magazine is not made with reference to those who buy their art by the yard and their reading by the pound. It could spoil twice the white paper it does, but it has no ambition to pad out cheap pages. ... It will grow as it can; but meantime it is soothed by knowing that it is already by far the most liberal dime's worth ever marketed in the West, and that in actual readable matter it gives more than some magazines of twice its size.[11]

Sharlot must have looked through *Land of Sunshine* with a great deal of interest and must have read the three short poems in that issue with an eye to whether her own poetry might fit the same pattern. In January she sent a poem to Lummis for possible publication. Lummis promptly fired it back to her, but he did not reject it out of hand; he made suggestions for improvement.[12] Sharlot returned the poem "with changes" and on September 15, Lummis accepted it for publication, paying her $1.50.[13] The publication of "Daybreak in Ventura"[14] marked the beginning of the most important literary relationship in Sharlot's life, her friendship with Charles F. Lummis.

Although none of Sharlot's letters have survived from 1896, she and Samuel Putnam undoubtedly corresponded; during the course of the year he sent her at least three books, including his own long epic poem *Prometheus.*[15] By Christmas time that year, however, the faithful followers of Samuel Putnam in the Prescott Free Thought Federation had received a terrible shock. Their mentor was dead, and under dreadful circumstances. The *Chicago Tribune,* obviously relishing the scandal, gave a full account of Putnam's death on December 11, 1896.

In a richly furnished flat of a stylish apartment hotel on St. Botolph Street [in Boston] a double tragedy was enacted this morning.... The victims... were Mary L. Collins, a pretty brunette, twenty years old, and Samuel P. Putnam....

After looking into the matter the police... found Mr. Putnam and Miss Collins were to have gone to New York this afternoon to attend a farewell banquet to be given to a number of their club who were upon the eve of their departure for the Old World. It was also found that the gas escaped from a valve at the back of the regular valve, which had been placed there for the purpose of attaching a lamp tube and it is thought that the cock of the valve was accidentally turned on when the other valve was lighted.

Putnam was a lecturer on "Free Thought" and President of the American Free Thought Federation, while Miss Collins acted as his traveling companion. They were what are commonly called socialistic exponents in its broadest meaning. The man was about 58 years of age and was deeply attached to his young companion. The girl, before taking up with Putnam, resided with her parents at Midway, Ky. She was a promising writer and lecturer on the same subjects as Putnam advocated....

... When the occupants of the house smelled the gas this morning and the door was broken in the bodies, fully dressed, lay upon the floor. That of Miss Collins was across that of Putnam. A half filled bottle of wine and another of benedictine stood on a table.

The case is one of the saddest that the police have investigated for a long time, as Miss Collins was just in the prime of life and had become prominent in her following. She was rather pretty, of good appearance, and had a handsome figure....

The article went on to state that Putnam had met Miss Collins at the National Free Thinkers' Congress in Chicago on November 13, just a month before.

... During the sessions of the Congress Miss Collins read an original poem and made an address. President Putnam was attracted to the young woman, who had a reputation as a public speaker in her own community before coming to Chicago.

The two became acquainted and the acquaintance grew. Mr. Putnam spent much of his time lecturing and he believed Miss Collins would do well to join him on his tours, speaking from the same platforms with him. He proposed the plan to her. She agreed, and since a few

days after the congress the two have been traveling and lecturing
together.... [16]

Putnam and his youthful companion had been about to go to New
York City for a farewell dinner for the British Secular leaders G. W.
Foote and Charles Watts. George E. Macdonald, a good friend, noted
sadly that instead of attending the December 15 dinner in New York
City, Putnam was cremated in Boston and his ashes interred
in Forest Hill cemetery. Of the banquet which Putnam missed,
Macdonald said,

> The Liberals, owing to Putnam's death, were not inclined to anything
> festive. It was a funeral. Young Dr. Foote, responding to a toast to
> "The American Secular Union," whose president had just died, nearly
> broke down.... I made my theme "The Departed Guest" and talked of
> Putnam, the partner and "pard," the poet, the orator, the man of
> intellectual gifts, the comrade, my friend "Sam." And I read a poem I
> had composed entitled "The Spot where He made One." I had written
> it with a feeling of resentment that some of Putnam's friends, suffer-
> ing from the timidity complex, were saying, "Let us wait for all the
> facts, before rendering judgment." The presumption of them, I
> thought, to judge Putnam!... [17]

"The life of Putnam," concluded Macdonald, "was a perpetual protest against puritanism. I never heard criticism of him on any other
score." [18]

What Sharlot thought when she learned of Putnam's death
and of his relationship with the young woman who seems to have
been so much like herself, she never said. Perhaps Putnam had made
her a similar offer while he was in Prescott. She seems to have
obliterated from her consciousness the circumstances of his death,
while for years she carried her aching longing for him like an open
wound. A letter written several years later congratulating an old
friend on her forthcoming marriage obviously refers to Putnam. Said
Sharlot:

> I've been a sort of heretic I know—it takes an awfully big lump of faith
> to believe in most that passes for love—but I'm going to tell you
> something that very few people know. For just a few months it was my
> privilege to know and love one of the grandest men that ever lived.

Perhaps our companionship was too perfect, our hopes and plans and happiness too great to be realized on earth,—at last he was taken away. But life has seemed sanctified since then. . . . [19]

Through the turning of the year into January's season of bitter cold and drifting snows that isolated the weathered brown house at Orchard Ranch, Sharlot lived in suspended shock, which at last found relief in verse:

> We crave no grief, my soul and I;
>   Each life enough of sorrow knows;
> Let none mourn darkly when we lie
>   In dreamless silence 'neath the rose.
> And you, gray wraith in cowl and gown,
>   Who "closer than a brother" pressed;
> Here on our last couch lay you down—
>   Together at the end we rest. [20]

January finally gave way to February, milder weather, and good news from the outside world. The editor of the *Journal-Miner,* who obviously admired Sharlot's talents, shared her first piece of news with his Prescott area readers: "Miss Sharlot M. Hall . . . won the first prize in the Midland Monthly's recent competition. Miss Hall seems especially fortunate in the matter of literary prizes, having won nearly a dozen in the past three years. . . . "[21] At about the same time she received word that a short article which she had written on blue-print photography as a home employment for women had been accepted by the *Delineator Magazine,* to appear in the May 1897 issue.

With the spring thaw of March Sharlot took the train to Congress on her way to visit old friends at Wickenburg, sixteen miles further. Tracks for the little narrow-gauge, wood-burning locomotive had been completed as far as Congress on January 29, the year before. The *Journal-Miner* editor had marveled at that time that it seemed "more like a dream than a reality" that one could leave Prescott at 10 A.M. and arrive at Congress at 1 P.M.,[22] certainly a breathtaking contrast to the two days in a buckboard that the journey had consumed up to this time.

After Sharlot got off the train at Congress, the buckboard took her the sixteen miles from the Congress station to Wickenburg in a couple of hours, in plenty of time to see the beauty of spring in the central Arizona desert that same day. The fields of yellow poppies that bloomed in March in those days near Wickenburg were famous. Travelers came for miles to see them during the short season that they set the hillsides ablaze with color. The lift that they gave Sharlot's spirits she put down in a happy lyric, "Poppies of Wickenburg," written March 27, 1897, which begins:

> Where Coronado's men of old
> Sought the Pecos' fabled gold
> Vainly many weary days,
> Now the land is all ablaze.
>
> Where the desert breezes stir,
> Earth, the old sun-worshipper,
> Lifts her shining chalices
> Up to tempt the priestly bees.

Mixed metaphors aside, it is likely that this poem celebrated a turning point in her will to go on with life. She submitted it to *Land of Sunshine,* and Lummis liked it well enough that he used it in the September issue of the magazine. [23]

Two other short lyrics, "The Thinker" and "The Bedesman of the Year," were written in June 1897. Sharlot must also have worked through the notes she wrote during her 1893 trip with the Davis family to the Grand Canyon at about the same time, for the first of her articles capitalizing on her experiences appeared in the September 1897 issue of *Travel Magazine.* [24] The article is illustrated with three photographs, which, since they are not otherwise identified, may be presumed to be Sharlot's own, taken on the trip.

In spite of this renewed activity Sharlot still felt Putnam's loss deeply. On June 29, 1897, she wrote the first version of a poem which she finally titled "Alone." [25] Although Sharlot left nothing specific in her writing to indicate that she ever had any spirit communication from Putnam following his death, her mystical Boblett heritage and later inclinations seem to have generated occult manifestations at times of extreme stress during her early and middle life. A cryptic quotation stands, without explanation, at the head of this poem. Perhaps this was an occult communication Sharlot felt she had received from Putnam as she mourned him to the verge of hysteria. It seems possible that the words both of the quotation and of the following poem are "Putnam's."

"Cease to mourn; thou hast thy memories—but for me Krishna decreed no friend—and though I wander all the worlds I am yet alone."

> ... What know you, though you grieve, of loneliness,
> Who count the days back—sure of smiles that were—
> And eyes that looked and loved and understood?
> Empty the arms, companioned still the soul—
> For souls once met blend all futurity
> Into that meeting. ...

Another long poem, "The Silent Leader," was written in its entirety during the night of November 19, 1897. It was published in the *Truth Seeker* to commemorate the first anniversary of Putnam's death. [26]

In the midst of a month of sub-zero weather came copies of the *Delineator* with Sharlot's articles, one in January and one in February 1898, on photography. The *Delineator* check bought Christmas cheer for all the Hall family, and the articles were renewed evidence of her ability to earn her way by her pen. In addition, recalling a story she had heard about a faithful dog who continued to guard his master and herd the sheep after the shepherd died with his flock in the San Francisco Mountains, Sharlot wrote the first version of one of her better narrative poems, "Sheep Herding," which after revision was published in *Land of Sunshine* in May 1901. Its final stanzas are:

> The collies halt, —the slow herd sways and reels,
>   Huddled in fear above a low ravine,
> Where wild with fright a herd unshepherded
>   Beats up and down—with something dark between:
>
> A narrow circle that they will not cross;
>   A thing to stop the maddest in their run—
> A guarding dog, too weak to lift his head,
>   Who licks a still hand shriveled in the sun. [27]

Sharlot Hall in 1898

Before winter had loosened its grip on Lonesome Valley the world intruded, with the February 23, 1898, *Journal-Miner* crying the destruction of the U.S. armored cruiser *Maine* in the harbor at Havana, Cuba. Although newspaper headlines told of continued tension, of more immediate interest to the Halls were their negotiations in March 1898 with the Prescott and Eastern Railroad for a railroad

right-of-way through their land, as the railroad pushed south to serve
the booming Yavapai County mines.[28] The railroad brought the world
to the Hall doorstep, to James Hall's distress; once again he was to
witness the closing in of the frontier environment that he loved, and
this time he was to seek vainly for another retreat into isolation.

In the midst of railroad-building and daily war news, Sharlot
suffered another bout of spinal trouble. For fifteen days during April
1898 she endured such agony of pain that she could not lie down or
turn her head. As she put it, she "had to sit straight up and look to
the front."[29] During this hard time she turned to what was always
the best opiate for her—reading and writing. Having time for reflection, Sharlot thought again of Samuel Putnam. On April 18, she
wrote a long poem in the rhythm and atmosphere of Coleridge's
"Kubla Khan," entitled "The Immortal."[30] the poem, which was
published in the *Truth Seeker*[31] and read at the meeting of the
Prescott Free Thought Society on December 11, 1898,[32] deals in con-
ventional terms with the nature of immortality and concludes that
in "noble deeds... may we / Build our immortality." Having finished
her public praise of the late Freethought leader, Sharlot could then
give herself up to her private grief, which found its outlet in a poem
called "A Lover in Spring," which begins:

> Come back, come back, beloved,
> Whither hast followed the star-road
> Out from my heart to the sky?[33]

Between July and December, 1898, a lengthy series of Sharlot's articles entitled "Amateur Photography" appeared in *The Delineator*.
Although none of the photographs which accompany the articles are
identified, it is probable that most of them are Sharlot's. The graphi-
cally simple explanations she wrote concerning each part of the
complex process of taking photographs in those days are extremely
interesting; they must have done much to popularize home photography as a hobby among *The Delineator's* readers.

December came, and with it the annual memorial service for
Samuel Putnam, at which Sharlot read the poem which she had
composed in pain in April. The services brought back memories;

two further poems are dated December 11, 1898, the anniversary of Putnam's death. One of them, entitled "Two Years After," begins, "Naught left, naught left of thee, my Beloved?" and concludes:

> . . . even Love, with finger laid to lip,
> Stands peering o'er the waste with tear-wet eyes
> That catch no hint of dawn or morning star. [34]

6

Charles Lummis and "Out West"

Winterbound at Orchard Ranch, Sharlot spent the first months of the twentieth century writing. She began to exploit her own experiences and personal observations of ranch life for her poetry. "The Range Rider," written February 19, 1900, is the first of her southwestern poems. It tells of a cowboy high in the chaparral country rounding up wild longhorn steers:

> Up and saddle at daybreak,
>   Into the hills with the light,
> While still on piñon and cedar
>   Linger the wings of night;
> Clatter of hoofs in the cañon,
>   Scatter of horns on the trail;
> Dim forms lost in the chaparral,
>   Fleeing like frightened quail. [1]

Charles Lummis was obviously intrigued by the young poet from the arid wastelands of Arizona. Sharlot had almost certainly paid him a visit in 1899 while on a trip she made to southern California. Lummis's impulse was always to help young artists and writers like Sharlot who were just getting started. In 1897 he had first noticed the work of a brilliant young San Francisco artist, Maynard Dixon, then working as an illustrator for the San Francisco *Overland Monthly*. When Dixon submitted some drawings and watercolors to *Land of*

Sunshine, Lummis liked his work. In a generous review in the January 1898 issue of the periodical he praised the young artist's paintings, stating that Dixon had great potential.[2] In 1900 Lummis suggested that Dixon break his newspaper routine to accompany artist Dana Bartlett on a camping-sketching trip to Arizona on commission for *Land of Sunshine.* Part of Dixon's assignment was to go to Orchard Ranch to see Lummis's Arizona contributor in her own territory.

Maynard Dixon was only one of many paying guests who stayed at Orchard Ranch with the Halls from time to time; providing room and board seems to have been one way that the Halls supplemented their meager income. His stay during the hot summer of 1900 was not long, nor did he ever return. But his brief visit to Lonesome Valley made a real impact on Dixon, both in his paintings and sketches of the area and in his meeting with the daughter of the house, Sharlot Hall.

First was the land. It had been a dry year, the third one in succession, and never before had Dixon seen (as Sharlot later described it)

> The fence posts blister in the burning sun
> And wisps of wind like hungry hunting dogs
> Sniff the dry corn that rattles and falls down
> Like dead bones gnawed and left long time ago.
> Dry bones are plenty on the water trails
> Where long before the sun comes up the dust
> Swings in the air like low-hung graying haze
> And staggering cows creep slowly in to drink—
> Hides taut and sere and hair like bleached-out grass.[3]

Then there was James Hall. "Old Man Hall," Dixon called him, noting Hall's contempt for Buffalo Bill, the "parlor cowboy," and his rambling tales of life on the old frontier when the buffalo ranged the plains and a man could do as he pleased with no neighbors just down the road. "If I knew where there was another country like that I would go to it, as old as I am," said Hall, pathetically eager to talk.[4]

Sharlot made the greatest impression on Dixon. As he said of her:

James Hall

It was at the fag end of July of the third dry year that I happened upon the "Orchard Ranch" in the Agua Fria, where Miss Hall, in a sunbonnet and working clothes greeted me—in no joking manner, made me welcome to the ranch house and begged to be excused from further immediate politenesses, as many things required her attention. And so they did. The cows must be milked, the loose stock watered, the windmill regulated, the pigs fed, the butter made, the garden (what was left of it) looked after, the chickens fed, the washing done, the dinner cooked, and a thousand and one other details cared for, and beside all this she must have time for reading and writing.

I watched and learned. It was all accomplished—all that fell to her hands to do, and it was practically the conduct of the whole ranch— but I do not yet know how it was done. . . . [5]

Dixon spent a week sketching in the Agua Fria area near Orchard Ranch. While he was there he had his first taste of an upland thunderstorm which with all its violence could be as devastating as the drought itself. As he said in a letter written to Lummis,

The country looks like hell—Dead cattle everywhere—punchers all gone out or gone to mining; all the "infallible" streams and springs gone dry; farmers on the verge of starvation. These people are about dried out, but we had a freshet down the creek 'tother day that will tide the old man's orchard over. I helped irrigate and still bear the scars of toil;—*that* was something *real*.

Miss Hall, too, is one worth knowing. In her quiet way she is a heroine.... [6]

Dixon gave an inscribed sketch of a cowboy on a running horse to Sharlot when he left. This sketch hung on her bedroom wall for years. But more important to Sharlot were the letters Dixon had written to Charles Lummis about her. The picturesque details of this "child of the wilderness's" life touched and intrigued the influential editor of *Land of Sunshine* in a way that would bring tangible benefit to Sharlot in the near future.

In November 1900, as Sharlot again mourned Samuel Putnam, she received a letter from Charles Lummis. Judging from

Sharlot Hall in her study at Orchard Ranch

Sharlot's response, Lummis must have written with understanding and encouragement. Sharlot replied:

> Dear Mr. Lummis: I don't quite know how to write—you've put my heart into my throat. Go back along your own years to the *Hardest Place*—and if a word came then you'll understand. . . .
>
> I'm glad too if you think me worth while—there's times when one word would be a hail in the night—for the truth of life as I have seen it here is a pretty big thing for bigger people than myself to handle. . . . [7]

As he had done for Maynard Dixon in 1898, Lummis was now anxious to help Sharlot along with a biographical "plug" in *Land of Sunshine*. He evidently had asked her for information about herself, for five days later Sharlot sent him an autobiographical sketch and a brief, happy letter:

> . . . I hope to pull your latch string next year for a little stay—I can't leave the folks here at home long—but I want to see you again—and I want your best doctors to see my unregenerate back—which of late gets worse faster than I like. . . .
>
> *This* is childish—but really I can't help wanting you to know . . . I have just won a fine typewriter in a short story competition[8]—not—as I know—for literary merit but for the sake of the truth I tried to make clear.
>
> Don't think I expect letters ever—I know what a busy life means—in a smaller way. And this one letter of yours is armor for the whole fight.
>
> But I thank you—and I shall never forget. [9]

By this time Sharlot's poems in *Land of Sunshine* were reaching a wide audience. In March 1901 Doubleday, Page and Company asked her to submit a collection of verse for consideration as a book. Sharlot, in the midst of gardening and bossing the ranch, was flattered but undecided. She wrote Lummis, asking his advice. Lummis evidently advised her to wait. On April 16th she responded:

> Dear Mr. Lummis:
>
> One word to thank you—I knew it all—but Mother wished so much to have your opinion.
>
> When I have a book worth your kindness I shall have done my best—and what the rest say is no matter.

For *fame*—as it goes now—I care nothing—and as little for money—except that one must eat and be clothed—and I'd rather not do either than be a tax on other people. But out here one has few needs so the waiting is easy. Believe me, I thank you for the word. . . .

Atlantic has a little prose scrap of mine to use presently—I could have thought your own hand was behind the more than kind letters they have sent me. Things sell a lot easier than they write. . . . [10]

The "little prose scrap" to which Sharlot referred with such excessive modesty must have been her charming autobiographical essay, "A Memory of Old Gentlemen," which appeared in the *Atlantic Monthly* in January 1903.

Lummis must have been impressed with his protegé's progress. A little later that year he invited her to come to California as one of the editors of *Land of Sunshine,* to take temporary charge of affairs while he made a fall business trip. In addition to Lummis, Frances Willard Munds, a Prescott woman whose activities embraced every feminist cause in the Territory, from woman's suffrage to WCTU and, eventually, to public office as the state of Arizona's first woman legislator (1914), also seems to have noticed Sharlot for the first time about now. The day before Sharlot was to leave for California, Mrs. Munds hosted a gala literary and musical entertainment in her honor at the Monday Club, Prescott's women's club, the most prestigious and most active social organization in the city. Sharlot was not a member, perhaps because she lived too far away to attend meetings regularly or because her Freethought Federation activity made her suspect among Prescott's more "respectable" women. But this afternoon, as the guest of honor, she read one of her newest poems, "The Trail of Death,"[11] and her latest short story, "The Price of the Star," just then out in *Everybody's Magazine.*[12]

With her Prescott triumph behind her, Sharlot took the train for Los Angeles and her new assignment as editor of *Land of Sunshine.* The world was beginning to open up, and Sharlot was ready to step into it. Los Angeles, *Land of Sunshine,* and Lummis were there to receive her.

Eleven years older than Sharlot Hall, Charles Fletcher Lummis was forty-two in September 1901 when Sharlot joined the *Land of Sunshine* staff. A Harvard graduate and newspaperman, Lummis first came to public notice when Harrison Gray Otis, pub-

*Charles Fletcher Lummis at the time of
his editorship of* Out West *magazine*

lisher of the *Los Angeles Times,* offered him a job as city editor of
the *Times* if he would walk across the United States from Ohio to
California and send weekly accounts of his adventures along the
way to the *Times.* Lummis left Cincinnati on September 12, 1884,
and arrived in Los Angeles, his left arm broken and in an improvised
sling, on February 1, 1885, having walked thirty to forty miles each
day across seven states and two territories.

    Lummis's continued output of books, articles, and stories in
the next eight years was punctuated by three paralytic strokes, probably brought on by overwork, and a year in Peru and Bolivia with
archaeologist Adolph F. Bandelier. He met and married Eva Douglas,
who helped care for him after his third stroke, and had four children.

    Back in Los Angeles from Peru in 1893, Lummis was asked to
take over the editorship of a struggling Los Angeles-based promotional

monthly called *Land of Sunshine*. Of all Lummis's causes, and they were many, *Land of Sunshine* (later called *Out West*) was nearest his heart and consumed most of his time and energy. In a real sense the periodical *was* Lummis; he solicited and edited contributions from prominent writers all over the United States, he wrote feature articles for almost every issue, and he took many of the photographs which illustrated the articles. Under his direction *Land of Sunshine* grew from a sunshine booster throwaway to a nationally recognized literary journal whose reputation for excellence was sustained until the termination of Lummis's editorship in 1910.

While Lummis was editor, he served as a generous mentor, father-confessor, and guide to countless aspiring young authors as well as a confidante and friend to many of the established writers of the Southwest. His Los Angeles home, El Alisal, was a mecca for California's literati; Lummis's social evenings, or "noises," as he called them, were famed for good food and good talk.

Physically, Lummis was small, weighing about 135 pounds and standing five feet seven inches. He was given to wearing green corduroy suits, a red sash, moccasins, and a wide-brimmed Stetson hat. He was an egotist and a ladies' man; in fact, as one author has put it, "until his fires banked in later years, a compulsive love life made him notorious."[13] As for his relationship with Sharlot Hall, though it seems to have been one of genuine mutual affection, it was almost certainly strictly platonic from first to last.

Sharlot's association with *Land of Sunshine* brought her into personal contact with the coterie of southern California writers who lived and worked near Lummis. Almost immediately she met Idah Meacham Strobridge, whose writings, like Sharlot's, portrayed the desert from the point of view of the first women pioneers. Sharlot also met Mary Austin and Eugene Manlove Rhodes during this period.

After Sharlot's arrival Lummis left for San Francisco, sure that *Land of Sunshine* was in good hands. His purpose in going was to see Mrs. Phoebe Apperson Hearst, wife of newspaper magnate William Randolph Hearst, in hopes that she would finance a new enlarged version of *Land of Sunshine*. After reaching an agreement with Mrs. Hearst, Lummis was back in Los Angeles on October 14, full of plans for the new magazine, which was to be called *Out West*.

A poem was needed for the first issue planned for January of the next year. Both Edwin Markham and Joaquin Miller had been contributors to the old *Land of Sunshine*; now Lummis asked them to write something for the first *Out West*. That done, he left Los Angeles on a ten-day trip through Arizona and New Mexico. But when he returned on November 1, there was no word from either Markham or Miller.

Meanwhile, Sharlot was preparing to return to Arizona. On November 12 Lummis in desperation told her that she would have to write the poem he needed, and that she must come up with it before she went home.[14] Not until November 24 did Sharlot begin her task. She was scheduled to leave for Prescott the next evening, and the poem Lummis needed for his new periodical was still not ready. With inspiration born of desperation she began to write.

> When the world of waters was parted by the
>   stroke of a mighty rod,
> Her eyes were first of the lands of earth to look
>   on the face of God;
> The white mists robed and throned her, and the
>   sun in his orbit wide
> Bent down from his ultimate pathway and
>   claimed her his chosen bride;
> And he who had formed and dowered her with
>   the dower of a royal queen,
> Decreed her the strength of mighty hills, the
>   peace of the plains between;
> The silence of utmost desert, and cañons, rifted
>   and riven,
> And the music of wide-flung forests where
>   strong winds shout to heaven.

Then high and apart he set her and bade the
 gray seas guard,
And the lean sands clutching her garments' hem
 keep stern and solemn ward.
What dreams she knew as she waited! What
 strange keels touched her shore!
And feet went into the stillness and returned to
 the sea no more.
They passed through her dream like shadows—
 till she woke one pregnant morn
And watched Magellan's white-winged ships
 swing round the ice-bound Horn;
She thrilled to their masterful presage, those
 dauntless sails from afar,
And laughed as she leaned to the ocean till her
 face shone out like a star.

And men who toiled in the drudging hives of a
 world as flat as a floor
Thrilled in their souls to her laughter and turned
 with hand to the door;
And creeds as hoary as Adam, and feuds as old
 as Cain,
Fell deaf on the ear that harkened and caught
 that far refrain;
Into dungeons by light forgotten, and prisons of
 grim despair,
Hope came with the pale reflection of the star
 on the swooning air;
And the old, hedged, human whirlpool, with its
 seething misery,
Broke bound, as a pent-up river breaks through
 to the healing sea.

Calling, calling, calling; resistless, imperative,
    strong;
Soldier and priest and dreamer—she drew them,
    a mighty throng;
The unmapped seas took tribute of many a
    dauntless band,
And many a brave hope measured but bleaching
    bones in the sand;
Yet for one that fell a hundred sprang out to
    fill his place;
For death at her call was sweeter than life in a
    tamer race.
Sinew and bone she drew them; steel-thewed—
    and the weaklings shrank;—
Grim-wrought of granite and iron were the men
    of her foremost rank.

Stern as the land before them, and strong as the
    waters crossed—
Men who had looked on the face of defeat nor
    counted the battle lost;—
Uncrowned rulers and statesmen, shaping their
    daily need
To the law of brother with brother till the world
    stood by to heed;
The sills of a greater empire they hewed and
    hammered and turned,
And the torch of a larger freedom from their
    blazing hill tops burned;—
Till the old ideals that had led them grew dim
    as a childhood's dream,
And Caste went down in the balance, and Man-
    hood stood supreme.

The wanderers of earth turned to her, outcast of
    the older lands—
With a promise and hope in their pleading, and
    she reached them pitying hands;
And she cried to the Old World cities that drowse
    by the Eastern main:
"Send me your weary, house-worn broods, and
    I'll send you Men again!
Lo, here in my wind-swept reaches, by my mar-
    shalled peaks of snow,
Is room for a larger reaping than your o'er-tilled
    fields can grow;
Seed of the Man—Seed springing to stature and
    strength in my sun—
Free, with a limitless freedom no battles of men
    have won."

For men, like the grain of the cornfields, grow
    small in the huddled crowd;
And weak for the breadth of spaces where a soul
    may speak aloud;
For hills like stairways to heaven, shaming the
    level track—
And sick with the clang of pavements, and the
    marts of the trafficking pack:—
Greatness is born of greatness, and breadth of a
    breadth profound;
The old Antaean fable of strength renewed from
    the ground
Was a human truth for the ages—since the hour
    of the Eden-birth,
That man among men was strongest who stood
    with his feet on the earth.

The next morning she handed her host a sheaf of hastily pencilled manuscript. Lummis was ecstatic; he noted that night in his diary "Sharlot Hall me traie poem magnifica para 1st OUT WEST!"[15]

Sharlot went out on the train at six that evening, having been in Los Angeles for two months. She left behind her a host of new friends and literary associates, and through the poem "Out West" she had established her reputation. Maynard Dixon painted a full-page illustration for the poem; Lummis issued the painting and the poem as a broadside on heavy cardboard which was sent all over the United States as an announcement of the change in the magazine's name.[16] What Lummis thought of the poem he stated in his editorial column, "From the Lion's Den":

> The Lion doesn't know much; but he thinks he knows the difference between a Poem and a Fritter. If not, it is his own fault, not Heaven's; for he was suckled on Homer and the Hebrew seers, and bred up on Chaucer and Milton and Shakespeare and chastened by reading, for the last seven years, an average of over 300 "poems" a month. But if he does, the noble stanzas which open this number (page one) are of a rare sort. Our Joaquin [Miller] ought to have written their like—but has not since the "Ship in the Desert." Kipling used to—and perhaps still can. But neither did—nor either has, in half his productive period. It was left for a little, round ranchwoman who never has been outside Arizona six months in all since she was a child; who never had "schooling" or "social advantages," who has never had a teacher more "up" in pedagogy and modern hysterics than God Almighty and the Illimitable Spaces; a backwoods girl who can still blush at a little compliment and turn white at a big one; a girl who milks cows and rides broncos ride-side-out, and is an Influence Unseeking in a frontier community, a Means of Grace to the amelioration of unlicked cubs from the metropolis who cross her quiet orbit—it was left to her to do this Imminent Thing.
>
> The Lion is quite content to pin his judgment to this poem. The armchair technicians can pick technical flaws in it—and so can he. But if it is not, in breadth and depth and every other creature that deals with the Long Count, a greater poem than any of them are writing who have had every chance save one to surpass this girl of the wilderness—why, he can endure being laughed at. And not only is this the sort of thing he expects of the frontier when it shall come into its own—the sort of thing this magazine is here to foster and give voice to—the precise reason why this Unadvantaged Young Person could write, is the same reason that decided the choice of name for "Out West."[17]

Not only did Sharlot's poem hold a featured place in the first number of *Out West,* but the same issue included her fifteen-page, illustrated article entitled "Arizona," chiefly about Prescott and the mining area around the city.[18] Furthermore, beginning with this issue, her name was added to the masthead of the publication as a staff member, joining such luminaries of the day as David Starr Jordan, Ina Coolbrith, George Parker Winship, and Frederick Webb Hodge.

Sharlot returned to Prescott in triumph. Her Prescott sponsor Mrs. Munds insisted that she recite her poem for the august members of the Monday Club the same week she got back. As far as Prescott was concerned, Sharlot had arrived.

7

The Quest for Arizona's Past

TAKING THEIR CUE from Lummis's praise in the January 1902 *Out West,* journalists all over the United States began to comment on Sharlot's verse and her colorful life as an Arizona ranch woman. The *San Francisco Examiner* gave her a spread on February 16, 1902, and the *New Orleans Daily Picayune* proclaimed, "A Western poet; Sharlot M. Hall and her life on the frontier; some of her verses have met with a widespread success—compared to Joaquin Miller."[1] J. C. Martin, editor of the *Journal-Miner,* was hardly likely to let himself be outdone; he declared that "her poems of the desert have... been received as the most remarkable verse that has come out of the west since Joaquin Miller.... Her stories of pioneer Arizona touch the finer, stronger side so little known beyond the hearts of those who have lived it and critics regard them as promising great things in the western literature of the future...."[2]

Sharlot wrote the first of her dialect story-poems in April 1902—"The Hash Wrastler," a story of a camp cook who gave his own life to save three cowpunchers who were sick with smallpox. In the last stanza he himself has the disease and is delirious:

> "Th' boys is comin'!" he says, quite wild; "An'
>   them beans ain't seasoned right—
> An' Jim'll kick at th' bread, an' say th' coffee's
>   a holy fright.
> You tell 'em"—he fingered th' kiverlid, an' his
>   words come choked an' thin—
> "Reddy jist 't th' minnit, boys. Grub pi-le!
>   Fa-all in! Fa-a-ll in!"[3]

During 1902 Sharlot developed a deep interest in preserving Arizona history by recording the experiences of the Territory's pioneers. While she was in Phoenix in June, Charles Poston died. Poston, called the father of Arizona because of his influence in lobbying for the bill which brought Arizona into being as a territory in 1863, had lived neglected and alone in a filthy, two-room adobe house in downtown Phoenix.[4] After Sharlot heard the news of Poston's death, she hurried over to his unlocked house and made herself at home. If the account of Poston's death in the *Tucson Citizen* is to be trusted,[5] the dirt-floored shack was a veritable rat's nest, with dirty clothing and newspapers strewn in untidy heaps on the floor, and feathers from a torn pillow mixed with the rest of the debris. Sharlot hastily pencilled some notes: "Col. Poston's effects—pkg old photos—by Brady—of Washington—Mostly of Senators and public men at date of Arizona's admission—valuable as historical data. Nearly all well known men—Seward—Sumner...." Perhaps these notes were meant as the basis for a future article, as was, possibly, Poston's private diary, found among Sharlot's effects after her death. It bears a note in her hand: "Charles Poston died in abject poverty in his house in Phoenix."

In July word came to Sharlot that one of her oldest friends, "Uncle" Dick Thomas, who lived about a mile and a half from the Halls on a ranch on the Agua Fria River, had fallen and injured himself. Uncle Dick and Aunt Nell had been near neighbors and close friends ever since the Hall family had been in Arizona. Childless themselves, they had been fond of the young Sharlot and Ted Hall; one of Sharlot's pleasant memories of her early years on lower Lynx Creek was Mrs. Thomas's pies and Uncle Dick's slipping Ted and her a big piece fresh from the oven on their way home from school.

Uncle Dick clung to life for a week and a half after Sharlot arrived at the Thomas ranch to help nurse him. Sharlot had time to think of some of the pioneers of Arizona who had died within the last year or so, some, like Charles Poston, who had been shapers of Arizona's destiny, and some, like the old man who lay dying on the bed beside her, who had lived simple lives, no less heroic for being uneventful. She vowed to do what she could to record the memories of old settlers like Uncle Dick who were too unlettered to set them down themselves.

As Sharlot watched the old man suffering in his last delirium, she pondered life and death and wrote "The Compact," one of her most universally appealing poems:

> O Life, let us make compact here, as men who set
> 　a bond between them;
> 　. 　. 　. 　. 　. 　. 　. 　. 　. 　. 　. 　. 　.
> When that stern call no mortal may gainsay rings
> 　in my ears,
> Do thou make generous haste—nor grudge my
> 　going—nor cling doggedly
> Till flesh and soul are riven with mighty pain, or
> 　worn with slow decay;
> But, as thou love me—as I have been true to thee
> 　and to thy service—
> Give me swift release, and lift our love up as a
> 　lifted torch to light my going.
> 　. 　. 　. 　. 　. 　. 　. 　. 　. 　. 　. 　. 　.
> Till from beyond those farthest heights of all my
> 　cheer rings down to meet your parting cheer—
> As some path seeker on untrodden peaks shouts
> 　backward to his fellows and goes on. [6]

The Arizona Federation of Women's Clubs held its first annual statewide conference in November 1902. Prescott was chosen as the meeting place. Although not at that time a member of any women's club, Sharlot was asked to speak at the conference. She addressed the morning session on Thursday, November 20, speaking on "A Story of Arizona Life." In addition, she recited several of her poems at an entertainment given for the delegates that same evening. That some of Arizona's influential women had begun to admire and respect Sharlot is obvious. These women were to support her on more than one occasion in the future when she needed substantial backing to achieve her goals.

During the spring of 1903 Adeline Hall, who had not been well for many years, suffered from heart trouble. Sharlot, alarmed for her mother's well-being, stayed close to the ranch to relieve her as much as she could. She worked only at odd intervals on her writing until May, when in a sudden burst of inspiration she finished off two poems which she had begun some time before, "Medusa to Perseus" and "Santa Fe Trail."

Sharlot's mother continued unwell that summer. Evidently her heart trouble was compounded by further misery. On September 13, 1903, she was admitted to Mercy Hospital in Prescott, suffering from an abscess on her neck. Sharlot was alarmed. She accompanied her mother to Prescott and stayed with her at the hospital for the entire month that she was confined, until her discharge on October 12.

What the men did on the ranch in Sharlot and Adeline's absence is hard to say, but it may be inferred that they did not overexert themselves. Sharlot's brother Ted, twenty-nine years old and still working as a cowboy and general handyman at home on the ranch, came into town on September 16, presumably to visit his mother in the hospital. The *Journal-Miner* editor thought there was another reason, however: "Ed V. Hall was in Prescott last evening for the purpose of letting the Indians of the Zuni Tribe [a men's fraternal organization] take his scalp. From the ominous sounds that were heard in the neighborhood of Odd Fellows Hall he must have fallen into the hands of the scouts."[7]

Sharlot had to roll up her sleeves and tackle domestic chaos when she and her mother finally got back to the ranch. It was two weeks before she could write Charles Lummis, even though she had a poem she wanted to send him.

> Dear Friend:
>
> Only to tell you that mother is out of danger at last and we are back on the ranch where I am working about such hours as you usually keep [Lummis made it a strict rule never to work more than twenty hours a day].
>
> The enclosed verses were finished just as we were going to the hospital.... If you don't want the poem send it back....[8]

The "enclosed verses" were the poem "The Eagle of Sacramento," actually finished May 31, considerably before Mrs. Hall went to the hospital. As for keeping the poem, this occasion was one of the few times that Lummis gave Sharlot a flat rejection. The poem gives a highly romantic version of the battle of Sacramento, fought on

February 28, 1847, during the Mexican-American War. Lummis told Sharlot:

> From a rhetorical point of view they are [acceptable] but from an ethical I cannot stand for them. There has been enough hate fanned on both sides in that contemptible Mexican War, the effects of which are not only visible today but are among the strong reasons why Arizona is not admitted to Statehood...the Mexican War was unjust, disgraceful, and atrocious. You will find in many contemporary histories an equally valiant account of the storming of Chapultepec — where, as a matter of history, half of the American army did manage to lick the schoolboy cadets of the Military Academy.... [9]

To Sharlot's credit, she accepted the criticism gracefully, although she needed three months to come around to it. She finally wrote to Lummis, acknowledging that "the verses were a bit of bad morals on my part — for though I don't *know* all there is about it I've always regarded that war as a sort of government free-booting expedition." [10]

*Adeline Hall in the kitchen at Orchard
Ranch (Sharlot Hall's photograph)*

Meanwhile, Arizona's club women had not forgotten Sharlot. It is evident that her speech at the meeting of the Arizona Federation the year before had been impressive. By the time of the second Federation meeting in November 1903, she had been asked to chair the Federation's department of history of Arizona, a position which she held until 1914.

Spring 1904 was a bad time for northern Arizona ranchers as another year of relentless drought settled in, stunting crops and killing livestock. When Lummis wrote Sharlot urging her to move her whole family to Los Angeles and join the *Out West* staff as a paid editor, the offer could hardly have come at a more propitious time. When he added that he had found a fine lot near El Alisal with a small house, adequate for two or three people, and a good stand of trees on it, at a "cheap figure,"[11] Sharlot was more than tempted, despite the fact that she could not leave the ranch at the moment to inspect the property.

All through the long, hot, dry summer Sharlot suffered agonies with her back. At length, on September 4, 1904, "tired beyond telling and miserable in health," Sharlot wrote Lummis to let him know that she and her mother would be coming in a week or so to California.[12] Sharlot had long wanted her mother to meet Lummis, and, with the possibility of a move to California, this seemed like a good time. They arrived in Los Angeles on September 16, spent a good part of the day with Lummis and his family at El Alisal, and then left for Ventura, where they visited Sharlot's friends George and Ida Richardson.

Sharlot and her mother remained in Ventura until September 29. The rest from ranch duties had done her mother good, but evidently Sharlot's problems were more serious. Concerned about Sharlot's health, Lummis took her to see his friend Dr. James H. McBride, a Los Angeles physician. Although McBride was not able entirely to correct the problem, Sharlot said later that he was "a truly great physician . . . who gave me a start toward recovery."[13]

A week later, on October 10, Sharlot and her mother took the evening train for Prescott, but not before Sharlot and Lummis had a serious talk. Sharlot's mother had not been happy in California; perhaps her feelings were the major factor in Sharlot's decision not to make a permanent move to Los Angeles. There is a sense of regret, however, in her brief note to Lummis written on her return to Arizona: "I feel as if a year lay between our going and return—a year made beautiful and inspiring by your friendship...."[14]

Sharlot did not spend much time at Orchard Ranch following her return from Los Angeles. By the first of November she was back in Prescott. At a meeting of the Monday Club she was elected the Club's official representative to attend the Arizona Federation of Women's Clubs meeting in Bisbee, November 16 through 18, 1904. The following Saturday, November 12, she set off for Bisbee so that she would have some time before the meetings started to collect data for further historical research.

While Sharlot was in Bisbee she met Mrs. W. F. Nichols, then president of the Phoenix Woman's Club and wife of the secretary of the Arizona Territory. Mrs. Nichols was charmed by Sharlot, so much so that she invited her to visit her in Phoenix at the end of the conference. The two women returned to Phoenix on Monday, November 21; Sharlot spent the next week with the Nichols family.

Judge Nichols, as he came to be called later, and Mrs. Nichols were to be Sharlot's lifelong friends. More importantly, Mrs. Nichols' daughter, Alice Olivia Butterfield, whom Sharlot met for the first time during this visit, was to be not only a friend but in years to come a stay against emotional disaster. Eight years younger than Sharlot, Alice Butterfield (later Hewins) was a graduate of Stanford University. When Sharlot met her, she was an instructor at the fledgling University of Arizona in Tucson, teaching physical culture and history and serving as assistant librarian.

Sharlot returned to Prescott the following Monday. The bonds of friendship she had formed were to stand her in good stead when she needed help in later years. Her decision to stay in Arizona and her growing interest in the Territory's living pioneers set the direction of her lifelong commitment to the preservation of Arizona history.

8

Triumph
and
Turmoil

SHARLOT PASSED THE WET, SNOWY WINTER of 1904–1905 in work
and writing at Orchard Ranch. On February 8, 1905, she entered a
homestead claim in her own name for 160 acres of land immediately
to the northeast of the 160-acre homestead which James K. Hall had
proved in 1896.[1] It is evident that she was still struggling with her
memories of Putnam, now dead more than eight years. She went back
at the end of January to finish a fragment of verse she had started long
before, "A Truce With Dead Souls."[2] That her "Truce" was not long
in being broken is evidenced by another poem, never published, "The
Passer," which she wrote on May 8. It reads in part:

> How could I know that I would miss
> A step across the floor?
> How could I know my eyes would seek
> A face there at the door?
> Can life catch up new rhythms so,
> Between the dusk and dawn,
> That still our hearts must sing the tune
> When all the theme is gone?[3]

Between February 1 and 3 Sharlot wrote "The Mercy of Nah-né,"
which has been singled out as one of the best of her ballads. It is
a romanticized account of how Felix Knox, a gambler, was killed
while holding off a party of bloodthirsty Apaches to give his family
time to escape.

> Ay! That was Knox! When the cowboys came
>   On that day-old trail of the renegade,
> Nah-né the butcher, the merciless,
>   This was the tribute the chief had paid
> To the fearless dead. No scarring fire—
>   No mangling knife—but across the face
> His own rich blanket drawn smooth and straight,
>   Stoned and weighted to keep its place. [4]

Heavy rains in January and February all over Arizona meant an unusually beautiful spring in the southern Arizona deserts. Sharlot gathered her camera and note pad and went south to see and write about it; she described it in her lyrical poem "When Spring Comes to the Desert."[5] Several short stories of rather indifferent merit must have been written about this time as well; the *Ladies' Home Journal* took her brief story "The Love That Endures," about a woman, old before her time and isolated on a desert ranch, who nobly sacrifices her life to the care of her half-witted husband.[6]

Although in real life Sharlot felt that Mexicans were far from romantic (indeed, along with most Arizona "Anglos" of that day she regarded them with ill-concealed contempt), she wrote twice that spring of the stereotypical Mexican girl with the "laughing eyes" and hand like a "gentle, brown-winged bird," the "soft guitar and low-hung moon," and the death that inevitably lay ahead for her, since she had been singled out for love by a white American male. "Cactus and Rose"[7] was written on January 23, 1905. A short story on the same theme, "Santa Teresita of the Shoe," probably followed the poem rather quickly. The story tells of an American engineer who falls in love with a Mexican girl, Teresita. Teresita is killed when her vengeful Mexican lover blows up the American engineer's railroad bridge. Lummis liked this trite bit of melodrama well enough to print it in the August issue of *Out West*;[8] not so "Cactus and Rose," which was never printed outside Sharlot's own book, *Cactus and Pine*.

On June 12, 1905, Lummis noted in his diary, "Sharlot M. Hall viene 8, para trabaja on Out West." Although none of Lummis's correspondence with Sharlot during this period has survived, it is not hard to guess what prompted Lummis to bring her to Los Angeles at this time. In April the Los Angeles Public Library Board had asked him to take the position of Los Angeles City Librarian. Lummis, despite his capacity for twenty-hour working days, must have realized that a full schedule as editor of *Out West* together with a full schedule as librarian of the Los Angeles Public Library was more than even he could handle. In order to ease the load, he promoted his assistant editor, Charles Amadon Moody, to joint editorship with him. Sharlot was brought in as assistant editor, with the understanding that she was to move to Los Angeles permanently. [9]

Had Lummis been able to foresee the result of his decision to accept the Los Angeles Public Library Board's offer, he might well have hesitated. For the capable incumbent, Mary Jones, refused to step aside in favor of her successor; she decided to fight for her job. The battle which ensued made headlines in the *Los Angeles Times* almost every day for the next two months. [10] When the last salvo had been fired, although Lummis and the Library Board won the day, the victory cost Lummis more than he could possibly have envisioned. In five years both his career as a library director and his personal life were to come crashing down about him, the former on account of the enemies he made during the library fight and the latter because of the man he trusted to carry on the editorship of *Out West*, Charles Amadon Moody.

In the meantime, Lummis was determined to launch his new assistant editor, Sharlot Hall, properly before he took over his duties as city librarian. Sharlot could not have been in town more than a day or so before a reporter from the *Los Angeles Times* was called to El Alisal to interview her. A two-column biographical article together with a two-column-width photograph of the "well-known poet and writer" appeared in the *Times* the next Sunday.

While Sharlot was still at Lummis's home, Professor Thomas D. Seymour of Yale University, president of the American Institute of Archaeology, came to El Alisal. Two years earlier, in November 1903, Lummis had founded the Southwest Society as a branch of the Archaeological Institute of America. The group was an active one, specializing in the collecting and recording of folksongs and the collecting of artifacts of the Southwest with the idea of establishing an archaeological museum in Los Angeles. Whether Lummis had thoughts at that moment of involving the Southwest Society in his new library venture it is hard to say, but it seems almost more than a

coincidence that the executive committee of the Society was invited
to meet with the president of the parent organization two days after
the official announcement of Lummis's new position.

A comment in Sharlot's journal for this period gives a clue as
to the tension which must have existed in the Lummis household
because of the library battle. As she had done with others of
Lummis's literary circle, Sharlot observed Professor Seymour closely
and noted her impressions of him in her journal: "He is a tall, fine
looking man with white hair and the kindliest face and gentle consideration of manner that is delightful. His clear blue eyes had a *good*
look and there was an atmosphere of harmony all about him. It would
not be easy to think of him buried behind a newspaper at breakfast
and snarling out criticisms of the food—as seems to be the accepted
literary way...."[11] Since Sharlot's opportunities to observe literary
men at breakfast had been limited to those she had met at Lummis's
house, she must have been referring in her last sentence to her host,
who, behind his free and easy public manner, was evidently quite
another man in the bosom of his own family. Sharlot and Eva had
become close friends by this time; some of the things Eva may have
told Sharlot, together with what she could observe for herself, were
undoubtedly enough to convince her that her hero had clay feet, even
aside from what she may have thought of his stance regarding the
embattled librarian, Mary Jones.

Curiously enough, though opposition to Lummis as city librarian was led by feminist members of the Friday Morning Club, the
largest and most prestigious women's club in Los Angeles, Lummis
seems to have maintained his friendship with a number of literary
women. Even Charlotte Perkins Gilman, at that moment herself a
hotly controversial figure in the Los Angeles area, was a guest at one
of Lummis's Sunday evening dinners. Mrs. Gilman was a radical
feminist, a revolutionary even among the feminists of her day. Unlike
such women as Susan B. Anthony, who chiefly devoted their efforts
to women's suffrage, Mrs. Gilman struck at the very foundation of
society, the family, believing that woman's traditional position as
mother and housewife kept her from realizing her full potential as a
human being. Her answer to the problem was to abolish the home.
She advocated the establishment of community centers for cooking,
cleaning, and the care of children that would free women to be

productive members of society by putting these admittedly necessary duties in the hands of "professionals."[12]

The two Charlottes, Sharlot and Charlotte, found much in common in their philosophy and experience. Sharlot paid Charlotte Gilman the supreme compliment of comparing her favorably with Samuel Putnam, stating, "I count her the most interesting woman I have ever known and probably the greatest intellect, unless I except Putnam—who would have revelled in a play of wit with her—and I don't think he would have had anything to his credit."[13]

Reminded once again of Samuel Putnam, then dead for more than eight years, Sharlot wrote "The Long Quest," which seems to be a sort of farewell to a ghost and a plea that she be left alone to go on with her own destiny. It ends, "I seek thee, seek thee—call to thee 'God speed!' / Go thou—nor wait—sure that somewhere I come."[14]

Certainly Sharlot had begun to see that a rich, full life lay before her. Her editorial work on *Out West* brought her into frequent contact that summer with the magazine's charming and erudite editor Charles Amadon Moody and other literary figures of the Southwest. In addition, because she was living in the same house with Charles Lummis she perforce became interested and involved in the projects that interested him.

Charles Lummis had plunged himself not only into the building up of the Los Angeles Public Library that August, but also into another major project. Lummis as president of the Southwest Society had determined to build a fine museum for the relics which the Society was collecting, and to build it that year. Lummis also prodded the world in general and the Southwest Society in particular to collect native folksongs of the Southwest, feeling that these were just as much archeology as the "digs" among the Indian ruins that the Society sponsored. Lummis had been badgering his Mexican friends in Los Angeles for years to record songs and stories on his Edison recording machine. To record Mexican folksongs was one thing, but to transcribe them in musical notation and to arrange accompaniments so that they could be sung and played by others was beyond Lummis. The summer before, he had called on Arthur Farwell of Newton, Massachusetts, a talented musician and composer, to arrange some of them. This summer he brought Farwell out to Los Angeles with his mother to do further work with the Mexican folk music. Arthur and Sharlot became good friends during the course of that summer; Farwell later set one of her poems to music, and it was through this contact that Sharlot in her turn became interested in the folk songs of Arizona sheepherders.

Sharlot enjoyed her friendship with Farwell. Judging from a comment in her journal, however, things began to go sour by the end of the summer. Sharlot wrote:

> He is a fine looking fellow, rather tall and broad shouldered and well built, with a very pleasant face and "soulful" gray eyes. I am no judge of his music, which is said to be very promising, and I am undecided whether the man himself is all pose or genuinely pleasant, as he sometimes seems to be. I liked him at first much better than the average of the men I meet here, mostly men who pose as of the "artistic temperament," but if some of the things I hear about him are true he is merely one more of the old brand. [15]

Just what Sharlot meant by that comment is hard to tell. It is curious that, although her original arrangement with Lummis had evidently been that she would come to Los Angeles on a permanent basis, she rather precipitously left, on October 2, 1905. Things were apparently going along well at home in Arizona in her absence: because the summer rains had been ample, the Orchard Ranch peach crop was so abundant that her father was feeding the fruit to his hogs. Perhaps something had gone wrong at El Alisal that upset Sharlot so badly that she decided to leave. Whatever the problem may have been, Sharlot did not record it. Lummis's comment in his private diary was restricted to "Voy Santa Fe Station y despido Farwells & Sharlot," [16] for the Farwells returned to their Massachusetts home on the same train that carried Sharlot back to Arizona. Sharlot's journal of her Los Angeles experience ends rather cryptically:

> A long course of severe training has made it practically impossible for me to take anyone at his "face value"—sometimes I regret that my bump of trustfulness was so early amputated or turned into a canyon, but on the whole I am glad. I find it vastly more comfortable to trust no one, but be kind to all and give them as much courtesy and ontuard [sic] friendliness as may be—while keeping them inwardly so far distant that nothing they do can hurt me much. A selfish thing perhaps, or would be if I did not give lavishly of kindness, but to live at all one must have some wall between one's heart and the world, and it is better to be a little lonely behind the wall than to stand the target of

many arrows outside. In truth I have been vastly better able to help people and make things pleasant for them than would have been possible had I cared much about the whole matter myself. [17]

Whatever may have triggered Sharlot's decision to leave Los Angeles, she did not mean to sever her professional connections with *Out West* and Lummis. After a couple of weeks at home, she set off again on her Arizona travels, this time in company with Charles Amadon Moody. The trip had been decided upon during the summer in conjunction with planning for a special Arizona issue of *Out West* scheduled for January 1906. The entire issue was planned to support the fight against the Hamilton Bill in Congress, a measure which proposed that Arizona and New Mexico come into the Union as a single state.

The idea of joint statehood for Arizona and New Mexico had been broached in Congress as early as 1902. Although it had been consistently opposed by citizens of Arizona and New Mexico, its congressional supporters backed the idea, principally because if the two territories were admitted as two states, it would upset the balance of eastern power in the Senate, with four rather than two new western senators being added. The congressional battle was waged, with more or less intensity, for the next decade before it was finally settled in 1912 with the admission of Arizona and New Mexico as separate states. It was an open question in 1905, however, though feelings in Arizona ran high in opposition to the idea.

Lummis, who was on most issues the champion of the underdog, had come out three years before in his "Lion's Den" column opposing joint statehood. [18] Editor Moody came to Arizona to see for himself what was going on. Sharlot accompanied him part of the way to introduce him, as he put it, to "hundreds of all men of all classes," [19] and, for her own purposes, to gather material for the important survey article on Arizona which she had assigned herself to write on behalf of the cause.

The main point of Sharlot's proposed article was to prove that though Arizona might be in the West, it was not Wild. After brief stops in Phoenix and Tucson, Moody and Sharlot headed for the Bisbee headquarters of the Copper Queen Mining Company and home of its millionaire owner, James Douglas. Douglas went out of his way to be hospitable to the two journalists and to be certain that they were fully impressed by the magnitude and sophistication of his mining operations at Bisbee and Douglas. He also showed them through his palatial home and the company-built Copper Queen Hotel.

Following her Bisbee and Douglas visits, Sharlot left Moody and returned to Phoenix, where she attended the third annual Arizona Federation of Women's Clubs meeting from November 22 to 24, 1905. She presented a paper, "The Makers of Arizona," which according to the *Phoenix Gazette* was one of the principal speeches at the convention.

Undeterred by heavy rains that had caused flooding in the Salt and Gila river valleys near Phoenix, Sharlot left Phoenix as soon as the convention was over, still on the trail of material for the Arizona article which she intended to write. Her next stop was the Tonto (later Roosevelt) Dam site. Here, after a hair-raising stage-coach trip over the newly built wagon road (the Apache trail) between Mesa and the dam site, she gathered material for a separate article on the new dam. She stayed long enough to inspect the temporary coffer dams which had been built up the Tonto River to divert some of the water so that the dam itself could be built. On Tuesday, a couple of days later, she went on to Globe, forty-three miles distant, where she toured the copper mines.

The weather changed suddenly by the time Sharlot traveled to northern Arizona for the last leg of her research trip. Snow covered the ground and snow was in the air as she reached Flagstaff, where Lummis had given her an introduction to Michael G. Riordan, owner of the Arizona Lumber Company. Because Sharlot was ill with a cold, she did not enjoy her visit as much as she might have otherwise. Nonetheless, she had come to Flagstaff to tour the lumber camp and tour she did, tramping through snow-covered forests and inspecting the saw mill, largest in the West, taking notes as she went. By the time she took the train for Prescott on December 8, she was feeling so ill that she feared she was coming down with pneumonia.

Sharlot was not so ill, however, that she could not read the *Arizona Republican* newspaper that she had carried onto the train with her. There, leaping out at her, were headlines telling of President Roosevelt's message to Congress on December 5, 1905.

JOINT STATEHOOD IS ORDERED
THE PRESIDENT DIRECTS ANNEXATION OF ARIZONA
CRACK OF THE WHIP

As she read the text of the President's message, recommending that Indian Territory and Oklahoma be admitted as one state and that New Mexico and Arizona be admitted as one state, and that these admissions be carried out immediately, she became more and more indignant. How could the President give such a directive in the face of solid opposition from both Arizona and New Mexico citizens?

It was a cold, tedious train ride from Flagstaff to Ash Fork, where Sharlot transferred to the Prescott and Arizona Central line. Getting off finally at the Verde station north of Point of Rocks near Prescott, she transferred once again to the Southern Pacific railroad line that ran through the Hall property. It was ten o'clock when she reached home. Her mother, frightened to see how ill Sharlot appeared to be, wanted to put her right to bed. But Sharlot was still excited. "Make a fire in the sitting room for me, Mother," she said, "and the rest of you go on to bed and leave me alone. I've got a poem to write before I turn in."

The opening lines had been singing through her head for hours. Her pencil moved with quick strokes that almost stabbed the brown paper. Line after line poured from her scornful indignation:

No beggar she in the mighty hall where her bay-crowned sisters wait;
No empty-handed pleader for the right of a freeborn state;
No child, with a child's insistence, demanding a gilded toy;
But a fair-browed, queenly woman, strong to create or destroy.
Wise for the need of the sons she has bred in the school where weaklings
     fail;
Where cunning is less than manhood, and deeds, not words avail;
With the high, unswerving purpose that measures and overcomes;
And the faith in the Farthest Vision that builded her hard-won homes.

Link her, in the clean-proved fitness, in her right to stand alone—
Secure for whatever future in the strength that her past has won—
Link her, in her morning beauty, with another, however fair?
And open your jealous portal and bid her enter there
With shackles on wrist and ankle and dust on her stately head,
And her proud eyes dim with weeping? No! Bar your doors instead
And seal them fast forever! But let her go her way—
Uncrowned, if you will, but unshackled, to wait for a larger day.

Ay! Let her go barehanded; bound by no grudging gift;
Back to her own free spaces where her rock-ribbed mountains lift
Their walls like a sheltering fortress; back to her house and blood;
And we of her blood will go our way and reckon your judgment good.
We will wait outside your sullen door till the stars that ye wear grow dim
As the pale dawn-stars that swim and fade o'er our mighty Cañon's rim;
We will lift no hand for the bays ye wear, nor covet your robes of state—
But Ah! By the skies above us all we will shame ye while we wait!

We will make ye the mould of an empire here in the land ye scorn;
While ye drowse and dream in your well-housed ease that States at your nod
　　　are born.
Ye have blotted your own beginnings, and taught your sons to forget
That ye did not spring fat-fed and old from the powers that bear and beget;
But the while ye follow your smooth-made roads to a fireside safe of fears,
Shall come a voice from a land still young to sing in your age-dulled ears
The hero song of a strife as fine as your father's fathers knew
When they dared the rivers of unmapped wilds at the will of a bark canoe.

The song of the deed in the doing; of the work still hot from the hand;
Of the yoke of man laid friendly-wise on the neck of a tameless land.
While your merchandise is weighing we will bit and bridle and rein
The floods of the storm-rocked mountains and lead them down to the plain;
And the foam-ribbed, dark-hued waters tired with that mighty race,
Shall lie at the feet of palm and vine and know their appointed place;
And out of that subtle union, desert with mountain flood,
Shall be homes for a nation's choosing, where no home else had stood.

We will match the gold of your minting, with its mint-stamp dulled and
　　　marred
By the blood and tears that have stained it, and the hands that have clutched
　　　too hard,
With the gold that no man has lied for, the gold no woman has made
The price of her truth and honor, plying a shameless trade:
The clean, pure gold of the mountains, straight from the strong, dark earth;
With no tang or taint upon it from the hour of its primal birth.
The trick of the Money-changer, shifting his coins as he wills,
Ye may keep—no Christ was bartered for the wealth of our lavish hills.

"Yet we are a little people—too weak for the cares of state!"—
Let us go our way—when ye look again ye may find us, mayhap, too great.
Cities we lack—and gutters where children snatch for bread.
Numbers—and hordes of starvelings, toiling but never fed.
Spare pains that would make us greater in the pattern that ye have set;
We hold to the larger measure of the men that ye forget—
The men who from trackless forests and prairies lone and far,
Hewed out the land where ye sit at ease and grudge us our fair-won star.

"There yet be men, my masters"—though the net that the trickster flings
Lies wide on the land to its bitter shame, and his cunning parleyings
Have deafened the ears of Justice—that was blind and slow of old;—
Yet Time, the last Great Judge, is not bought, or bribed, or sold;
And Time and the Race shall judge us—not a league of trafficking men,
Selling the trust of the people, to barter it back again;—
Palming the lives of millions, as a handful of easy coin—
With a single heart to the narrow verge where Craft and State-craft join. [20]

Still full of indignation but completely cured of her cold, Sharlot
went down to Phoenix on December 10, manuscript in hand, to visit
her friend W. Frank Nichols, secretary of the Territory and Alice
Butterfield's stepfather, to see how she could help in the fight.

Tension was mounting in the territorial capital. A delegation
of twelve prominent Arizona men had been appointed to plead
Arizona's cause before President Theodore Roosevelt and the House
Committee on Territories. Secretary Nichols took Sharlot's poem to
Dwight B. Heard, publisher and owner of the *Arizona Republican*
and one of the twelve delegates. Heard printed the poem in full on the
editorial page of the *Republican*. Perhaps more could be done with
this poem, which Heard was astute enought to recognize for what it
was, a cadenced polemic, passionate with righteous indignation. He
and Secretary Nichols took the poem to Governor Joseph H. Kibbey.
Might Sharlot's poem help turn the tide of congressional reaction
against the joint statehood bill? It was worth a try. At Heard's expense, the poem was printed as a broadside in enough copies for every
member of Congress. Shortly after the first of the year the Arizona
delegation left for Washington, taking Sharlot's poem along. A copy
was placed on the desk of each member of both houses of Congress.

It is difficult to say what influence Sharlot's poem had on congressmen who may have read it while they debated the joint statehood measure. On January 25 the Committee on Territories voted the bill onto the floor of the House, where, despite the Arizona delegate's impassioned plea and the reading of Sharlot's poem into the *Congressional Record* for April 10, 1906, the Hamilton bill was rammed through the House, 192 to 165.

Sharlot's poem and other material she had written in opposition to joint statehood gathered momentum and a wider audience outside Congress. Almost the entire issue of *Out West* for February was devoted to the Territory. It included Sharlot's by now widely known poem and her sixty-four page article "Arizona," illustrated with black-and-white photographs, the result of her activities the previous November. This frankly promotional essay told of Arizona's mining, forest, agricultural, and cattle industries and stressed the fact that, although transportation difficulties had hitherto isolated the Territory, these problems had largely been solved by the coming of the railroad.

To the relief of most Arizonans, Arizona and New Mexico were stricken from the Hamilton bill before it passed the Senate. By an amendment attached to the bill, the decision on joint statehood for Arizona and New Mexico was to be made by popular referendum. As it turned out, after the November election that year, the measure was defeated. Oklahoma and Indian Territory were admitted in March 1906 jointly as the state of Oklahoma; Arizona and New Mexico remained as territories until they were finally granted separate statehood in 1912. As to Sharlot's share in the happy outcome of the matter, we have no conclusive proof. It is obvious, though, that her work had impressed the editor of the Du Bois, Pennsylvania, *Morning Courier,* who said: "The people of Arizona, who are rejoicing over the defeat in the Senate of the measure that would have joined them in Statehood with New Mexico, should not fail to give credit in their jubilation to Sharlot M. Hall, as well as the senators who mustered enough votes to save them. Sharlot M. Hall perhaps put out the strongest papers that were issued to show why Arizona should, when admitted to statehood, be admitted as a great commonwealth singly...."[21]

9

Catching History Alive

History is more than a record of events—more than an accurate compilation of dates and names and places—true history is the most vivid picture of past conditions which we can project into the present and preserve for the future... preserving to us the living men and women of the past and the scenes through which they moved, the difficulties they met and the materials out of which they built their tier in the great wall of life. No generation lives for itself alone, but tomorrow rests upon the shoulders of today— as today rests upon the shoulders of yesterday....[1]

CHARLES LUMMIS'S EFFORTS to collect the stories and songs of the Indians and Mexicans of California stimulated Sharlot's long-standing interest in Arizona history. Why should she not do for Arizona what Lummis was doing for southern California? Obviously it never occurred to her that it was one thing for Lummis, being a man, to travel about the countryside interviewing indigenous inhabitants and quite another for a proper lady to do the same thing. Sharlot was never one to let restrictive social conventions hamper her, however. She had already proved that she was capable of taking care of herself, traveling alone or with Charles A. Moody on public conveyances to collect material for her Arizona article the previous fall. Now the fast-vanishing desert and upland wilderness of western Arizona called her with all its unexplored human resources— miners, sheepherders, and pioneers, who would share their memories if only she could get there to talk to them.

At this juncture Charles B. Genung entered the picture. Charlie Genung, a prospector and rancher, was not only a fountain of firsthand material himself but also a friend of many other old settlers of the western Arizona mountain area. Charlie proposed to take Sharlot with him in his traveling wagon, to retrace with her the route by which he had entered Arizona from California in 1863. It is obvious that Charlie was attracted by Sharlot's intelligence, ambition, independence, unconventionality, and good looks. As for Sharlot, she found Charles B. Genung, then a man of sixty-nine with a wife, seven grown children, and a ranch southwest of Prescott, a richly entertaining companion. The friendship which blossomed between the two of them endured until Charlie's death in 1916.

Sharlot and Charlie spent most of the month of May 1906 on the wagon trail in the wilderness area between Ehrenberg and Date Creek, where Charlie had camped more than forty years previously. The miners and sheepherders whom Sharlot met on this trip became her friends and supporters, furnishing her with much background material for a history of Arizona which she already was planning to write.

During the remainder of the year Sharlot traveled, wrote, and ruminated on ways to fulfill what was increasingly becoming a fixed idea with her. Lummis had established a museum in Los Angeles which would house and protect the vanishing artifacts of the California area. He had shared with Sharlot his dream that his Southwest Museum be the parent organization to an endlessly expanding number of similar museums all over the United States, each collecting artifacts and documents from its immediate area. Why should not Prescott have such a museum?

Sharlot knew that this was too big a job for one person, so she turned to the women of the Prescott Monday Club. The Monday Club needed a clubhouse; a museum might be built in connection with it. All that need be done to finance the combined museum-clubhouse was a benefit program at the Prescott Opera House, which Sharlot would be glad to organize.

On January 15, 1907, a gala "Hassayamper's Evening" was produced at the opera house. The evening was all Sharlot's. She began the program by reviewing Arizona's earliest history, with the coming of Governor Goodwin and the establishment of the first territorial capital at Prescott. "There still stands one rare monument of those early days," said Sharlot, "the old Governor's house—on the little knoll just above Granite Creek. It is a priceless relic and should be preserved for the future." Not for some years, however, was Sharlot to think of the Governor's Mansion as the building for the museum she was urging the Monday Club to sponsor. The plan as she saw it in 1907 was for the Monday Club to include a museum of Arizoniana in its clubhouse, a museum which club members would care for. She concluded, "That a fine and valuable collection can be obtained there is no doubt—already a number of things of more than local interest are pledged to the Club, when it shall be ready to care for them."[2]

By the following week Sharlot had other things on her mind. She returned to Phoenix to witness the opening of the twenty-fourth Arizona Territorial Legislature on January 21, 1907. It was no casual visit, nor in this instance was Sharlot on the trail of article material. She had determined to seek the only political position then open to women, a clerkship in the legislature.

It is not difficult to understand why Sharlot sought this position. Her interest in Arizona politics was evident from her 1906 efforts to block the joint statehood bill. These efforts had made her acquainted with Arizona politicians from Governor Kibbey to local precinct officers. She had also made a lasting impression on such influential Arizonans as Dwight B. Heard and a prominent Prescott man, Colonel A. J. Doran, who had just been elected as Yavapai County's delegate to the Council, the upper chamber of the legislature. Furthermore, since Sharlot was interested in history, the legislature, to use Lummis's phrase, was a place to "catch history alive." Here also was the opportunity, if she could get the post, which was appointive, to make what was a good salary for a woman in those days, $300 for two and a half months work. On the first day of the legislative session Sharlot's friend Colonel Doran was elected president of the Council with practically no opposition. Sharlot was pleased, for with Doran's backing she was sure of the success of a couple of her own pet ideas, as well as virtually assured of a place as one of the Council clerks. Indeed, as the friendly editor of the *Journal-Miner* put it, "It is generally conceded that she will have no opposition for the place. She is engaged in writing a story of the Territory, some of the features of which are connected with the actions of the Legislature of the early days, and her experience in this session will be of much value to her."³ No one was surprised, least of all Sharlot, when she was named Bill Clerk for the Council. In this position she helped Council members draft bills in proper form and correct English. She immediately found herself involved in helping to word prospective legislation which both Governor Kibbey and the legislators hoped would impress Congress with Arizona's readiness for statehood.

Sharlot also worked with Doran to put through some bills which reflected her interest in the preservation of Arizona's pioneer past. One was the Doran Bill, which established a home for aged and infirm Arizona pioneers. No one quarreled with the idea of setting up such a home, but some of the legislators felt it inappropriate to locate the home in Doran's home town of Prescott, with its high altitude and distance from the major population centers of the Territory. The bill was passed during the last days of the legislative session, on March 16, 1907. The fact that Frank Murphy of Prescott promised to donate a handsome tract of land for the home probably influenced the legislators in their decision to locate the Arizona Pioneers' Home there.

At the end of the legislative session Sharlot and the legislators scattered to their homes. Sharlot was hurrying home to a family reunion. Her brother Ted, who had left home some time before to try his hand at mining engineering in southern Arizona, was visiting his parents at Orchard Ranch for a couple of weeks before leaving for a new mining job in Chihuahua, Mexico. Ted and Sharlot seem to have been genuinely fond of each other, and Sharlot saw him leave for his new position with real regret, realizing that it would be a long time before she would see him again.

Sharlot began a formal diary on January 1, 1908. Rather casually, she noted on January 29 that she had a letter "from D. M. Riordan wanting to take me to the mountains of northern California."

Denis Matthew (Matt) Riordan, born in 1848 in Troy, New York, was, like most of Sharlot's admirers, nearly as old as her father. He came to Arizona in the 1870s, worked in the mines, and became acquainted with Governor F. A. Tritle. The governor was impressed with Riordan enough to offer him the position of Navajo Indian Agent at Fort Defiance in 1882.

D. Matthew Riordan

Riordan resigned his post after a year and a half, in frustration and anguish at the lack of sensitivity of the United States government toward the needs of its Indian charges. Sometime during this early period Charles F. Lummis must have met him; twenty years later, writing in *Out West,* Lummis said of Riordan: "We have had in all our history of Indian affairs, very few Indian agents who would know a scruple if they met it on the street. . . . At that time (twenty years ago) there was a young man in charge of the Navaho agency in Arizona who had both brains and heart. Also 'nerve.' . . . His courage is a proverb throughout the Southwest. . . ."[4]

In 1884 the Chicago capitalist Edward Everett Ayer hired Riordan to supervise his lumber mill at Flagstaff; Riordan brought in his two younger brothers, Timothy and Michael, to help him and had considerable success. After Ayer sold him the mill in 1887, it was reorganized as the Arizona Lumber Company.

By the time Sharlot entered the picture, Riordan had sold his interest in the lumber company to his brothers. Matt Riordan by this time was engineer and mine superintendent for the copper mining interests of the General Electric Company. Sharlot may have met him through their mutual friend, Charles F. Lummis. The first of many letters which have survived from Riordan to Sharlot Hall is dated July 22, 1905. It is obvious from the tone of this ten-page letter, which tells of his travels and describes the California mines he was supervising at the time, that theirs was a friendship of long standing. Said Riordan: "I often think of you in many and in fact most of the experiences I have and enjoy and wish you were with me to share them. . . . Your faithful, though sadly neglected, admirer, D. M. Riordan."[5]

What Riordan's three grown daughters and his estranged wife thought of Sharlot and Matt's relationship is not known. Whether their relationship was more than a friendly father-daughter intimacy is also unknown. As for Riordan's latest offer, that she should visit him at the big General Electric-owned copper mine in northern California, Sharlot discreetly planned her affairs so that she could make the trip in combination with a visit to Charles Lummis that summer, with no one in Prescott knowing of it. On June 26 Sharlot noted in her diary, "Ranch in good order. Large fruit crop." The next day she took the train for Los Angeles.

The stated reason that Sharlot went to Los Angeles that month was the news that a special summer course was about to begin at the Cumnock School of Expression with the well-known Dr. Richard Burton as special lecturer.[6] The Cumnock School had been started in 1894 by Addie Murphy Grigg, cousin of Frank M. Murphy, railroad magnate, mine owner, long-time Prescott resident, and a friend of Sharlot's. The summer course included lectures on literature and the drama, voice culture, reading lessons, and breathing lessons from various members of the Cumnock staff. During the afternoons Sharlot worked in the editorial office of *Out West*.

Sharlot was determined to make the most of this opportunity for formal training, but, judging from a wryly humorous account of her experience written some years later, she may have felt somewhat ill at ease with Addie M. Grigg, who taught elocution. Recalled Sharlot,

I was her despair. "Why don't you relax—now just relax" were her constant plaints to me. "Put some life into what you are saying— express, express—don't repress all the time." And once—"O you country women are my despair—you are tense as fiddle strings—you are colorless as skim milk—you never let anything out—you never let holds go and flop—How can you, being among all the beauties of nature, be so tense and expressionless?"

Then I expressed. I laughed till they thought I was crazy. Then I rose up and said, "Dear lady, it is true we live among all the beauties of nature, but if we relax one instant the cry comes—"Sa-a-ay—have you seen the old horse collar?" "Sa-ay, sa-ay—where's the hatchet? Maaw—I kaint find the kitchen ropes—Ma-aw them damned blue jays is gittin' all the peas fast as they come up. . . ."[7]

Whether this account is factual is open to question, for judging from newspaper reviews of her appearances before women's clubs and elsewhere, Sharlot was a naturally gifted speaker. It is obvious from her brief diary notes that her days during the month of July were full of exciting, happy, intellectually stimulating activities, from Dr. Burton's lectures to her editorial work at *Out West* and a planned course of reading at the Los Angeles Public Library directed by Charles Lummis.[8] Only one discordant note marred the diary account of her July activities. On July 10 she wrote, "Word from Ted today. End of all but sad memories." Ted Hall, who had gone as a mining engineer to Mexico in 1907, had met a Mexican woman, Petra Acosta. He had written Sharlot to announce their engagement. They were married on October 19, 1908, near Mexico City and soon thereafter came to Tucson to live.

Sharlot reacted with horror and indignation to this news. There was at that time no interest among most Anglo-Americans in Mexican history or culture. Lummis, with his adoption of Mexican dress and his lifelong friendship with several southern California Mexican families, was an exception to the general pattern; indeed, Lummis's liberal views on people of other cultures were regarded by most southwestern middle-class whites as eccentric at best, if not downright dangerous. It would seem from Sharlot's written comments on the matter that her contacts with Mexican ranch hands and miners in the Lynx Creek area had reinforced her prejudice against Mexicans. Of the Mexican as a ranch hand Sharlot said that he "lasted about as long as a snowball in Hell" on a Yavapai ranch. "White cow hands generally rode separate from Mexicans in those days [the 1880s]—the color line was as real as the Hassayampa Highway is now."[9]

The Mexican, the "squaw man," and the "half-breed" alike were regarded with a contempt that had its origins in the days of the rugged frontier when the first American trappers, traders, and miners made casual alliances with Indian and Mexican women. Naturally, these informal living arrangements were frowned on by the more strait-laced settlers from the East who followed with their wives and families to make homes on the frontier. The idea that Sharlot's own brother would enter into any kind of relationship with a woman of the race that Sharlot had been brought up to feel was inferior to her own was unthinkable. After Edward Hall and Petra Acosta married, Sharlot never mentioned her brother again. Giving out a story that he had been killed in a skirmish with Mexicans, she completely ignored him, his wife, and his growing family in Tucson.

On August 23, at the end of the Cumnock summer session, Sharlot left Los Angeles for San Francisco, where her friend Matt Riordan met her, as he had proposed in his January letter. This was Sharlot's first trip to San Francisco, a city still showing tragic evidence of the great earthquake which virtually had destroyed it in April 1906. As she described it, "Everywhere among the new buildings were heaps of burned bricks and piles of twisted iron. Scattered over its sand hills the city did not seem to be beautiful or real—it was like rows on rows of toy houses scattered over a big sand pile."[10]

Riordan and Sharlot apparently left San Francisco immediately for the copper mine at Bully Hill, about a hundred miles north of Sacramento, where Riordan was superintendent. Sharlot spent the month of September at Bully Hill and in other parts of the California Mother Lode country, soaking up impressions of early California mining for a three-part article, "In the Land of the 'Forty-niners," which appeared in *Out West* between December 1908 and March 1909.

That Matt Riordan thoroughly enjoyed his guest's visit is evident from his letter to Charles Lummis, written while Sharlot was still with him at the mine: "I will mention in passing that Miss Hall is here holding down a large portion of Bully Hill to our great joy, and I will let her tell you all about it when she gets back, which she never will if we can help it. So there."[11] By mid-October Sharlot was in Los Angeles again, busy with editorial duties and happily mining the resources of the Los Angeles Public Library. She remained in Los Angeles a month before returning to Arizona.

Sharlot's October 1908 visit to Los Angeles marked the termination of her association with *Out West,* either as editor or as contributor. It would seem from a letter which she wrote Charles Lummis a year later that she and Charles Amadon Moody had a parting of the ways that month which was hardly amicable. Sharlot had found out that Moody had been gambling at the California Club, and she had reason to suspect him of disloyalty to Lummis.[12] Lummis, who was increasingly troubled with problems at the Los Angeles Public Library, had for some time left the running of *Out West* in Moody's hands. At about this time he joined Sharlot in withdrawing from further editorial connection with the magazine. By the end of the next year Lummis had sold his stock and severed his connection with *Out West* entirely.

10

Historian
Makes
Headlines

SHARLOT HOPED TO BE APPOINTED once again to a clerkship in the
Arizona legislature, which began its twenty-fifth biennial session in
January 1909. Regardless of the backing of the *Arizona Republican* [1]
and even a bit of subtle prodding by Republican Governor Kibbey, [2]
however, Republican Sharlot's chances of obtaining a position in that
solidly Democratic legislature were about as good as that of the pro-
verbial snowball in hell. Sharlot did not receive one of the coveted
clerkships.

Despite her disappointment Sharlot remained in Phoenix,
lobbying and writing in the local newspapers on behalf of her dream:
the preservation of Arizona's historical artifacts. As she said:

> Today the student of Arizona history must go outside of Arizona to
> consult the one collection of books and references complete enough to
> command attention, a collection which might have belonged to us had
> we been able to care for it and awake to its importance [the Munk
> Collection, Southwest Museum, Los Angeles]. There is one other
> collection, which has cost the writer of this article nearly twenty years
> to gather, which is more intimate and not less valuable than the great
> Munk collection referred to. This will belong to Arizona as a free gift
> if she is ever in position to care for it properly, and if not it will go with
> the Munk collection to the Southwestern Museum at Pasadena, where
> so many of our Arizona records and relics are going. . . . [3]

Obviously, Sharlot felt that the gift without the giver would be bare,
and that if the legislature should establish a museum or other office

for Arizona history, one Sharlot M. Hall ought by all rights to be appointed as its first incumbent.

Although the legislators did not approach Sharlot for advice, they were far from unaware of the desirability of preserving Arizona's vanishing history. As the *Arizona Republican* announced on March 9, "Among several bills brought in to the Council yesterday... was one creating the office of territorial historian.... The bill was introduced by President Hunt.... It is said that in the event of the enactment of the bill into a law Mulford Winsor, assistant chief clerk of the Council, who has for some years been interested in the early history of the territory, will be put forward for the appointment to the office of historian."[4]

Mulford Winsor was best known in 1909 as an Arizona newspaperman who, because of his interest in politics and his personal friendship with George W. P. Hunt, president of the twenty-fifth Arizona Territorial Legislative Council, had been named assistant chief clerk to the Council. Born in 1874, Winsor began his newspaper career at the age of eighteen, working as a typesetter for the *Prescott Courier*. The next year found him in Yuma, which was to be his home base for much of the rest of his life. Here, eventually, he managed two Yuma newspapers as well as, for a time, the *Tucson Citizen* and the *Phoenix Enterprise*. In 1904 he moved his family to Phoenix, where he turned his attention to politics. A Democrat, he was rewarded on more than one occasion for his loyalty to the party and to future Arizona governor Hunt. Another of his concerns was the preservation of Arizona history; that his interest was real is attested to by his later career as state librarian (1932–1956), in which position he had the reputation of being "more interested in collecting Arizoniana and in furnishing legislative reference than he was in library extension."[5] As the twenty-fifth Territorial Legislature began its 1909 session, Winsor counted on his party affiliations to help him to a position which would allow him to indulge his desire to collect material about Arizona history.

He was not to be disappointed. On March 13 the bill establishing the office of territorial historian was sent forward from the Council to the House, quickly passed, and transmitted to Governor Kibbey for his signature. It was a foregone conclusion that Arizona's first territorial historian would be the assistant chief clerk of the council.

Mulford Winsor in 1909

At this point the Phoenix Woman's Club filed an official protest with Governor Kibbey. Referring to Sharlot Hall's years of research in Arizona history, the statement asserted:

This material is almost ready for moulding into shape for publication and it has been gathered and prepared with the intention of producing a thoroughly accurate and reliable history, as well as a work of attractive literary quality and permanent scholarly worth.... The club women who have followed its growth with closest interest feel if the historical needs of Arizona are to receive recognition at last some attention should be given to selecting the official writer of Arizona's history. [6]

In case anyone should be in doubt as to whom they had in mind as the best-qualified candidate for the new position, the combined Phoenix Woman's Club in a second statement nominated "Miss Sharlot M. Hall, who for fifteen years or more has carried on the systematic collection of historical data along the very lines suggested by the bill in question, for your consideration for the position of historian of Arizona." [7]

Governor Kibbey faced a dilemma. It is obvious that he wanted to sign the historian bill. It is also obvious that he admired and respected Sharlot Hall and that he was well aware of her fitness for the position. Because of a commitment he had made to President Hunt and others on the Council, however, he had gotten himself into an extremely awkward position. He finally did the only honest thing possible: he wrote a long letter to the Phoenix Woman's Club and the Arizona Federation of Women's Clubs explaining just what had happened. It was printed in the *Arizona Republican* along with the statement from the clubwomen. Said Kibbey:

> Some two weeks ago, Mr. Mulford Winsor... came to my chambers and broached the subject of the creation of the office of territorial historian.... I approved the plan and suggested that Miss Hall would be admirably qualified to fill that position. He then told me that the legislature would not create the office if Miss Hall... were to be appointed to it. He said that the legislature would, however, pass a bill creating the office if he, Mr. Winsor, would be appointed to it.... The alternative presented to me was to have no such office at all, or consented to appoint Mr. Winsor to it.... If I had insisted on Miss Hall we would not have had the office established, so that my action in no event can be deemed to be a want of recognition on my part of her worth and fitness.
>
> Very Respectfully, JOS. H. KIBBEY, Governor [8]

On March 18, 1909, the last day of the twenty-fifth and last Territorial Legislative Assembly, Governor Kibbey signed the bill establishing the historian's office. Even as the territorial legislators scattered from the capitol to their homes in various parts of Arizona, Mulford Winsor moved into his new office. He told an *Arizona Gazette* reporter that he would be in Phoenix for three or four months "working over some material that he has collected, before starting out on his travels over the territory. Before he can even begin this work, he will have to get a list of the best sources of information, the names of old-timers.... The immediate need of the office was to obtain the facts from these early settlers, who are fast passing away."[9]

Winsor would probably have liked to borrow Sharlot's notebooks and the files which she had been accumulating over the past fifteen years. He hardly had time to get himself settled in his office, however, before events on the national scene transpired which were to make a change in his plans. As soon as William Howard Taft was inaugurated as President of the United States in March 1909, he exercised his prerogative to appoint a new governor for the Territory of Arizona. On May 1 Kibbey returned to private life. Sharlot's good friend Richard E. Sloan from Prescott was sworn in as territorial governor.

Mulford Winsor might well have experienced some uneasy moments as he saw Governor Kibbey leave the capitol and a new governor, who had no reason to favor him, take office. If he suspected his tenure as territorial historian might be affected by the change in administration, it was not evident. He put together a rather brief progress report for the governor and then left for Charles Lummis's Southwest Museum in Los Angeles, to acquaint himself with the material in the Munk Collection of Arizoniana there.

Sharlot, meanwhile, was not idle. She spent the month of May near Salome and Quartzsite, interviewing old settlers and locating and marking graves of Arizona pioneers. Not to be outdone, Mulford Winsor, soon back from Los Angeles, was also beating the bushes for old-timers. As the friendly *Arizona Gazette* reporter put it, "Mr. Winsor will get right out there among the people and stay there until he obtains what is needed."[10] Shortly after Winsor returned from his trip to Los Angeles, Sharlot took herself off to California, where she spent the rest of the summer studying at the Southwest Museum.

Winsor meanwhile occupied himself in scouring southern Arizona for pioneers whom Sharlot might have missed. On September 2 he was back in Phoenix with a suitcase full of old manuscripts and records from Pima and Yuma counties. But Mulford Winsor, though he was a friend of George W. P. Hunt's, was not a friend of Governor Richard Sloan's. Precisely what Sloan thought of Winsor is not known, but Winsor, who was known as a person who "had rather make a wise crack than get through a bill," and one who "cracked his friends, and cracked his enemies, and often made enemies of friends,"[11] may have antagonized Sloan. Certainly Republican Sloan had no obligation to keep Winsor in office, and he may have resented the Democratic legislative deal that put Winsor there in the first place.

Late in September Sharlot Hall returned to Phoenix from Los Angeles. On October 1 the *Arizona Republican* headlined: "Historian of Arizona: Miss Sharlot Hall succeeds to that office today; replacing Mr. Winsor." In the next few weeks Sharlot's appointment as territorial historian grew to the proportions nearly of a *cause célèbre.* James H. McClintock, Arizona correspondent to the *Los Angeles Times,* wrote a full account of the appointment which appeared on October 2, headed "Woman Gets Public Office." The article stated that "Miss Hall's appointment is the first of any woman to a territorial salaried office, bringing up a challenge of legality, but the Governor, a lawyer of long acquaintance with the territorial statutes, has concluded that his action will stand review." That some of the members of the territorial legislature were less than happy with Governor Sloan's choice of a woman may be inferred by the abortive effort to insert a plank in the constitution of the new state of Arizona which would effectively have barred women from public office.[12] Sloan received a letter from New York City lawyer Frank Rudd, thanking him for appointing Sharlot to the position: "I know enough of Arizona men and affairs to know that this appointment represents the outcome of a severe struggle in your mind between private and public interests, and that in that struggle your sense of public duty has won a decisive victory.... [Sharlot Hall's] appointment under the circumstances was a piece of clear political courage...."[13]

Sharlot did not spend much time crowing over her good fortune. Almost immediately she set off on the travels which were to take her to nearly every corner of the Territory. July 1910 found her in Flagstaff. Just after her arrival, Al Doyle, a Flagstaff man who made a business of guiding parties of campers and travelers through the Arizona wilderness, came to town, laying in provisions for Dr. J. Walter Fewkes's study and exploration of the area south of Black Falls on the Little Colorado River, near what is now Wupatki National Monument north of Flagstaff. By a lucky chance, Sharlot encountered Doyle; as she wrote Matt Riordan, "I promptly packed a suitcase and planned to come out."[14] Fewkes, a nationally known ethnologist, had first explored the ruins near the Black Falls of the Little Colorado before the turn of the century. He had returned during the summer of 1910 with his wife and twelve-year-old daughter, still hoping to prove his theory that this area was the ancestral home of the Snake clan of the Hopi Indians of Walpi.[15]

The area near Black Falls is a desolate expanse of black lava and fissured, red sandstone buttes where sagebrush and a few stunted cedars with gnarled roots fight for life in sandy gullies and cinder plains. After traveling all day with a horse and wagon, Sharlot and Doyle reached the Fewkes camp, two little tents and a shade of cedar boughs and poles at the foot of a black lava mountain near the Little Colorado River. Sharlot was welcomed to camp and assigned to share a tent with Fewkes's daughter. It was hot; the water, hauled in from Indian Tanks, was alkali; and Sharlot found that "the smooth side of a cinder pile shared with a few blankets and a strenuous twelve year old girl [was] no luxury to linger over." Yet her letter to Riordan is full of the joy of the whole adventure.

> Yesterday we drove to the Little Colorado where Dr. Fewkes hoped to find some ruins not previously explored. There was only a trail down over the cinder mesas, and low canyons in which the black ash drifted like some uncanny snow. The horses' feet sank deep at every step and the wheels "scrunched" and ground in the sand. The river was dry except for little red, thick pools... sand banks, clinker-like, burned-out sandstone cliffs and buttes, and black cinder piles over all.
>
> The ruins had been looted long since, but as we came back we saw again a most picturesque big ruin built on a huge mass of red sandstone, standing high above the earth like the back of some Hopi monster god—the ruin itself very well built of sandstone and quite like a towered castle....
>
> The desert was wonderful again under turbulent storm clouds and wind-blown rain, and later from the tent door I watched a furious sand-storm blot out the far-away walls of the "Painted Desert."...

Arizona territorial officials in 1910. Governor Sloan is the second man to the right of Sharlot Hall.

The party broke camp and returned to Flagstaff on July 26, in time to drive to the Walnut Canyon cliff dwellings southeast of Flagstaff, a group of well-preserved cavate rooms and a well-known souvenir-hunting area at the time for Flagstaff citizenry. Sharlot wrote that they "came back in a beautiful rainstorm that beat over Elden Mountain like a whirlwind of water and turned all the pine trunks a glowing brown.... The road was lined with that pinky-lavender spider plant all abloom and whole flocks of humming birds swarmed over it, just like bees or butterflies."

A final short note appended to Sharlot's long, continued letter to Riordan hinted at the depth of their feeling for one another, a love which obviously had grown in the days since Sharlot's 1908 trip to Riordan's mine at Bully Hill in northern California.

> It rests me just to think of you, the one man on earth in whom I have perfect faith, you're so strong and wise and tender, so clean and true.
>
> God keep you safe, dear best friend, and ease the hurts that must touch your great heart. You are so much to so many people, so many of us love you and pray for you—let that make sunshine for your darkest days.
>
> Goodnight. Great comrade—I thank God for you, as, next to Mother, the best gift of my life. [16]

Sharlot was increasingly concerned about her mother's failing health. She had spent a few days at home just before coming to Flagstaff. It is quite probable that Adeline, always her daughter's proud literary supporter, urged Sharlot to think again about the possibility of issuing her poetry in book form. Sharlot had demurred, telling her mother that she would like still more time to write. "I am afraid," her mother had answered, "that you are going to wait until I will not be here to see the poems in print." So Sharlot gathered her poems together, some previously published and some not. After all, as she said later, "All of the poems were written to please mother...or to put into written words things she had suggested.... Many times it was her own thought or her experience that I shaped into verse."[17] The manuscript was sent to Sherman, French and Company of Boston.

With her poems off to the publisher, Sharlot turned her attention once more to her duties as territorial historian and her pursuit of the raw material of Arizona history. She had set as her goal for the summer of 1910 a thorough coverage of northern Arizona: the Arizona Strip country north of the Grand Canyon, the Hopi and Navajo reservations in the northeastern corner of the state, and the Little Colorado area colonized by the Mormons. She must have realized how unrealistic this program was, because the journey to the Strip was postponed until the following summer. The rest of her activities, particularly in the light of her occasional mention of ill health, are little short of incredible in their variety and in the strenuous traveling involved.

Sharlot's first encounter with the Mormons of the Little Colorado settlements came almost by accident. In Holbrook the first part of August to interview pioneer residents and to see the great petrified forest northeast of the town, she and her guide were caught by a surprise rainstorm that turned the Río Puerco into a roiling, unfordable torrent of "thick red water rolling along like an angry mud bank in motion." Said Sharlot, "Our supper and beds were in sight, but we had to turn the tired horses and ask them to go twelve miles to the village of Woodruff, where the kindly-faced but weather-beaten second wife of 'Brother Fish' gave us lodging."

"Brother Fish" was Arizona historian Joseph Fish (1840 – 1926), one of the Mormons sent by Brigham Young in 1879 to colonize the Little Colorado area of Arizona. Fish, who lived for many years in the vicinity of Snowflake, shared the same passion for collecting information about Arizona history that consumed Sharlot. It is probable that Sharlot knew of Fish's 700-page manuscript history of Arizona, since a copy of it was in the J. A. Munk Collection of Arizoniana at the Southwest Museum. Fish stated in his autobiography that Sharlot spent about a week with him, looking the manuscript over with the idea of buying it for publication by the Territory of Arizona. [18] Sharlot found the manuscript interesting, although she noted that it was only partly original work; a great part of it consisted, she said, of "the oddest inweaving of extracts from various authors—with no quotation marks for the most part—yet well enough chosen." [19]

Fish, who had tried previously without success to have his history published, offered to sell the manuscript to the Territory for five hundred dollars. Sharlot wrote to Governor Sloan, asking for authorization. Sloan's reply was cautious:

> With regard to the purchase of Mr. Fish's manuscript I think with you that it is desirable that the Territory have the benefit of Mr. Fish's work and that he should be paid for it. I am not sure, however, that there is any fund at the disposal of the Historian for this, at any rate to pay five hundred dollars from your contingency fund might seriously deplete the latter and embarrass your work. You will be able to judge of this better than I. I leave the matter for your decision. . . . [20]

Sharlot returned shortly to Fish with the Governor's go-ahead. Fish told what happened next.

> I let her have it and she agreed to have it published, with the understanding that she was to group the items together a little different, that is separate the Indian wars from the other matter a little more. She asked permission to make this change which I, of course, granted. In the settling up for the work she wrote me that there was but $350 in the treasury and that was all they could give. She had the work so I let the matter go. In a short time there was a change of governors, a Democrat coming in and Miss Hall resigned.
>
> Mr. T. E. Farish came in and he now started to write up the history of Arizona. He used my work as reference, etc. He soon reported to me that there were 210 pages out of the center of the work gone, he supposed that it had been stolen and wanted to know if I had a copy and could replace it. I did not have a copy but sent him a few items that I gathered up that might help him out some I thought, but it was impossible to make the story complete. I never knew where the 210 pages went to but there was one thing pointed to the late historian. She had contracted to write a history of Arizona for a firm in the east soon after her resignation or about that time. She, however, took sick and was unable to write and Mr. McClintock wrote the work and it is possible he fell heir to the missing papers as he doubtless got all of Miss Hall's papers to work from. These were some of my conjectures. [21]

Fish's suspicions seem to be well-founded: the missing pages of the manuscript were found in Sharlot's collection of Arizoniana after her death.

Sharlot was back in Holbrook by August 10, where she received a message from the already legendary Navajo Indian trader

John Lorenzo Hubbell (1853 – 1930), inviting her to visit him at his Ganado trading post in the heart of the Navajo Indian Reservation. Sharlot wrote Riordan about her visit:

> You know better than I can tell you what I saw — the wild, beautiful country, strange buttes and cliffs of red-brown sandstone in fantastic carvings — the wide, high valleys and the low cedars that look like little apple trees. . . . You know Ganado — the fort-like pile of rough stone buildings on the red hill-slope with the wide river bed below, full just now of red mud from the recent rains. Mr. Hubbell welcomed us royally — the gracious manner making us seem old friends. . . .
>
> Already the Indians were crowded around the store — wagons, dogs, ponies, babies, men and women — a very quiet crowd, so little talking that the silence was marked. The best clothes were airing you can guess — velvet shirts in all colors — some velvet trousers open to the knee, and a few shirts of bright plush — all worn with the tails out. And belts and beads and buttons of silver and charms of turquoise and big turquoise earrings tied on with string.
>
> The sports were held in a little round valley with hills all about and one like a tier of reserved seats at the end, on which the Indians grouped themselves as thick as sardines in a box. . . . [22]

Sharlot enjoyed the whole affair: the all-night dancing ("mostly *noise*"), the cock-pulling, the horse-racing, the betting, the milling crowds of Navajo Indians ("about 2,000" was her estimate), and the few non-Indian guests: "Indian Dept., artists, collectors, and mere cranks of various brands." Most impressive of all was Hubbell, "all in a class by himself."

The following day Sharlot joined a party going out from Hubbell's post to Oraibi to see the famed snake dance of the Hopis. The journey west from Ganado fifty miles in a buckboard over sandy trails to the Keams Canyon trading post was a continued delight. She sat next to the Mexican driver and plied him with questions. The only woman in the party, she was accompanied by a young government physician coming to his Indian agency post at Oraibi, a German artist, and a seventy-two-year-old Vermont banker. Despite her enthusiasm, however, Sharlot found the trip exhausting. The rest at the Keams Canyon trading post of Lorenzo Hubbell, Jr., was a welcome relief. She ended her letter to Riordan by stating, "I shall be out till October — unless this old illness shoves me over the line to Los Angeles—I sometimes fear I shall have to give up but I'll fight as long as possible."[23]

When the party was ready to go on to Oraibi, Hubbell sent his own team and his clerk, Mr. Thacker, as driver. Sharlot continued her "log book" to Riordan, describing the trip:

> You remember those great, broken mesas rising out of a sea of sand blown into strange dunes that almost seem wet with salt water. The rich colored buttes and cliffs cut into fantastic shapes were like a fitting frame to the irregular green valley through which the road wound—now over pale yellow sand and again, past patches of corn and melons and squashes, vivid green on the yellow dunes in which they grew. Sometimes a just-gone flood had left a sleek, wet coating of mud among the corn—for these Walpi fields are planted in the canyon beds and spots that the rains may flood easily.... Recent sand storms had taken literally miles of the good land—that strange, yellow sand blowing over the valley and up the canyons like drifted snow. As we came to the cliff-foot at Walpi I saw big peach trees buried all but their topmost branches—great, whaleback dunes running from tree to tree.... We had the noon lunch in an orchard only beginning to be buried, and then Mr. Thacker took me up the sky-hung trail to see the swallow's nest houses of these curious people....

Sharlot and the others reached Oraibi on Third Mesa at nightfall, where they were housed overnight in some vacant pueblos. Sharlot, usually so ready to describe her surroundings in the most colorful terms, was strangely silent about Oraibi. Possibly it was beyond her to be as lyrical as was her wont over the ancient and odoriferous pueblo which greeted her eyes that September evening. Because of a feud in 1906 between residents who wished to cooperate with the Indian Agency and those who clung to the old ways, Oraibi had lost much of its population. The "hostiles" had moved nine miles west and established another village, while the "friendlies" had stayed behind. Leo Crane, who came to the Hopi Reservation as Indian agent the same year that Sharlot was there, described the pueblo:

> Old Oraibi is not a pretty picture, although its setting relieves much of squalor and debris. The narrow streets were filled with rubbish and worse; fowls scratched in the offal, burros herded in doorways, and lanky, half-starved dogs were legion. Many of the houses had crumbled and others were being demolished. These were the abandoned homes of the defeated factionists.

There were short alleys and blind courts, while around a central plaza the dwellings arose to the height of three stories, reached by little ladders, where a few of the inhabitants were sunning. The roofs were piled with drying peaches. The place of the ceremonial kiva sloped away to the mesa edge, and from it one looked away, many miles, to the dimming river-country....[24]

The 1910 Snake ceremony at Oraibi had been sadly depleted by the removal of the "hostiles." The preliminary running of the Antelope clan priests to the valley early in the morning of the dance was, said Sharlot, "tame and of children mostly." The dance late that afternoon was also a disappointment. Because of the defection of many of the Snake priests, most of the snake handlers in the dance were boys from eight to ten years of age.

More interesting to Sharlot than the Indian dances were the few Anglos who came in to Oraibi on the day of the dance. Among them was Arizona's current delegate to Congress, Ralph H. Cameron. Sharlot and Cameron's wife, Ida May Spaulding, had been schoolgirl friends. Sensing an opportunity to further her own interests, Sharlot made sure that she and Cameron sat together in the buckboard that took the group back to Ganado. As she told Riordan, they "had a big talk that I think will bear fruit later — he had not known me at all, you know." Sharlot's association with Cameron was indeed to bear fruit, but much later, and in a context which in 1910 would have surprised her.

Most of the rest of the summer and early fall Sharlot spent with the Mormons of the Little Colorado River area, traveling from here through Show Low, Pinetop, and Fort Apache back to her office in Phoenix in time for the opening of the Constitutional Convention on October 10. She immediately made herself available to reporters, who were glad to run a long story of her summer's adventures in the pages of the friendly *Arizona Republican*. Ever the Arizona booster, Sharlot closed the interview with a quick summary of the untapped natural resources she had seen: the fine ranges and grasslands of the Mormon country, the fish and timber of the White Mountain area, and the coal belt of the Navajo country were all assets to be exploited, according to her account. In addition, concluded the reporter, "The Globe-Durango railroad, which is now a certainty, will do a great deal to open up this country and Miss Hall expects in a very few years to see thousands of people where there are scores now."[25]

Sharlot's private reaction to her summer of travel she saved for her friend and correspondent, Matt Riordan. Realizing that only by remaining single was she able to see and to experience the world as she had done that summer, she said,

> I do enjoy everything—just the sunshine on the sand is beautiful enough to keep on giving thanks for eyes to see with. And all day long I'm so glad, so glad, so glad that God let me be an out-door woman and love the big things. I couldn't be a tame house cat woman and spend big sunny, glorious days giving card parties and planning dresses— though I love pretty clothes and good dinners and friends—and would love a home where only the true, kind, worth-while things had place.
>
> I'm *not* unwomanly—don't you dare think so—but God meant woman to joy in his great, clean, beautiful world—and I thank Him that He lets me see some of it not through a window pane. [26]

Yet, had Riordan, her "dear, dear, dear Great Comrade," been free to remarry, Sharlot's story might have ended differently.

Sharlot remained in Phoenix for the sixty-day session of the Constitutional Convention and then returned to Orchard Ranch. Her book of poems, *Cactus and Pine,* was published on November 30, 1910, [27] a proud moment for Sharlot and even more so for her mother. As Sharlot told Lummis, the book "fared wonderfully well at the hands of reviewers, especially in the East." [28]

In February Sharlot resumed her travels, lecturing to groups all over southern Arizona on "Unknown Arizona," illustrated with lantern slides of her own making from her summer's travels. She joined the official party at the March 18 dedication of the Tonto (now Roosevelt) Dam by Theodore Roosevelt; she dodged bullets of the Mexican Revolution in Douglas, Arizona, near the Mexican border; and she seems to have captivated both young and old in Tombstone, Clifton, Morenci, and Safford as she scoured the area for historical materials. June 16 saw her back in Phoenix after almost two months in southeastern Arizona. She remained in Phoenix until the end of the month, organizing her notes and preparing an official report of her activities for Governor Sloan. [29]

Home at Orchard Ranch by the first of July, 1911, Sharlot went with her mother to the South Rim of the Grand Canyon, where they spent a few days at the El Tovar Hotel. After seeing her mother

Sharlot and Adeline Hall in 1910

back safe at the ranch, Sharlot set off again for Flagstaff, to start what was to be the longest and most exciting expedition of her tenure as territorial historian, a wagon trip north of the Grand Canyon into the area known as the Arizona Strip.[30]

The Strip, when Sharlot made her almost unprecedented journey, was virtually unknown territory, isolated from the rest of Arizona by the nearly impassable barrier of the Colorado River. Although the South Rim of the Grand Canyon had been opened to tourists by the building of a spur of the Atlantic, Pacific, and Santa Fe Railway in 1901 from Williams, the North Rim still remained, for all but the most intrepid adventurer, remote and nearly unattainable.

Sharlot's interest was, as always, to see, to know, to experience, and to collect historical data from the few people who had made their homes in the Strip. In addition, she had a more patriotic motive. In May 1866 part of the original Territory of Arizona, a triangle of land west of the Colorado River, had been transferred to the new state of Nevada. The loss of this area still rankled; the matter was not helped by annual agitation in Congress by Utah delegates who pressed the logic of the annexation of the part of Arizona north of the Colorado River by the state of Utah. As the Utah delegates regularly pointed out, a person living in Fredonia, Coconino County, Arizona, who needed to get to the county seat at Flagstaff, must travel three hundred miles and make a hazardous crossing of the Colorado, whereas Fredonia was only eight easy miles from Kanab, Utah.[31] Was the Arizona Strip worth keeping?

It is clear that among Sharlot's reasons for making the trip was the desire to publicize the economic worth of the Strip and to rouse the interest of Arizonans so that they would fight Utah's continued attempt at annexation. Sharlot's report emphasized the untapped wealth of the Strip and minimized the difficulties involved in getting there. As she stated, with considerable restraint, "There are several roads leading into this region from the south side of the Colorado River, none of them good, and none so bad as to be impassable for a good team and strong wagon. Any one of them will emphasize the need for a wagon bridge somewhere on the Colorado River."[32] It was not until January 1929, with the completion of the great iron span across Marble Canyon south of Lees Ferry, that a bridge finally opened the Strip to travelers.

In 1911 the journey was a hazardous one indeed. In 1935 Sharlot recollected how it had been.

> July of 1911—no highways running north across Arizona—only the wagon roads worn and rutted for fifty years back and just then fading and dim from infrequent travel—no great bridge swung out across Marble Canyon—to link northern Arizona with the south all the way to Mexico—only the water-soaked floor of the old ferry-boat, teetering back and forth as the river sucked around it.

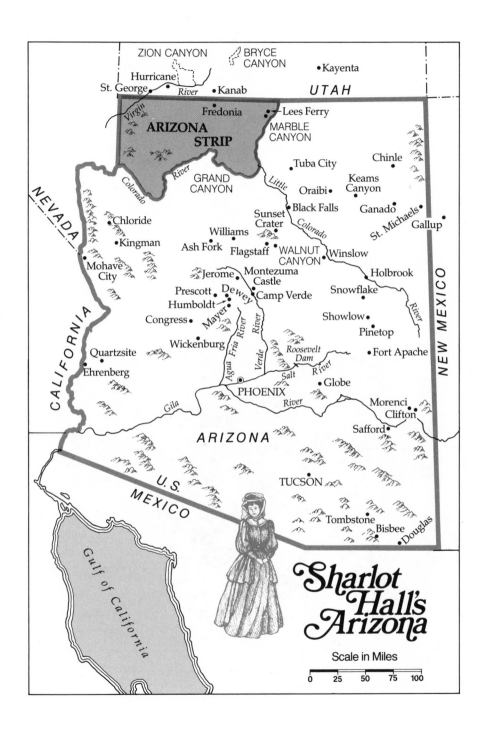

ZION CANYON   BRYCE CANYON   • Kayenta

Hurricane
St. George •   River   • Kanab   *UTAH*

Fredonia   —Lees Ferry

ARIZONA STRIP   MARBLE CANYON

Virgin

NEVADA

Colorado   River   GRAND CANYON   Little   • Tuba City   • Chinle

Keams Canyon

• Chloride   Sunset Crater   • Black Falls   Oraibi •   Ganado •

Colorado   St. Michaels •   Gallup •

• Kingman   Williams •   WALNUT CANYON   • Winslow

Ash Fork   • Flagstaff

Mohave City   Jerome •   Montezuma Castle   Holbrook •

Prescott •   Dewey   • Camp Verde   Snowflake •

Humboldt •   Mayer   Showlow •

Congress •   Pinetop •

Agua Fria River   Verde River

CALIFORNIA   Wickenburg •   Roosevelt Dam   • Fort Apache

Quartzsite •   Salt   River

Ehrenberg •   Gila   PHOENIX   River   • Globe

Morenci •
Clifton •

Safford •

ARIZONA

NEW MEXICO

U.S.
MEXICO   TUCSON •

• Tombstone   Bisbee •   Douglas •

Gulf of California

Sharlot Hall's Arizona

Scale in Miles

0   25   50   75   100

"The Strip" was a No-man's land, a place apart—and only sheriffs crossed the river to hunt for criminals who were trying to lose themselves in that big no-where.

At Flagstaff old Al Doyle waited with a light Studebaker mountain wagon and span of cream-colored, red-spotted Arabian horses that had been raised in Cedar Valley, Utah. The wagon was already partly loaded, water barrels in place—barley and bales of hay in the back. We hurried in a two month's supply of grub and pulled out on a trot to lose ourselves as soon as possible....

Doyle had never been north of Tuba City...but he had friends here and there among the Mormons and among the Indians—and if the road was dim and time-worn it most likely had another end on which we could come out—if we kept going long enough.

Camped in a hidden little park in the cedars we were wakened at midnight by the roll of heavy wheels, the crack of bull whips, and the sighs of yoke-tired cattle—the bull teams of the Lee's Ferry Mining company....

Sharlot Hall and Al Doyle on the Arizona Strip

Dugway at Lees Ferry (Sharlot Hall's Photograph)

The Little Colorado was in flood far beyond its banks—no bridge to see us over in those days, though current opinion held that the quicksandy bottom had sucked down enough freight wagons to bridge it twice over. Long strings of yoked bulls were cut loose from the wagons and driven across and back until the bottom was firmed—then one at a time, with twenty yokes of bulls to the wagon, the big freight went across—

The quicksand sucked and wheels dropped out of sight—but all got over. We headed the "paint ponies" in—with big bulls yoked by long ropes to the end of the tongue—and though water flowed into the Studebaker we made the other bank.

Tuba next day—and Sam Preston's big log hogan that housed the trading post—Tuba that was the range of Lot Smith and the Mormon settlers—and next day Moen Ahvi, the roofless, abandoned retreat of John D. Lee and the courageous women who shared his wanderings after Mountain Meadows.

Plum trees of his planting had dropped their red fruit thick on the ground and grape vines which he brought from Utah had climbed over the red sandstone wall and purpled them with thick clusters—only the Navaho women now and then camped under the trees and spread the fruit to dry in the sun—for long since the Mormons have gone elsewhere and this is all Indian country.

On up the long, sandy trough which leads towards Lee's Ferry—on the right hand those strange cliffs like broken pie-crust, which are the up-tilted edge of the "great fault" where long ago the earth's crust broke up and tilted back. At water camps we found old dates and names scratched on rocks—where Mormon families passed a half century before. And once in a while the grave of a child or woman too tired to go on.

At last the long, red-earthed "dug-way," like a sluice box leading down to the river.

In the red-rock houses of the mining company they were watching for the bullteams and soon the ferry boat came crawling over. All the bulls except the yokes needed to put the wagons on the boat, turn by turn, were to go over to pasture on Pahria creek.

The bulls thought not—that sullen, dirty water looked bad to them. The bull-wranglers pushed and shouted—on they crowded—then in midstream one wide-horned Texan swung his head high and went over like a bird. Bravely he swam toward the green cottonwoods—and straight into one of the strange, greasy whirlpools that suck and gurgle all along the river bottom. He went under as if pulled by some relentless monster—and never came up. . . .

In the house [John Lee] built—burned down some years ago—I visited with the Johnson women who were brave keepers of the ferry after the day of Lee was done. In the tiny graveyard lay the grown son which these lonely women had buried when he died of an accident—and the four children who died of diphtheria brought by passing travellers. They told me of Emma Lee whom neither the strange river, the Navaho prowlers, nor the wild and savage land could frighten—who led out her little children and put them to sleep beside the night fire of the warriors who had threatened to kill her and them.

On over a dim and tangled thread of road where now the fair highway goes—camping in House Rock Valley and photographing the buffalo in a rain storm while the biggest bull pawed and bellowed his anger—and later Uncle Jim Owens said it just proved that the Lord looked out for fools—because that bull was worse to meet than a mountain lion. . . .

Across the Buckskin mountains by old cow trails when roads were lacking—digging out a dying spring and catching drops of water in a tin cup to save the paint ponies of dying of thirst—putting the Studebaker down cliffs like stairsteps—and myself walking to save the horses an ounce of extra weight—so we came at last to Kanab—and to Fredonia. . . .

And to Uncle Jim Owens and his mountain lion dogs—and to the ghost towns along the Virgin river, beautiful stone houses vacant for fifty years because the river took away the land for farming.

Then to St. George, holding the fiftieth anniversary of its founding—and to Hurricane with its big sulphur spring and its orchards and vineyards surpassing California.

To Zion Canyon, and Bryce, and to many a still unheralded natural wonder—to the Grand Gulch mine, a "funeral" copper mine of the highest richness in Arizona, in the midst of an old placer gold region where once Joe Porterie, the old Greek assayer, was lost and nearly died for water.

So, looping the half-obliterated roads for more than three months, while the Studebaker grew dusty and the paint ponies thin and hard—then with a cedar tree dragging on a rope to keep the wagon on the long unused road and with poor old Doyle deathly sick in the back on the bed rolls, I held the team down the seven mile Lincoln Hill which was once part of Pah-Ute County, Arizona—and came again to the Colorado. . . . [33]

Sharlot spent two and a half months on the road, between July 23, 1911 when she and Doyle left Flagstaff and October 2 when she finally reached Kingman and civilization again. In spite of all the publicity given her trip, though, it was strangely ignored by government officials. On July 10, 1914, another reconnaissance was made of the Strip, this time by A. M. McOmie of the Arizona Agricultural Experiment Station; C. C. Jacobs, District Engineer, U.S. Geological Survey; and O. C. Bartlett, Assistant State Entomologist. One statement made by Professor McOmie is particularly startling; of his own trip he said, "Up to this time, no officials of any institution or departments of the state had made even a cursory survey of that country." [34]

Sharlot's fortunes as writer and official historian peaked with her spectacular summer in the Arizona Strip and its attendant publicity. A contract from Sherman, French and Company for her proposed

book of short stories, to be entitled *The Price of the Star,* was waiting
for her when she reached Phoenix late in October.[35] It is obvious
from the terms of the contract that the publishers were impressed by
the critical acclaim of *Cactus and Pine* and were anxious to issue
more of the author's work. Although manuscript for a half dozen
stories was prepared for this collection, Sharlot never managed to get
the material to the publishers.

Not surprisingly, Sharlot took advantage of the interest
which her trip had created to travel and to lecture wherever she was
asked. As Arizona's days as a Territory drew to a close and George W.
P. Hunt was elected the first state Governor, Sharlot may well have
been uneasy. Mulford Winsor, who had been ousted by Governor
Sloan to make way for Sharlot, was a personal friend of incoming
Governor Hunt's. Democrat Hunt had political debts to pay, none of
them owing to Republican Sharlot. As Hunt himself had said, "one of
his cardinal principles was to reward those who had battled for his
cause."[36] The announcement of Winsor's appointment as Governor
Hunt's personal secretary did nothing to allay Sharlot's uneasiness.
Setting out to create a groundswell of support for her own retention,
Sharlot enlisted the help of her friends throughout Arizona. The
members of Arizona's women's clubs rallied to her support. Even
before the Arizona Federation of Women's Clubs meeting in Phoenix
later in January, the clubwomen began writing letters to the governor
and circulating petitions. In addition, Sharlot's friends among the
miners wrote on her behalf to state legislators. The rival newspapers,
all partisans of one political party or the other, picked up the question
of Sharlot's retention as state historian. "Nothing Doing, Miss Hall!"
shrieked the *Arizona Democrat* in an editorial January 10, 1912.
"Is there nothing doing?" returned the *Arizona Republican* on
January 12.

In the midst of the letter-writing and campaigning appeared
the February number of *Arizona, The New State Magazine,* a special
women's issue, "the editorial force [being] ably assisted by Sharlot M.
Hall, Territorial Historian, and a magazine writer and editor of prom-
inence."[37] Featured with the lead article, "Women Who Broke the
Trails for Us," was a large photograph of the charming editor and her
beloved mother, the picture which had appeared as a frontispiece in
Sharlot's *Cactus and Pine* the year before.

Admission Day dawned at last, and with it the passing of the old order under Sharlot's friend, Governor Richard E. Sloan. Sharlot made sure that she had a conspicuous role in the day's activities; she must have come close to burning out her stereopticon slides if not her voice with her illustrated lectures, one given on "Travels Through Unknown Arizona" on the eve of Admission Day and a second, "Reminiscences of Our Territorial History," given as part of the official activities at Tempe Normal School the next day. Then, along with all the other appointive officials of the old administration, she dutifully tendered what she hoped would be a pro forma resignation to the governor.

The first legislative assembly of the state of Arizona met between March 18 and May 18, 1912. There was much to be done, and as the end of the session drew near, it was obvious that Governor Hunt would have to call an extra session. This he did; the extra session met between May 23 and June 22, 1912. Among the bills put forward then was one proposed by Pima County Democratic Senator John T. Hughes, a good friend of Governor Hunt's. This bill, which passed the Senate but died in the House, was "An act to create the office of State Legislative Reference Librarian for the State Library, authorizing the appointment of a librarian, defining his duties, fixing his compensation and making an appropriation to carry out the provisions of the act, and abolishing the office of Arizona Historian and Assistant Librarian."[38]

It is impossible to state if this new bill was, as was hinted in a rather scurrilous newspaper account of Mulford Winsor's activities, drawn up expressly for Winsor's benefit and with Winsor in mind. The newspaper account stated that "Winsor was to be made the state historian and librarian under an arrangement which contemplated the consolidation of the two positions under a rather munificent salary...."[39] This rumored activity of the legislature on Winsor's behalf is the only thing which can explain what Sharlot did next. She composed a letter which she laid on the desk of every member of the legislature; in addition, she sent a copy for publication to the *Arizona Republican*. The letter spelled out in minute detail the condition of the historian's office when she took it over from her predecessor, stating not only that she had found the office in a state of confusion, but that her predecessor had taken twenty-one books and one map that belonged to the office when he left. In contrast, she pointed to her own meticulous *Report,* issued on December 31, 1911, which detailed with careful accuracy each item in the historian's office and which gave a detailed account of her own travels and activities.[40]

Sharlot must have been realistic enough to foresee the governor's reaction to this attack on his friend. As the newspaper copy of her letter commented, "Miss Hall does not expect to regain the office which she left on the transition of Arizona from a territory to statehood." But she may not have anticipated the prompt and icy response she received from the Governor himself:

> Frankly, I do not commend your taste, nor admire the spirit evinced by your letters.... I was the author of the bill which created the office of Arizona Historian, and lent my best support as a member of the Twenty-Fifth Legislature, to its passage. I was an earnest advocate of Mr. Windsor's appointment to the position, and considered the Territory most fortunate in Governor Kibbey's selection of him. And I venture to say that had he not been interrupted in his work, the office of Arizona Historian would today be in a position to make a most creditable showing for the considerable amount of money which has been expended....
>
> On the whole I must express keen regret that you have seen fit— whatever your motive or whoever inspired it—to go out of your way to attack, needlessly, gratuitously, and as I believe, without any basis of fact, a gentleman who has always spoken of you with respect and consideration; who is one of the most conscientious and able officials I have ever known, and whose sin apparently consists of nothing greater than having for a time held an office to which you aspired.[41]

After this exchange, obviously, Sharlot's pro forma resignation was to stand.

11

ℛetreat
to
Orchard Ranch

SHARLOT'S INITIAL REACTION to her peremptory dismissal was evidently shocked outrage, but it could hardly have been surprise. As a matter of fact, several weeks before she wrote her open letter about Winsor's activities as territorial historian, she had signed a contract with a Chicago firm, the S. J. Clarke Publishing Company, agreeing to produce a history of Arizona, to be completed by February 1, 1913.[1]

Sharlot did not consider that her preparations for writing the proposed history for the Clarke Company were complete. She had never visited the area north of the Hopi villages on the Arizona-Utah border, an arid region on the vast Navajo Reservation of much interest because of its little-known Anasazi cliff dwellings. It is possible that she had made arrangements while she was still territorial historian to visit the ancient ruins of northern Arizona the following summer, and that she had at that time chosen her traveling companion, Charles Lummis's friend and hers, Arizoniana collector Dr. J. A. Munk of Los Angeles. Now that she could no longer draw on state funds for her travel expenses, she solicited the Clarke Company for an advance of two hundred dollars "to enable her to carry on the work of preparing for the writing of [the] history," money pretty obviously needed to finance her trip.[2]

Sharlot met Munk on the train en route from Los Angeles to Gallup, New Mexico, catching it at the Ash Fork station north of Prescott at 3:10 A.M. on Sunday, July 28. Her mother had not been well when she left but had urged Sharlot to go; Adeline's illness seemed no worse than many others which she had had over the years. So Sharlot was off, with no more than her usual worried concern for her mother's welfare.

At Gallup, Sharlot and Dr. Munk left the train and took the stagecoach for Ganado. Here once again Sharlot was made welcome by the ebullient and hospitable John Lorenzo Hubbell, who had agreed to outfit them for the trip to Kayenta in the far Navajo country. He furnished them with provisions, a wagon and team of horses, a saddle horse, and a Navajo Indian guide by the name of Grover Cleveland. [3]

With Grover Cleveland on horseback scouting ahead of the wagon, Sharlot and Dr. Munk struck out from Ganado on the road to Chinle. The summer rains had preceded them; grass covered the prairie, and water for the horses was easy to find. They had trouble only once, as they attempted to cross a seemingly dry flat: "The surface seemed to be dry and hard, but underneath the soil was soft and boggy. Suddenly the horses broke through the crust and sank to their knees in quicksand, and the wagon plunged in after them up to the hubs. After some effort and considerable maneuvering the horses found firm footing and pulled the wagon out of the slough onto dry land...."[4] From Chinle they headed over the sometimes almost indistinguishable wagon road to Kayenta, home of Navajo traders Louisa and John Wetherill. Sharlot's notes recalled the desolate, untraveled route, with the road winding over long slopes, past huge red cliffs and down into sand washes. At length they caught sight of Agathla, the huge rough tower that guards the entrance to Monument Valley, "a detached world on top of which all the dreams of romance might be real." They shortly came to the trading post at Kayenta, where the Wetherills had lived since 1909. John Wetherill was already known in archeological circles for his discovery of Rainbow Arch and the Betatakin cliff dwellings. He had agreed to take them to the Laguna (Tsegi) Canyon cliff dwellings.

Munk told of the trip to Betatakin:

> We left the wagon road at Marsh Pass, twenty-five miles beyond Kayenta, and with a pack train, took the trail which led into an exceedingly wild and rugged country. The main canyon is winding and has many lateral gorges, all hemmed in by high walls of red sandstone.

Its floor is irregular and broken and our progress was slow and confusing as to location and direction. There was scarcely a foot of good road on the trail and we were compelled to pick our way through deep sand and dense brush thickets, and over rocky barriers that were almost impassable.[5]

Up the canyon they struggled, visiting Anasazi cliff dwellings which had been given fanciful names such as Ladder House, Forest Glen House, and Pine Tree. Betatakin Canyon, six miles from the entrance of Laguna Canyon, led to one of the largest and most spectacular Anasazi ruins Sharlot had ever seen; hidden in thickets of aspen and scrub oak, the ruins had been discovered by John Wetherill in 1908. The party moved next to Kiet Siel, the House of Broken Pottery. Here they marveled at one hundred and forty-eight rooms under the cliff.

While Sharlot was still in the Marsh Pass area, an Indian runner came with a telegram from the Tuba agency for her. Her mother had been brought, critically ill, from Orchard Ranch to the Mercy Hospital in Prescott on August 14. Wasting not a moment, Sharlot made preparations to intercept the train at the nearest station, Winslow. Commandeering the buckboard and the Navajo guide, Grover Cleveland, she started out late that afternoon 'to make an all-night dash over the all but invisible wagon track between Marsh Pass and Winslow. A violent storm broke during the night, turning a dry wash on the way into a raging torrent of muddy water. Terrified, the Indian driver refused to go on. Sharlot pulled a gun on him, forcing him to take the buckboard through the swirling waters and on down the nearly obliterated trail until they reached Winslow and the railroad station. Sharlot told the story later to her friend Alice Hewins, who recalled, "she did not know which he was most afraid of, the road or Sharlot."[6] Somehow Sharlot had managed to reach the station in time to catch the westbound train for Ash Fork, where she transferred to the local line for Prescott.

In time and yet not in time. Sharlot's feelings as she stepped off the train at Prescott Tuesday morning, August 20, and hurried to the hospital on the hill may be imagined. The few days that remained of her mother's life Sharlot spent by her side in the hospital room. Her father was also there; in later years Sharlot recalled how he sat on the side of my mother's bed in her last illness and chewed and chewed in this dull way—though her illness had brought a terrible nausea—and all his life he had known that the smell of tobacco made her sick—yet there he sat and drooled and spit while she turned her face to the wall and the farthest side of the bed to escape him. Yet his stolid, tobacco drugged dullness was so complete that I am sure he had only a pleasing sense of doing exactly the most comforting thing.

On Saturday, August 24, 1912, Adeline Hall died. A clipping from the *Prescott Courier* stated the cause as "abscess of the peritoneal glands." Sharlot said later that the cause of death had been an inoperable bleeding stomach ulcer and heart failure.

The next hours passed in a haze of numbed disbelief as Sharlot made the necessary arrangements to carry out her mother's last wish, that she be cremated. The body had to be taken to Los Angeles, as there was no crematorium closer. But death brought with it also a compelling spiritual experience which steadied Sharlot in her hour of agony. She told Alice Hewins of it when she returned from the trip with her mother's ashes.

> Because we are so near in heart I am going to tell you that this great, great experience has had its living revelation—stronger even than the sense of loss. As I sat by my beloved mother in the last hour and all alone with her for nearly an hour afterward I had the overwhelming knowledge that she was only free—not lost to me but out of pain—out of the bondage of the flesh and the sorrows of the primary school of life.
>
> I could not shed a tear—would not have dared to call her back into the worn and weary body—the dear face was too peaceful and the soul of her seemed to enfold me with such joyous assurance of well being.
>
> All the journey to Los Angeles she seemed to go beside me and to show me new beauty in every shrub and tree and hill—as if pleading with me to realize that she was more free than ever before to feel and enjoy every beautiful thing.
>
> Here in the home even the great absence does not lessen my feeling that she is only away—only going out to the natural progress into free and full and glorious life. I feel nearer to her than ever—as if her very soul was living part of its life in my body. . . . [7]

The urn of ashes which Sharlot had brought back from Los Angeles she installed in a niche in her bedroom wall. Here it remained for the

next thirteen years, a tangible reminder of the spiritual union that
was to furnish the strongest motivation for her life in the next decade. Thirteen years later, as Sharlot watched at her father's death-
bed, she thought back to the long days that had seemed so much like
a dream after her return to Orchard Ranch in 1912.

> There is something very strange about coming back to a home from
> which someone has just passed—I think it is perhaps the astral life
> which clings more closely to the living for a time. Anyway, it seems as
> if the one nearest of those living in the home really lives and suffers for
> two, no longer individual but double. . . . [8]
>
> Life seemed all blurred like woods blown full of smoke, the fall she
> died. . . . [9]

It is clear that the shock of her mother's death drove all thought of the
history of Arizona which she had promised to write for the S. J.
Clarke Company out of Sharlot's mind for several months. Her father
also seemed bewildered, too bewildered to oppose any plans for
change as he ordinarily would have done. Sharlot decided that the
ranch must be sold, and that she and her father would build an adobe
house on five or ten acres of land near Phoenix, where her father
would have enough space to putter but not so much that he would tire
himself out, and where she could get in to Phoenix easily to see
friends and professional associates. As soon as she advertised the
ranch, several prospective buyers approached her. Things seemed to
be moving along; Sharlot busied herself cleaning the house and pack-
ing their belongings to be ready for the move to Phoenix.

Sharlot had mentioned in a September 1912 letter to Alice
Hewins how terribly tired she was. This exhaustion, coupled with
the emotional strain of her mother's death, seems to have triggered
another siege of her spinal disorder; the next three months blurred
into a haze of pain which further drove from her mind all thoughts
of her contract with the Clarke Company for a history to be completed by February.

It is obvious, though, that the Clarke Company agents had not
forgotten. They were busy fanning out over Arizona taking orders for
the projected work and collecting laudatory biographical sketches of
the subscribers to make up a third volume of the work. Sharlot's old

friend Sidney DeLong of Tucson may have been the first to tell her what was going on when he wrote to her in December that he had placed an order for her history of Arizona with a Clarke Company agent. [10]

Sharlot was stunned. There she was, with a signed contract obligating her to furnish the Clarke Company with 200,000 to 400,000 words of Arizona history in the next six weeks! What to do? She read the contract carefully. At last she noted a clause which stated, "Sharlot M. Hall also agrees in case of illness or other inability from any cause to carry on the work of completing this said history, that the publishers reserve the right to complete the work under their own supervision." [11] There was the answer! She would plead illness and break the contract. She wrote to the company, telling them of her bad health and suggesting that a friend of hers, journalist and Phoenix postmaster James H. McClintock, might undertake the history in her stead.

In response to Sharlot's letter, the Clarke Company sent their local representative, L. C. Davidson, to talk to her. Sharlot's reputation obviously made her a valuable commodity to the publishing firm; Davidson pleaded with her to reconsider, stating that the Clarke Company would give her an extension on the original February deadline if she needed it. Sharlot rather reluctantly agreed to hold off on her final decision, at least until March 1. In his turn, Davidson promised to cease canvassing. It would seem, however, that he continued his activities. Furious, Sharlot wired Chicago.

As she told Alice Hewins, she "evidently stirred them up," for on February 19, while she was in the midst of domestic chaos with a whole backyard full of just-washed bedding stretched on the clotheslines, none other than Mr. S. J. Clarke himself "strayed in, coming in the back way past all the lines of wet things." As Sharlot described it to Alice, obviously relishing the entire incident, "He got to the pantry door and I called from the wash tub 'Come in,' thinking it to be one of the [hired] girls. I was awfully cross and told him plainly what I thought of him.... He promised to drop my name at once.... I could make it unpleasant for him but I don't want a row...." [12]

This arrangement would seem to have been a satisfactory conclusion to the matter, except that Clarke's agents evidently did not know about it. At least one man continued to canvass. At last, exasperated, Sharlot fired off a statement which was printed in the Phoenix *Arizona Gazette* under the heading:

WITHOUT AUTHORITY

I wish to state that no material gathered by me at any time is to be used in the history of Arizona for which the S. J. Clarke company of Chicago are now canvassing in Arizona. Many misrepresentations have been made concerning my connections with these canvassers, none of whom had any authority from me to approach any person and use my name. Such material as I have I expect to use myself in the future, and in case of my death before I am able to make use of it I expect it all to go to the great collection of Arizoniana in the Southwestern museum at Los Angeles, or to some suitable place in Arizona.

SHARLOT M. HALL[13]

This short paragraph, inconspicuously tucked at the bottom of the *Gazette's* editorial page, was to cause serious trouble for Sharlot.

The Clarke affair would have been trying enough had Sharlot been in good health. She had difficulty sleeping and was suffering periodic bouts of spinal pain. She struggled through the spring of 1913, with the Clarke Company agents' activities simply one of many annoyances. A Mr. Hancock expressed interest in buying Orchard Ranch; the negotiation progressed to the point that Sharlot packed their things and took her father to Phoenix, leaving Hancock temporarily in charge of the ranch. But when they returned, Hancock pulled out of the agreement. Sharlot never really unpacked again until she finally left the ranch some fifteen years later.

In the meantime she busied herself cooking for hired hands, canning, and making pear preserves from the fruit on the ranch, and watering 120 head of cattle. The watering in itself was a major operation; as she described it, "There are so many strays that I open and shut the gate, turn water out of the tank into the boxes, and set the dogs on the ones that wear the wrong brands. But when it is all done I saddle Limb o'Sin and ride—Indeed I do no house work except the cooking and dish washing and just enough sweeping to live with."[14]

"I am alone all day long," said Sharlot in a letter written probably to her friend Matt Riordan, "except that father and the two Mexicans now come home from the cane field for dinner—swallowed in three gulps and off again—and I have tried to miss no beauty of the autumn coloring and no bird or animal visitor. The yellow leaves are a glorious litter everywhere and I like to walk among them and love their rich tones — mother loved them so. . . . " Now forty-three, Sharlot was alone, alone with her memories of the mother who had been the inspiration for her writing and the spur for her ambition, alone with excruciatingly painful muscle spasms the length of her spine which came more and more frequently, alone with her father who once again had turned surly and refused to budge when she suggested they should try once more to find a buyer for the ranch.

Winter settled in on the isolated ranch in Lonesome Valley, and on its inhabitants. With the snows which obliterated the wagon road that led from the ranch to Prescott and Dewey, isolating Sharlot and James Hall, a brooding, deadening inertia sapped Sharlot's strength. As she told her friend Alice Hewins:

> Usually I never see a person from breakfast till supper day in and day out. . . . The cold days I spend in a big upstairs room where I have a stove and am very comfortable — with the funniest old tag ends of long discarded furniture — boxes — and evidences of my genius like the typewriter table [which she had constructed from two old chairs, two cheese box lids, and an old bread board]. . . . I have not tried to do anything yet but some fragments of essays — the atmosphere of this place is very painful to work in — a powerful opposing force always to be felt — of which I will some day tell you. Sometimes it makes me really ill — then I gather strength to dominate it for a time and work a little. It is not a *new* thing — but the more sad because it is part of the old problem which I tried so long to solve for my mother — merely the psychic manifestation of it is new.
>
> I take refuge in the hills when I can endure the house no longer and hope to find some avenue to permanent control presently. . . . [15]

Sharlot could expect to find no intellectual or spiritual companionship with any of the men and women of Dewey; as she told Alice in January 1914:

> I had some faint thought of trying to start a little club of Dewey women, but Mercy! yesterday I asked my old neighbor, Mrs. Thayer, about it and she said they all but came to blows at the dances and used "violent and abusive language" that wouldn't go in print. I knew there was hardly a respectable one there and none of even moderate intelli-

gence so I concluded that some more material *club* was what they
needed. My cedar trees and hills are too peaceful. I won't try to mix
with the human kind up here.[16]

Nonetheless, though Sharlot may have joked to Alice that her Dewey
neighbors needed a literal club rather than an association for mutual
betterment, she felt a sense of moral obligation to them. By the first of
February 1914 she had not only started a "Friendly Improvement
Club" for the women ("about as hopeless a bunch as you ever saw")
but had also organized a boys' club of the "regular little toughs" in her
neighborhood. She seems to have been an immediate hit with the
boys; as she told Alice, "I got a smashing compliment from one of the
boys. He rounded up a chum and made him help wash the dishes and
as we talked he said, 'You bet we'll have fun—you are just like a boy,'
so I've got to live up to that, of course."

   The women appealed to her less. As she told Alice:

Their need is so great—only God knows the dull life—broken only
when hubby beats up some one of them with a club—no uncommon
thing—And they are *so* ignorant and so timid. They regard me with
solemn awe because I could get up and talk to them—it would have
been funny if it had not been pathetic.... I hated like the dickens to
mix up with the outfit—I must confess—for many reasons—but
at last felt I must do what I could whether it was any visible good
or not....[17]

So Sharlot gritted her teeth and plunged in. Ignoring the pain of the
all too frequent muscle spasms in her back as best she could, she gave
her boys a picnic one week and took them to the local picture house
for a movie the next.

   Even the dull countrymen of the Dewey area must have been
aware of the Mexican Revolution led by bandit chief Pancho Villa
early in 1914. Border towns such as Douglas and Nogales were often
in the news; even Tucson had an invasion scare that spring. So when
Sharlot mentioned "the Mexican Revolution in my spine" to her
friend Alice a couple of weeks after her attempts to organize programs
for the boys and women of the Dewey area, Alice knew things had
reached the critical stage. Alice had been urging her all winter to take
a break from her daily round of drudgery and isolation and to come

down to visit her old friends in Phoenix, but Sharlot had resisted, claiming that she could not leave her father alone. Now she realized that something had to be done. She arranged to be admitted to a small hospital directed by Dr. E. C. Gillette in Phoenix on March 17, 1914. It was fortunate, as she observed in her letter to Alice, that their new hired man, Carlo Cantello, a "nice Italian boy," was working out so well. "He is such a kind pleasant fellow," she told Alice, "and comes close to walking the floor when my face gets too much tangled up with the revolution—did the churning beautifully last night and hovered around while I took up the butter just like an anxious hen with one sick chick.... Fortunately father is quite well and the work is moving along so they can spare me better than later in the spring...." Sharlot closed her letter with a comment which had more significance than she could have realized at the moment. "I won't be quite able to see *people* for a few days," she warned, "—only you two and the Gillettes."[18]

What Sharlot did not know was that U.S. Marshal J. P. Dillon was waiting for her in Phoenix. On March 2, 1914, the S. J. Clarke Company had filed a bill of complaint in the federal court in Phoenix against her. Sharlot had scarcely been dismissed from Dr. Gillette's hospital before she was served with a summons. The complaint alleged that the little notice, "Without Authority," which she had inserted in the *Gazette* more than a year previous, was "a false, scandalous, malicious and defamatory libel" which had "greatly injured" the Clarke Company. Fortunately her friend Richard E. Sloan, the former governor, was now a member of a Phoenix law firm. She sought him out. She remained in Phoenix until April 14, when the required legal answer was filed through her lawyer with the court.[19]

By the last of April Sharlot was back at the ranch, where her life would have been bearable except for increasing evidences of her father's mental instability. When Alice and her husband came up early in the summer of 1914 for a visit, James Hall took them aside and complained, very confidentially, that Sharlot was watching him. Sharlot tried to explain the situation to Alice:

> Last September I wanted to begin and keep a careful account of what we spent up to the first of this coming September, but this irritated him so much that I gave it up—and it had much to do with his irritated feeling that I watch him.

... Father's feeling is something that probably was born with him—it is characteristic of Southern men who always resented the effort of women to share in any way in business. . . . I have watched him seem to suffer physically as well as mentally when mother tried to plan for our education with him, and even more so if it was a matter of safeguarding us from associations which she feared. It was impossible for him to take action till danger was forced unmistakably upon him—and I have seen him burst into tears when she urged him to warn my brother about certain associates—as he often did with me when I tried to show him that mother was overworking, and plan to make things easier for her. It is some deep mental weakness, or as I have often felt, a mental immaturity, like his boyish delight in telling stories and joking with his hired men or any man he is with. . . . It is pathetic and in later years mother and I dropped all effort to discuss anything seriously with him and just did the best we could and let things go for the rest. . . . I am seriously and earnestly trying to do my best and especially to do what I know mother would want me to do—but with my lifelong understanding of the situation there are many limitations which no one on the outside can see. . . . [20]

At about this time Sharlot received word that the S. J. Clarke suit was to come to trial.[21] In September she went to Phoenix to confer with her lawyer, Richard Sloan. Probably fortunately for Sharlot's emotional well-being, the case was settled out of court. But the agreement must have cost Sharlot years of anguish; the Clarke Company agreed to drop the suit if Sharlot promised never to write a history of Arizona. She kept her word.

12

*Years
of the
Locust*

SHARLOT RETURNED TO THE RANCH following the meetings with lawyers and the Clarke Company representatives weary in body and spirit. Her father was deteriorating mentally almost before her eyes; his senility took the form of increasingly surly and suspicious withdrawal punctuated by insane outbursts of rage. She dared not leave him alone on the ranch, even with the hired men; he was incapable by this time of making even the simplest decisions.

In addition, Sharlot came to realize in the weeks that followed her trip to the Phoenix hospital that something more serious than her chronic spinal problem was affecting her health. She began to suffer the same low-grade fever, nausea, and dull abdominal pain which had plagued her mother during her last years. Resolutely Sharlot told herself that her mind was playing tricks on her, that this was simply a further physical extension of her acute spiritual sensitivity, her awareness that her mother was somehow still close by, watching over the affairs of the Hall household. So Sharlot tried to ignore her discomfort, the overpowering weariness that made even the few household tasks she undertook almost more than she could manage.

In January 1915 Alice Hewins invited her to come to Phoenix to attend the annual meeting of the Federation of Women's Clubs. Sharlot refused to leave the ranch. "To tell the truth," she said,

going away is so painful that I shall only go when urgent business demands—there isn't one particle of pleasure in anything—knowing

[142]

the conditions of my life absolutely fixed here. I felt like a corpse risen from the dead as I went about Prescott [before Christmas] and the meeting with one-time acquaintances was more painful than I can tell you. I'm not morbid, dear, I simply recognize that I can only live in some degree of peace by giving up absolutely everything—the least suggestion of sharing or in any way bettering any part of ranch life rouses such sullen fury and stubborn resistance.[1]

A further complication was their hired man, Carlo Cantello, an Italian immigrant. As Sharlot put it, "Hired men are the chief diversion of my life—we had a Mexican last year on whom I had to pull a gun—and a red headed American this summer who stormed and cursed and used 'dope' and tried to boss the whole ranch, indoors and out." Carlo had proved to be a refreshing change in this regard from his predecessors; he was clean, willing to help both inside and out of the house, and anxious to improve his English. "However," said Sharlot ruefully, "he has complicated the good he might do by falling crazily in love with me—and if you think it is any fun to have a fiery-eyed Italian tell you every day that he wants nothing more in life than to do the work for you because he worships you 'All same madonna in the church at home'—just *try it.*" Of course there was no use mentioning any of these problems to her father. As she told Alice, "His hired men are always his closest chums and he wouldn't understand either danger or annoyance to me."[2]

By the first part of February Sharlot realized that something was seriously wrong with her health. She knew she should seek medical help in Los Angeles; Dr. Gillette had advised her not to delay an examination by specialists there. Yet she procrastinated the journey in an agony of indecision. Unable to sleep and in constant pain, she told Alice on February 27 that

I read just as one takes a drug—to stop thinking.... Just now I admit that my nerves are pretty well upset.... I have reached the point where I do not feel that any short or slight change will meet the trouble and I quite recognize the signs of a complete breakdown unless I get into a different atmosphere and among people again.[3]

It was early May before Sharlot took the train for Los Angeles. Once there, she sought out Dr. P. Gregory Cotter, a specialist in surgery and gynecology, who had examined her once before when she was in Los Angeles. For the first three weeks Dr. Cotter treated her as an outpatient, keeping her in bed on a diet of cornmeal, gruel, chicken broth, and bread. By early June, however, it was obvious that this treatment had not solved the problem. Sharlot was admitted to Dr. Cotter's small private hospital, where she underwent two operations five weeks apart for an ulcerated colon, a problem very similar to the difficulty which had killed her mother three years previously.

Not until September 23 could Sharlot write to tell Alice that "I have walked on my own two feet alone and now come to the table like a grownup and this morning took a real bath in a real tub and put on my corset over a thousand dollar straight front which I expect to wear for the rest of my life." She was shortly discharged as a patient, "with the comforting assurance that *in a year* I would be quite well."[4] On October 14 Sharlot wrote her friend Charles Lummis that she was "to be sort o' packed in cotton and shipped to Oakland." Here she was examined by another surgeon and then, still in a wheelchair, she visited the San Francisco-Panama Exposition of 1915, one of the most exciting events happening in the West.

Sharlot had been warned by her doctors not to lift any weight, climb stairs, or do any work that would pull on her abdominal muscles, but she was appalled by the shambles which greeted her at the ranch house when she returned to Arizona in November. Carlo had been away during part of her absence, and "the most notoriously dirty and 'low down' family in the whole region" had moved in to "help" her father. Said Sharlot ruefully to Alice,

> I don't think anything on this place was not prowled over this summer and much destroyed by the miserable trash whom father let do just as they pleased with everything. . . . When Carlo finally got back he had to use as nearly hospital methods on everything washable as possible and was still "hoeing out" when I came. I looked the wreck over and felt that unless we camped out under a tree there would have to be some repairing done and the lumber and shingles were nearly all on the ground when thirty inches of snow overtook us. . . . [5]

In January 1916 a concerned letter from her old friend Charles Lummis prompted Sharlot to make a thoughtful analysis of her current status. She wrote:

As yet I am not making very swift progress toward health—such generous free-hand cutting has left an aftermath of pain and much difficulty in walking that I will need about a year, they tell me, to overcome. . . .

It hardly seems likely now that I will write much more—perhaps far in the future I may do so. For the present there is nothing but to stay on the old ranch with father. . . .

. . . I think frankly that about all that was alive in me died with mother. . . .[6]

Physically, Sharlot hung on, but her emotional hold on life was tenuous. A second letter from Lummis midway through the year prompted a report from Sharlot which must have wrung his heart:

After much thinking and some experimenting I have settled immovably into this spot while my father lives—and have long since become just the typical woman of the isolated little ranches. I often think of Mrs. Alcott's reply—"Only one woman"—when someone asked her if Brook Farm had any beasts of burden. . . . My poor old father is a bit less strong year by year—and he is one of the typical country men whom the slightest intrusion of anything outside the life-long routine irritates and annoys almost to the point of physical suffering. To stay with him I must accept life as he can live it—and eliminate even my friends when they irritate him. I want to stay—I want to be as good a soldier as my precious, wonderful mother was—and so I do not even keep in touch with friends—and know no more of life outside the ranch and . . . this tiny community than if I were locked in a dark cell. I sometimes dream—as I fly from feeding chickens to watering cattle or cooking or painting the house, of little things I would like to write —especially about the conditions that warp and mar the very souls of country people—but I fly to the next job and no word ever gets on paper. . . .

I have no thought of anything but the life here for the present, nor of being away for years to come. . . . I have arranged that in case of my death here my curios and collection of manuscripts go to the [Southwest] Museum—to be part of the Arizona collection there. . . .[7]

Carlo, anxious to relieve Sharlot, did the necessary chores, both inside and out of the house, staying out of James Hall's way as much as he could. Most days the old man brooded in his big easy chair in the front room, working his jaw incessantly over his quid of chewing tobacco and eyeing his silent daughter and Carlo suspiciously. The slightest provocation brought on an insane fury of shouted obscenities which shook the very fiber of Sharlot's being. Sleepless, tense, pained with neuralgia, overwhelmed with fatigue and depression, Sharlot found for the first time in her life that when she sat down at the typewriter no words came.

Symptoms such as those manifested by Sharlot between 1912 and approximately 1922 proliferated among sensitive, intellectual women of the nineteenth and early twentieth centuries. It is believed that these varied ailments were often outward manifestations of the women's frustrated rebellion against their societally assigned roles. Henry James's sister Alice, for example, suffered from an illness diagnosed as "spinal neurosis"; of her unhappy life, James commented that her "tragic health was, in a manner, the only solution for her of the practical problem of life."[8]

Alice James was never able to work her way out of her difficulty. Two other brilliant women, Charlotte Perkins Gilman and Jane Addams, like Alice James a few years older than Sharlot Hall but still of approximately the same generation, also suffered devastating psychosomatic breakdowns as young women. In each of these instances, the women had been encouraged to study, to educate themselves, but not specifically to aim for any particular intellectual or career goals. Barbara Ehrenreich and Deirdre English speculate that "illness was perhaps the only honorable retreat from a world of achievement which (it seemed at the time) nature had not equipped [them] to enter."[9]

Adeline Hall, to whom Sharlot had an intense emotional attachment, suffered from undefined "ill health" certainly from the period when the Hall family moved to Arizona. How many of Sharlot's mother's problems were real and how many were the result of nervous hypochondria cannot be known. Adeline Hall, from Sharlot's telling, was brilliant, ambitious, and completely frustrated by her husband's lack of sensitivity to her needs. Yet she seems to have had a loyal attachment to James Hall, an attachment which Sharlot interpreted in a neurotic fashion after her mother's death to mean that she, Sharlot, must fall heir to her mother's role of caretaker and companion.

With the coming of spring Sharlot did not again take up her earlier efforts at socializing with her Dewey neighbors. A letter written several years later to Lummis suggests why:

This little community is a slum such as even New York would have to hustle to show—and it has a snobbery of ignorance worse than the bluest Boston snob ever dared exhibit. Here an educated man is absolutely hated and a well-dressed or well-mannered man marked as a crook the first thing. No rich man is honest or good—no professional man knows anything—all trained men in any line are fools—the Lord's anointed are all ignorant, poor, and oppressed by these high-toned rascals who have an education and want to live without honest work....

The most terrific jolt came when I found that if any of my former friends showed an interest in me here it was immediately felt that they did so because I had had immoral relations with them at some time— the idea that anyone ever felt any interest in my writing or any work I had done was laughed to scorn.

Think of that!! Me myself! Who had travelled all over the Southwest and commanded the respect of the very worst men as well as the best! Even my harmless little book of verse is a subject strictly tabu—and I have had ignorant farm hands come to me to write a letter for them and then tell me that I didn't know enough to write good English.... [10]

The people of Dewey left her alone, though they did not cease to gossip about her. The young schoolteacher, Edenia Richardson, saw Sharlot with other people of the Dewey neighborhood only once, at one of the infrequent church services held in the Dewey schoolhouse. "She came in alone, dressed in black, sat by herself; her head was slightly bowed, her hands in a prayerlike clasp in her lap. When the service was over she left immediately without speaking to anyone." [11]

Charles Lummis, meanwhile, was pushing a project which a decade earlier Sharlot had enthusiastically supported: the building of a museum for the preservation of Arizona history. Several of Lummis's letters written to friends during the spring of 1917 described a new association he was attempting to launch, the short-lived "Institute of the West."

The Southwest Museum is growing every day; and the Southwest Society is now incorporating as "Institute of the West"—and plans to establish local chapters in every considerable population throughout that million square miles. We want to have one in Flagstaff, for instance; and one in Williams, and one in Phoenix and Prescott and Tucson and Albuquerque and El Paso—covering the places not already provided with adequate means and scientific authority for saving its regional history.... The central organization is to give authority and uniformity to the plans and installations and cataloguing. But we want each of these many populations (which need such thought more than any big city does) to get busy with saving their own relics and records.... [12]

It seems almost too coincidental that even as Lummis was writing his letter, the Arizona state legislature passed a bill entitled "An act to provide for the purchase and restoration of the old gubernatorial mansion at Prescott, Arizona, providing for the care thereof in perpetuity and providing for an appropriation therefor." The bill was signed by Governor Campbell on March 8, 1917, and $7,000 was appropriated. The State Board of Control was authorized to purchase the Mansion, provided the city of Prescott should guarantee "in perpetuity full care and maintenance of said Gubernatorial Mansion." [13] In this way the old Governor's Mansion passed from private hands to the care of the city of Prescott. Sharlot apparently had nothing to do with the transaction, and may not even have been aware of the event.

A few friends from the outside world, such as the faithful and concerned Alice Hewins, kept in touch with Sharlot. Alice and her husband, L. E. Hewins, came to Orchard Ranch several times during the year; James Hall seemed to enjoy Hewins's company, and Sharlot relaxed, glad for the harmony which these good friends always brought with them. Alice's letters arrived regularly, and packages came often to the little Dewey post office with books, clothing, and one spring even a pair of peacocks which proved to be a source of delight to Sharlot for several years.

The United States declaration of war against Germany on April 6, 1917, had little immediate impact on the isolation and monotony of life at Orchard Ranch. But soaring copper prices meant prosperity for the little smelter town of Humboldt south of Dewey and a good market for beef and fruit from the ranch. Carlo made regular trips peddling meat and fruit with the wagon and team. In addition, Sharlot bought some investment property in Humboldt, borrowing the money from an old friend of her mother's, Mrs. Lottie Hartsfield,[14] who came to Orchard Ranch to stay from time to time when her daughter and son could not care for her.

Mrs. Hartsfield, whom Sharlot characterized as "company— even if little help" was with her in the summer of 1918, when Carlo, an Italian citizen, returned to Italy to visit his mother. He was promptly drafted into the Italian army for the duration of the war, leaving Sharlot to carry on the ranch chores in his absence with the aid of his old cousin, John. Nothing daunted, Sharlot took herself into Prescott, where she bought a Studebaker truck. On September 24, 1918, she reported to Alice that she was "a pretty fair driver— with now and then some small mishap to teach me more of mechanical things." Once a week she made the long drive over the hills through Dewey and Humboldt all the way to Mayer and the Blue Bell mine to sell fruit. By December that year she was able to report that "I have made a great fruit peddler and can run the car quite well and take a good bit of the care of it."[15]

The news of Germany's surrender on November 11, 1918, lifted Sharlot's spirits; better days must be ahead, she felt sure. The deadly influenza epidemic which swept through Arizona during the fall and winter of 1918–1919 spared Orchard Ranch, possibly because of its isolation. By February 1919 Sharlot was able to write to Alice Hewins, "For the first time since I came back to the ranch I really 'see daylight' through the work and dare to plan for things I enjoy doing."[16]

When the Atlantic Monthly Press had included her essay, "A Memory of Old Gentlemen," in its second series of *Atlantic Classics* the year previous,[17] it had cheered Sharlot as nothing else could have. John McGroarty's praise of her poem "In Old Tucson," which he called his favorite of all the literature of southwestern writers and reprinted in 1919 in the *West Coast Magazine,* gave her courage to sit once again at her old Blick typewriter, suddenly full of ideas for chatty essays and articles. In June 1919 the first of a regular series of informal essays under her name appeared in the *Prescott Journal-Miner.* An odd combination of Yavapai County history, scenic description, Chamber of Commerce boosterism, and straightforward advertisement for Prescott merchants, the essays continued with some regularity through the summer and fall, culminating on

December 10, 1919, with a reprint of her short story, "The Price of the Star," first published in September 1901.

The most interesting of the series was the article which appeared in the *Journal-Miner* on November 11, 1919, under the title "The First Romance-tragedy of Governor's Mansion: Plea for Preservation of Relic." The Governor's Mansion had been placed in the care of the city of Prescott more than two years before. Sharlot wrote:

> There have been many suggestions looking to the safeguarding and use of this interesting old relic of early days but the only really acceptable one is . . . that it be restored as nearly as possible to its original appearance and used as a museum for objects and articles related to the early life of this region and associated with its early history.

Carlo Cantello returned to the ranch during the summer of 1919, but even with his help Sharlot found her daily round of activities increasingly, as she told Alice, "a staggering load." Winter once again brought isolation along with the hard, monotonous work. Sharlot's fragile hold on mental stability slipped as the blackness of depression once again engulfed her.

It was February 1920 before she surfaced. An unanswered letter almost a year old from Charles Lummis prompted her to describe her situation:

> This winter the work and isolation so got on my nerves that I had a huge battle with nervous break-down, but the worst seems past and no doubt I shall be all right. I have at last settled completely into the rut that is inevitable while father lives and shall find things easier by reason of making no effort to better them. [18]

A letter to Alice Hewins written about the same time gives a clue to something which had helped that winter and which was to become increasingly a saving comfort to Sharlot in the next few years: Christian Science. Though Alice was not a member of the Mother Church, she seems to have been interested in Christian Science doctrine. Probably hoping that Mary Baker Eddy's teachings would help Sharlot, Alice had been sending her Science literature since 1916. Sharlot acknowledged the good her reading had done:

"I came to a very bad piece of road this winter—and I turned as never before to Science and the life of Christ—and I am getting great things out of it.... I am trying to study constantly and I feel sure that the only limit to the good is my own slowness of understanding. Not, dear girl, that I may ever be an orthodox Scientist but I am certain they have this truth—that the real Christ will meet all our needs—answer all our puzzles. [19]

13

Cactus,
Pine, and
Coolidge

SHARLOT'S AFFIRMATION of the principles of Christian Science was a radical reversal from her belief in the Freethought tenets which she had embraced so warmly as a young woman of twenty-five. This turnabout from Freethought advocacy of "observation, experiment, demonstration—beyond that nothing"[1] to an agonized grasping for something beyond the tangible and the finite has an interesting parallel in the life of one of the most stalwart early advocates of the Freethought movement, Annie Wood Besant (1847–1933), a woman whom Sharlot admired and respected. Mrs. Besant entered the Freethought movement at the age of twenty-seven as the brilliant associate of the English Freethought leader Charles Bradlaugh (1833–1891). Before Bradlaugh's death Besant had turned from atheism and materialism to the theosophical mysticism of Madame Helena P. Blavatsky.

The same dissatisfaction with the basically negative concepts of Freethought that led Besant to develop a faith in Theosophy's doctrines of eternal progression and development may have motivated Sharlot's search for something beyond the unpleasant physical realities of life at Orchard Ranch during this period. Having rejected the prescriptive dogmas of orthodox Christianity as well as the atheistic materialism of Freethought, she investigated Spiritualism, Theosophy, Rosicrucianism, Swedenborgian mysticism, and the New England Transcendental philosophy of Ralph Waldo Emerson and Bronson Alcott. Then, at a point in her life of mental as well as

Sharlot and James Hall at Orchard Ranch

physical crisis, Christian Science held out a helping hand, through the good offices of several members of the church in Phoenix and Prescott.

Sharlot made a trip to Phoenix in January 1921. Evidently she visited with a Christian Science practitioner while she was there, for she returned to the ranch at the end of the month brimming with optimism, sure that science "demonstrations" on her behalf had been helpful. The aura of happiness which she brought with her from the trip affected even her father, who seemed glad to see her. But the glow which Sharlot felt faded all too soon. By the next week she wrote Alice Hewins:

> I guess the first week of February must have been bad medicine for all of us. Father had one of his worst spells. . . . He took it out in treating Carl to all the cussedness he could think of. . . .
>
> These awful scraps leave me too tired to work and numb all over. And I doubt not that father suffers too—and it affects Carl so seriously that I

don't wonder that he wants to leave. He said this time that I had to stand it but that he himself would be dead in another year of it. So I am right at the end of my rope—except to stay here alone by selling all the stock....[2]

Still shaken, Sharlot continued her letter the following day:

You will wonder if Science helped me this time—I think it did, greatly, though I admit that at first I was too sick at heart to try consciously to use it much—but I feel sure that the short duration of the "terror" as compared to past times, and the peace which seems following, has been an unconscious demonstration. Whatever comes I shall feel sure that it is leading toward harmony—even though over a rough road....

It is clear, however, from a letter which Sharlot wrote Alice at Easter time that her reading and study was taking her far beyond the bounds of orthodox Christian Science. She speaks of getting help

from Science, from Theosophy, and similar sources... the healing and protecting power is open to anyone and belongs to no one creed or race.... I continue to read every night the various books relating in one way or another to occult subjects and am beginning to get some very interesting flashes of vision.... I am neither curious nor afraid, neither doubtful nor eager, and it seems to move along much as my daily routine does—which, I feel sure, is the only way in which one can come into any real understanding....[3]

About the middle of April Mrs. Emma Smith Noyes, half sister of Charles Genung's wife and ill with cancer, came to stay with Sharlot. Still full of her new "power of positive thinking," Sharlot vowed to "help her forget a supposed sentence of cancer of the stomach. I shall try my brand of Science for her," she told Alice.[4]

Nonetheless, things slipped badly for Sharlot in the next weeks. Toward the end of May a telegram came from the University of Arizona, signed by President Rufus Von Kleinsmidt. The faculty of the university had voted to award Sharlot the honorary degree of master of arts at commencement on June 1. Could she come to Tucson for the ceremony? Sharlot told Lummis what happened next.

All I could do was laugh at the idea of my being able to go to Tucson— the old lady [Mrs. Noyes] roused enough to say a kind word—the only one I had in my family as to the event. Oh yes, my father had had one of his worst tantrums of temper that day and the hired men had come in to say they couldn't stand it another hour and were going to leave — *leave* and the wells almost dry, cattle bawling for water — and windlass ready for sinking deeper after the receding water.... All I've had time to think about the degree is to wonder why they gave it to that long dead woman who once was myself.... [5]

"Indeed," concluded Sharlot, "I did not bother to tell my father about it — he would not understand and would be contemptuous of any institution that thought I had any sense."

Sharlot's optimistic assurance of better things ahead that she had felt earlier that year seemed like a half-remembered dream by August. Mrs. Noyes's cancer did not respond to treatment. That month Sharlot sat by her bed in the Prescott Hospital, where Mrs. Noyes died. It was the ninth anniversary of Adeline Hall's death. Telling Alice of her sorrow, Sharlot concluded, "At this anniversary mother seemed almost visibly present for several days." [6]

The year 1922 opened much as 1921 had closed. Arizona residents hardly needed the *Tucson Citizen* on New Year's Day to tell them that the previous year had been one of economic depression, throughout the nation as well as the state. They probably saw little that rainy January to convince them that conditions would be better in 1922 than they had been the year before. Mrs. Lottie Hartsfield stayed most of the winter with Sharlot; the two of them studied Christian Science lessons each day. Sharlot, as always, read omnivorously, beyond Science, from popular psychology through spiritualism. In April she reported to Alice that

I am moving on as usual — except that a good many things are sort of "coming through" entirely without will on my part — like things whispered from behind a curtain. There is a growing set of poems of ranch life from the woman's viewpoint, none poetry of a high order, but all true to life.... The crudeness of some may repel you — others will remind you of mother. I am frankly interested to see what more will come for I feel as if I were just recording them, not creating them. [7]

Nonetheless, almost in spite of her, the curious current of Sharlot's life was about to carry her back to the mainstream of Arizona activity. Her teeth had been bothering her for several years, but it was not until the spring of 1922 that she managed the courage, the money, and the time to go into Prescott to have them removed. Her Good Friday letter to Alice gave the news. "At last the offending teeth are out," Sharlot wrote, "and a good (bad) job it is for they were in a bad state. The new ones are yet to come—in a few weeks I suppose and no doubt it will be another experience to learn to endure them. But if other people can do it I know I can."[8]

Before the new teeth arrived, however, Sharlot found herself snatched from her life of obscurity and propelled before the public as a wholly impromptu (though not totally reluctant) "toothless orator." A letter to Alice probably written in May 1922 told the tale. "In the first place," said Sharlot,

> the past three weeks have been peculiarly strenuous. Very hot and dry, Carl working almost day and night at his meat selling in a great effort to establish a paying business—and father and I working all day long to save potatoes and squashes and melons from millions of bugs—fighting them with torches of gunnysacks dipped in kerosene—which as we use it does not seriously harm the plants but does cause a hasty exit of bugs. Also we had sprayed orchard and a lot more strenuous things when father drank too much cold water and came down with summer complaint which lasted ten days and got his strength. During that time I did double duty—and in the midst of it the gang [Jerome City Health Department] closed in on Carl's business like a lot of wolves... to prohibit all meat selling outside a shop except under impossible restrictions....

Off went Sharlot to Prescott to get some legal advice. "I certainly had a headful of trouble," said she, "as I climbed into the car to start home." But her legal worries paled beside what happened next:

> Before we could step on the gas the County Farm Bureau president jumped on the running board and said: "Be there before twelve tomorrow—you've got to supply for Gov. Campbell." He jumped off and ran after a man whom I recognized as the state president before I could ask him what he meant. But as he jumped one way a big fellow from the Prescott Dry Farm Station jumped on the other side and said "Don't fail to be on the ground on time to confer with the state and University men—our main speakers have failed us and you've got to fill the time." He was gone sprinting after a bunch of men as he spoke. Our county farm agent spied the car at that minute with Carl frantically jerking the starter — and as he landed on the running board I grabbed his shoulder and told him to say what he wanted like a sane man before he did any jumping off.

He yelled "I wrote you a week ago—Northern Arizona Farm Extension Annual Meet"—then he sprinted—just about leaving his shirt collar in my hands.

So Carl and I tackled the unfinished grades on Lynx Creek hill, that look like a shell shocked mountain having a fit—and got the mail. They had really written me a week back that the State Farm Bureau president asked them to feature me on their program. Nice news for a sunburned potato bugging lady faced with a ton of dirty dishes at home and supper to get and an early start to Jerome in the morning to tackle the medical czar.

Carl went to bed vomiting up his heels, I started father through bath and shaving by lamplight because I wanted to take him to the farm meet and had to take him on the Jerome trip to do so—got supper, washed dishes, and went to bed planning the assault on the doctor— mere farm men lost in the distance.

Jerome was all the lawyers promised and then some—at quarter to eleven left there for Granite Dells, in the outskirts of which the letter stated the meet would be held, preceded by a barbecue dinner and adorned with various celebrities, state and local. They neglected to say which outskirts.

A drunken autoist on our side of the road and going like mad on a terrible grade nearly relieved us of all further responsibility to get anywhere—Carl's skill at the wheel saved us and we scooted on. Got in O.K. in time to see the County Farm president armed with shovels and running to aid the band autos stuck in a sand bar on the wrong road.... Celebrities arriving in squads and Dry Farm man, a young and plain dirt farmer yanking toothless lady out of car and shoving her ahead of him to welcome them. Bear in mind that I had snatched a hasty bath at four A.M.—anchored hair in a solid braid under a net for a forty mile drive in a keen wind...fed chicks, turks, and family and faced hours of grilling in Jerome. I sure looked like being hostess to a celebration in an unfamiliar cottonwood grove.

When everybody was beaned and beefed and pickled and cantaloped it was seen that a speaker's stand was lacking. The band safely rescued covered the grunts of a time worn Ford truck as it was coaxed into position and from it the speakers in turn held forth.

If you think it was fun to face that crowd and hold them with toothless oratory till the other folks got ready you mistake—but I made them all laugh the first twenty words, and kept them laughing, and wound up with two of the ranch poems that came in along with the potato bugs—and climbed out of the Ford while they yelled for more. I felt tired as a kerosened potato bug when it was done—but the other speakers were fine and the meet was a great success.... [9]

Even more than in her public triumph did Sharlot glow over a private victory. As she told Alice, "The meeting and my part in it seemed to impress father and Carl very much—neither had ever heard me speak in public—and both are themselves so ill at ease among people outside their own class."[10]

More was to come. The previous year, a group of Prescott businessmen had formed an organization whose original purpose was to raise funds for the annual Fourth of July Frontier Days celebration. Calling themselves the Smoki People, they had presented a program of Indian dances at the Prescott fairgrounds on May 26, 1921. The program was so well received that the men decided to make it an annual affair; in order to give credibility to the "Indian tribe" of Smoki, some ancient history was needed. Who better to concoct the history than Sharlot Hall? Shortly after the Farm Bureau meeting, two of the members of the Smoki Executive Committee, Neil C. Clark and Chris Totten, drove out over the rutted dirt road from Prescott to Orchard Ranch to exercise some friendly persuasion on Sharlot. They must have been extremely convincing, for in June 1922 an attractive sixteen-page pamphlet, "The Story of the Smoki People," was printed by the *Prescott Courier*.[11] The text, including six poems about the Smokis and a pseudo-legend telling the origin of the mysterious "tribe," was by Sharlot Hall.

Despite some urging by Neil Clark, Sharlot did not write again for the Smokis. But the success of "The Story of the Smoki People" seems to have broken the last of the psychological barriers which had virtually stopped Sharlot's pen during the previous decade. She retired again to the isolation of Orchard Ranch but not with the same depression and despondency.

The rest of the year passed uneventfully; farm chores and weekly trips to peddle Orchard Ranch fruit kept Sharlot too busy to write much, but by spring she was thinking of writing a new book of verse. In addition, she was ready to become active again in the Arizona Federation of Women's Clubs. She had not been forgotten by clubwomen in the years since her 1914 resignation as Federation historian. When it was announced that the 1923 meeting would be held in April in Prescott, Sharlot decided to attend. She told Alice what happened.

I got in late Thursday afternoon—with the darned old auto on fire from a crossed wire—and before I got my breath in the dark corner into which I tried to slide—the presiding officers called me to the platform. I was so plumb dazed I didn't know they expected me to speak till the president shook me and slid me out in front.

My hands were all auto grease, my nose smeared with black from the fire (I didn't know that just then however), and my old jersey suit showed exactly how I had crawled under that darned old machine hunting trouble. I hadn't any more speech in my system than a walnut tree has maple syrup... but I just shut my eyes and opened my mouth and they all laughed and then sniffled and cried and I don't know yet what I did say. They had a big banquet that night but I had to scoot back to father and the chickens.[12]

The Federation women were not finished with Sharlot. She was asked to return the next day to plant an official club tree; at the final luncheon on Saturday, April 7, in Jerome, she was named official Federation poet.

Sharlot obviously enjoyed the attention she was receiving from her Federation friends and Smoki admirers, but she shrank from ending her self-imposed decade of seclusion at Orchard Ranch. Still feeling the need for allowing the powerful psychic currents which she had tapped to use her as they wished, she went back to her solitude, waking each morning with a sense of tingling curiosity as to what the day might bring. Increasingly, almost of their own volition, lines of poetry surfaced, images in words forged of the despair of the past decade. "I seem to be 'sublimating' all my ranch life in these later poems," she wrote Alice, "and I am very curious to know what will come along later."[13]

The year 1924 was ushered in with snow, wind, and heavy fog that kept Sharlot, her father, and Carl housebound. Sharlot's father grew more feeble; he seemed so bewildered without her that she hesitated to leave the ranch, even to go in to Prescott. But go she did, whenever the roads were clear, to sell farm produce, since the Humboldt smelter's closing meant few sales to the west of Dewey.

Another of James Hall's vicious outbursts of temper that spring made Sharlot wonder if she dared leave the ranch to participate in the annual Federation of Women's Clubs convention, held that year in Tucson. But at the last moment, Sharlot took the train south to read her own poetry on the Thursday afternoon program, April 2, 1924. Following her reading, the Federation adopted a resolution "requesting Miss Hall to bring out a second edition" of her book of poetry, *Cactus and Pine,* first published in 1910.[14]

Sharlot was elated. The poems which had been pouring from her pen, almost as if they had been dictated by voices from the astral sphere, cried out for publication. Now the way was opened to her. The poems from the first edition, long out of print and the publisher out of business, would be reprinted with the new poems in a separate section. Before she left the meeting, Maie Bartlett Heard, wife of Dwight B. Heard, owner of the *Arizona Republican,* offered the services of the newspaper's presses for the printing. Everything was moving in Sharlot's favor.

While she was at the Federation meeting, Sharlot and her friend Norah Hartzell were chosen delegates to represent northern Arizona at the General Federation of Women's Clubs biennial conference in Los Angeles. The last day of May saw Sharlot and Norah on the train heading for Los Angeles. The Federation meetings were interesting, but for Sharlot the high point of the trip was her reunion with her old friend and mentor, Charles Lummis, for the first time in more than a decade. Sharlot was now fifty-three and Lummis sixty-four, ill and with failing eyesight.

Songwriter Charles Edson had nominated Sharlot to honorary membership in the Gamut Club, an exclusive Los Angeles men's club. Lummis was asked to make the nomination speech. He described the evening in his journal, saying,

> And Charlie Edson made some remarks and called on me for the nominating speech to make Sharlot an Honorary Member, which I did with great gusto and some success; and nothing that I could say was enough to say, so I had Edson bring me a reading lamp; and while I had no business to do it, and couldn't do justice either, I did read her magnificent poem "Out West" and in spite of these handicaps it swept the room.... And we elected Sharlot with a roar. And she made a little talk of such exquisite, childlike directness and simplicity that half the men in the room were half ready to cry, and to my joy, they applauded Sharlot heartily and longer and more fervently than anyone else in all the long night of many features....[15]

To Lummis's sorrow, Federation meetings and other business kept Sharlot from returning to El Alisal until Sunday. At that time she had dinner and a short visit with her old friend. It was Wednesday of the next week before she communicated again. Said Lummis,

> Greatly pained by a phone from Sharlot saying goodbye—has to run right back to Prescott tonight. Is terribly worried about her old father. I hope to God she finds him dead when she gets there—he has made her a wonderful character, with as much virtue on his part as the fagot and the stake had in ennobling the early martyrs. Some famous woman watching Sharlot the other night cried softly to herself just looking at her and not knowing a thing about her. She said, "She has all the Sorrow of Womanhood in her Face," which I guess is so.[16]

Lummis's heartfelt wish had not materialized when Sharlot reached Orchard Ranch. James Hall was still a factor to be reckoned with, though he no longer had the power to overwhelm his daughter. Sharlot's spirit had grown beyond his reach.

During the summer of 1924 Sharlot finished the last typing of the manuscript for the second edition of *Cactus and Pine.* She had scarcely gotten the manuscript off to the *Arizona Republican* print shop when she had an unexpected caller, ex-governor Thomas Campbell. The Republicans of Arizona wanted to place her on the Republican ticket as one of the electors for the presidential election in November. President Calvin Coolidge, filling out the term of his predecessor, Warren G. Harding, was running for a second term against a relatively unknown Democratic opponent, Wall Street lawyer John W. Davis. If Coolidge should be elected, Campbell told her, the Republican party would send Sharlot to Washington with the electoral vote from Arizona. Sharlot was flattered, but the forthcoming book was more on her mind than any possible political successes. She told Alice, "I let his flowery remarks go out at the other ear but as it will advertise the forthcoming book I let him go ahead—any sort of publicity being good for sales."

It is obvious, though, that the idea of the Washington trip had caught Sharlot's fancy. A note at the bottom of her letter to Alice confided, "This is strictly private—if the Party does win and I go it is probable that I will be presented with a gown of Arizona copper cloth to wear while officiating—no small ad for Arizona copper and also solving the dress problem for me in a unique way.... However, I consider all that pipe dreams."[17]

The next weeks were filled with literary activity. As more verses came to Sharlot, she began planning a second book, which she

decided to call *Poems of a Ranch Woman*. One of the poems intended
for this collection was "When Summer Rains Begin," about a "gentle
wife" and tender mother who keeps a rendezvous with her dead lover
during summer thunderstorms:

> She listened down the canyon trail
> For hoofbeats stilled a dozen years,
> And as a lightning flash leaped out
> Her heart went cold with long-past fears.
> With trembling hands she turned a key
> And opened wide a long-locked chest,
> And took a dress mud-stained and dark,
> Where once a drown'd, dead face was pressed.
>
> She put it on with eager haste,
> The gray rain fell like blades of steel,
> From cliff to cliff the thunder roared;
> The hillsides seemed to shake and reel.
> She left the cabin, door flung wide.
> She did not hear her children cry—
> She thought a struggling, foam-choked horse
> Screamed in the water whirling by.
>
> The riding drift churned madly down
> And spewed a sodden log to land—
> She stumbled, falling to the brink,
> And leaned to grasp a phantom hand.
> The seething bubbles held a face
> With yearning eyes loved first and most,
> And wild, by that wild flood she ran
> To keep her faith with one pale ghost.
>
> At dawn she climbed the canyon trail,
> And locked the mud-stained dress away,
> And lingered softly by the bed
> Whereon her sleeping children lay.
> Day-long she tended her small home,
> And swept the floors and made the bread,
> But kept within her gentle eyes
> The look of one who seeks the dead. [18]

When Calvin Coolidge won the presidential election in November, Sharlot was pleased. Coolidge's election, in theory, depended on the actual vote of the electors pledged to support him, and Sharlot was one of the three Republican electors on the state ballot. However, only one elector, carrying the three electoral votes, would be sent to the electoral college ceremony in Washington the following spring. The more Sharlot thought about it, the more desperately she wanted to be the one. Not only would she be a participant in all the excitement of a presidential inauguration, but, once in close proximity to the great museums and libraries of the East, she would be able to do research toward the fulfillment of her life's ambition, a dream deferred during her long decade of solitude but not forgotten: the creation of a historical museum for northern Arizona. As she traveled to Phoenix late in November to attend to final details necessary to the distribution of *Cactus and Pine,* she thought about what she might do to be sure that she would be the elector chosen for the trip.

On December 1, 1924, Sharlot decided to take some action. She wrote to Judge John S. Campbell, one of the three electors, asking his support should he not wish to make the trip to Washington himself. Meanwhile, her other rival for the coveted electoral trip, George O. Ford, a secondhand furniture dealer from Phoenix, was doing a little campaigning on his own behalf. About the middle of December, Judge Campbell received a letter from Ford, protesting Sharlot's solicitation of Campbell's support and requesting that the three of them draw straws to see who would go. Campbell responded on December 27, suggesting that the three electors meet at the capitol in Phoenix on January 12 and stating that he had no objection to having the selection of the favored elector being made by chance.

On January 12, at the appointed hour, Sharlot Hall, Judge John H. Campbell, and George O. Ford met in the office of James H. Kerby, secretary of state, in the state capitol. The *Arizona Republican* account of the meeting unfortunately was silent as to the fireworks which probably exploded when Judge Campbell as chairman of the group decided against the "selection of chance" which Ford had advocated. The newspaper report said only, "Judge Campbell was chosen as chairman of the Arizona electors and Miss Hall as secretary. The electors then voted on the envoy to carry the certificate of election from Arizona to the president of the senate. Judge Campbell nominated Miss Hall for the position and the vote disclosed Judge Campbell and Miss Hall voting for Miss Hall, while Mr. Ford voted in the negative. Miss Hall was declared the envoy."[19]

On January 18 Sharlot took the train for Washington and the start of her big adventure. She arrived in the capital at 9 A.M. on Thursday, January 22, 1925. Senator Ralph Cameron and his wife, Ida Spaulding Cameron, Sharlot's friend from their school days, were waiting for her at Union Station. They drove immediately to the Senate Office Building, where Sharlot saw "senators in squads." At noon she met President Coolidge, who kindly questioned her about Arizona. That afternoon Sharlot accompanied Cameron to the Senate chamber where the electors were to present their sealed envelopes, their states' votes for one or another of the three presidential candidates (Coolidge, Charles Davis, and Robert M. La Follette). "The Lady from Arizona was the first woman to arrive with the vote of her state, and as Acting Vice-President [Albert] Cummins reached out his hand to take the historical letter, cameras were snapping and we were caught in the act," Sharlot wrote in a long letter prepared for Arizona newspapers.[20]

At 9 P.M. Sharlot attended a reception at the White House to meet President and Mrs. Coolidge. She told her Arizona audience, "I felt like Cinderella.... I can scarcely believe yet that I really did move forward in that long, long line—nearly four thousand people, it is said—into the storied rooms...." And at last Sharlot was shaking hands with the president, who was "not at all like the descriptions of him which we have read...he is kind, not cold, a little grave, but with keen humor in his eyes and the quiver of his lips. He may not joke but he sees all the fun...."[21]

With Ida Cameron as hostess, guide, and promoter, Sharlot found herself the object of considerable attention. She was, as she said, "photoed to a finish" and entertained in high style at the Congressional Club, the Senate Luncheon Club, and the Pen Women's League. On each of these occasions she was asked to speak and read her poetry. At the Smithsonian Institution she renewed her acquaintance with Dr. J. Walter Fewkes, the anthropologist with whom she had visited in the summer of 1910 while he was exploring prehistoric Indian ruins on the banks of the Little Colorado River. It was the Library of Congress which seems to have been Sharlot's most frequent stopping point in Washington. Having discovered the historical resources of this great institution, she set herself a nine-to-five schedule of reading and research about her childhood hero Captain Bucky O'Neill, a Rough Rider from Prescott killed at San Juan Hill during the Spanish-American War. [22]

On February 11 Sharlot witnessed the formal counting of the ballots submitted by the state electors on January 22. She found the ceremony, held in the House chamber, an impressive one. Senator Cummins, preceded by two pages carrying mahogany boxes which held the returns from the states, came down the middle aisle followed by the rest of the senators to join the congressmen already seated in the chamber. One by one, the envelopes were opened and the votes called off and tallied. When all were read, the final result was 382 ballots for Coolidge, 136 ballots for Davis, and 13 ballots for La Follette. Calvin Coolidge was now officially elected to office. As Sharlot commented, "In the early days of the young republic this was no doubt a much more important part of the governmental procedure, but it is still one impressive and interesting to witness." [23]

The long-awaited copper mesh overdress arrived from the manufacturer on February 24, along with a handbag of copper mesh and a hat ornamented with cactus. Sharlot had worried about how this outfit would look; she reported to Alice with some relief that it "is really very pretty and not a bit freaky." [24] She wore the copper gown for the first time to a luncheon given for Senate wives honoring Mrs. Coolidge by her friend Ida Cameron the same day.

The day of the inaugural ceremonies came at last, March 4, 1925, with cloudless skies and clement temperatures. Sharlot and the Camerons listened to the President's inaugural address at the capitol. Then they hurried off to the Post Office Department, where they found a good vantage point from the upper windows of the building to watch the inaugural parade. "It was not a very big parade," said Sharlot, "for the President had earnestly begged that there should be as little as possible and that there should be no lavish expense or display anywhere." [25] Mrs. Coolidge, Sharlot was happy to note, wore the Arizona necklace of silver and turquoise sent by the Smoki People to the inauguration.

After the inauguration Sharlot left Washington for New York and Boston. In New York, Myron Westover, vice-president of General Electric and a friend of long standing, introduced Sharlot to the

Sharlot Hall wearing the copper gown, 1925

Metropolitan Opera and the museums, parks, and art galleries of the city. In Boston she was met by friends of Westover's, Mr. and Mrs. Byron R. Houghton. The Houghtons gave her a whirlwind tour of Boston, but best of all, learning of her still troublesome spinal problems, they took her to a specialist, Dr. Sheehan, who told Sharlot he thought he could correct the difficulty. A week later, she wrote to Alice to report that she was "strapped into an instrument of torture and told to stay there for a year or so—I am very lucky it is no worse. It is merely a brace at the lower part of the body to hold in place some bones that he put where they belonged by some very skillful yanking."[26]

Sharlot had planned to make a leisurely journey back to Arizona through the Midwest, with stops in Chicago and Kansas to give readings. During the first week of April, however, her father became very ill, so ill that he was brought from the ranch to stay with the Hartzells in Prescott. On April 8 Norah Hartzell wrote to Alice Hewins that James Hall had requested that no one write to Sharlot about his illness.[27] One of Sharlot's Smoki friends, however, must have told her. As soon as Sharlot got the news, she left Chicago and hurried straight to Prescott, arriving on Tuesday afternoon, April 14. James Hall, who for years had made Sharlot's life a living hell with his surly temper, had been "wretched all the while"[28] she was away.

14

First Lady
of the
Governor's Mansion

SHARLOT FOUND HER FATHER WELL ENOUGH after her return that she took him later that week to Phoenix, where they attended the two-day Arizona Pioneers' picnic sponsored by the *Arizona Republican* newspaper. With a strange turn of mind, James Hall not only was glad to see his daughter, but, as Sharlot told Alice, "he has a pathetic feeling that I ought to be there [at the Pioneer picnic] and I think he longs to see some fuss made over me, to tell you the truth, poor old man."[1]

James Hall had been suffering from Bright's disease for some months. His doctor gave him medication which seemed to control the pain and swelling, but Sharlot had been told that the end was possibly only months away. After the trip to Phoenix, Sharlot took him back to the ranch, determined to make his last days as comfortable as possible. She let him do whatever work he felt able to do; despite her earlier attempts to keep him on a simple diet, she now let him eat anything he wished. Planting time in May aroused his interest as nothing else had done. As for Sharlot, she slipped back into her old routine, "choreboy for the ranch, sewing a little in snatches, and generally putting to rights," as she told Alice.

James Hall's condition steadily deteriorated. A new prescription seemed to help, however, and by June 20, Sharlot's father felt so much better that he insisted on going out to help irrigate the orchard. Sharlot told Alice, "He so enjoys working in the orchard and garden and spreading floods when they come that I let him go—it seems no use to deny him the one thing he can really enjoy."[2] The improvement was only temporary. By the end of August James Hall was bedridden, fretting in his delirium at the sound of the thirsty cattle, a sound which he imagined was the bawling of the trail herds of long ago, those good times when the frontier was new and a man could be as free as the wild herds of buffalo that roamed the plains. Just past midnight on Thursday, September 3, James Hall died.

The next day Sharlot buried her father on a hillside on the ranch. The funeral was a double ceremony, for she buried her mother's ashes in the same grave. Many friends and neighbors came to the outdoor service, in which Sharlot spoke of her parents' lives on the frontier and read her own poem. She wrote to Alice: "I never saw a crowd so awed and impressed—yet there had been no emotion, everything as quiet as a dream. . . . It was just the sort of funeral mother would have wished and the double grave is where she and I often stood and looked out over the orchard."[3]

Sharlot determined to hold on to the ranch until more definite plans could be made for the future. As she said to Alice:

Never have I had so strong a sense of being upheld and of moving toward a long-destined work—of being selected by forces quite beyond myself to do something that needs doing. . . .

. . . I cannot regret one hour of this ranch life—if it has taxed my physical strength it has opened doors that I think seldom open to human eyes—to me now, past and present and future are one continuous stream of life—all moving to great and sure purpose.[4]

Sharlot's sense of other-worldliness remained with her through the end of the year. The failure of the Prescott State Bank just before Thanksgiving in 1925 concerned her only remotely. Many of her Prescott friends, however, were hard hit. Between the bank failure and the depressed condition of the mining industry in northern Arizona, local business was particularly stagnant; Sharlot was almost giving Orchard Ranch fruit away. Better that than let it rot unsold, she reasoned.

Sales of her book, *Cactus and Pine,* were also slow. Each woman's club in the state had pledged to sell a certain number, but even these copies were not moving. The worried Alice, who served as Sharlot's sales manager, told her that she must break out of her self-imposed isolation at the ranch, must get out among the club-women of the state, must accept speaking engagements so that she would be better known.

At this juncture Grace Sparkes entered the picture. Grace Sparkes (1893–1963) had come to Prescott as a child, graduating from St. Joseph's Academy in 1910. As soon as she graduated, she began working for the Yavapai County Chamber of Commerce as assistant secretary. In 1913 she was appointed secretary, a position she held until 1938. As part of her Chamber of Commerce duties, Grace Sparkes was in charge of the Annual Northern Arizona State Fair, the Prescott Frontier Days celebration, and the *Yavapai Magazine*.[5] Her one-time assistant, Evelyn Carnapas, remembered her as a driver and a crusader.[6] She seems to have adopted Sharlot, beginning about 1926, as one of her "causes"; Sharlot, sensing the value of Chamber of Commerce backing, was not at all unwilling to be adopted. On January 19, 1926, Sharlot wrote to Alice that, despite a return of her chronic spinal trouble, she had agreed to go to Phoenix to give a major address to members of the Phoenix Woman's Club.

A few days later, still in Phoenix, Sharlot was taken in tow by members of the Phoenix Junior Woman's Club. Pointing out historical sites, she drove with them over the Apache Trail which she had described so well in 1906 in her *Out West* article, "The Great Tonto Storage Reservoir."[7] The Apache Trail jaunt seems to have been too much for Sharlot's health. She had planned to go next to Tucson, where President Cloyd Marvin of the University of Arizona had invited her to speak. Instead, she stayed in Phoenix with the ever-solicitous Alice for about a week, before returning to Orchard Ranch.

Carlo had been anxiously awaiting her return. He had gotten word of the sudden death of his father in Italy, and was making arrangements to go home. Determined to get the ranch in good condition first, he and Old John had begun the spring plowing. Sharlot rolled up her sleeves and joined them in the work. As she told Alice later that spring,

> Busy is a misleading term—I am cycloning along these days.... I helped Carlo start mowing rye hay taller than my head.... Mower broke and I brought home repair piece—also a Hartzell donation of A-1 seed potatoes and after five o'clock Carlo and I cut them and planted six rows before dark—ate our supper at 8:15 and hiked out at 4 this

morning—he to mow again and I to shoot "Aphicide No. 10" out of a dust gun over all my young squashes.... Have planted hundreds of very small hubbard squash that sells well and keeps well—shall plant a very big lot yet—and pumpkins also—if the season is good shall have many, many tons. Every inch of ploughed land on both places must produce this year unless rains fail us entirely.... Carlo is as eager as I to make a big yield of marketable stuff and we are both in harness 12 to 15 hours a day.... The place looks wonderfully well and the cattle are fat already. A big fruit crop which we shall thin to the point where it will be large—and if water fails—rain I mean—I shall hire an emergency crew and sink a well in the middle of the orchard and put the gas engine on it. Shall put one man plowing the minute the hay is off the ground and plant alfalfa after the first summer rain. My neighbors are now worrying for fear there will be no summer rain this year— but Carlo and I are going to let them worry while we keep right on working.... [8]

Sharlot, Carlo, and Carlo's cousin John worked through the month of May and the first week of June. Then, carrying her copper dress, a bag of Arizona copper ore, and a load of copper craft items, Sharlot left the ranch for Los Angeles. The Arizona Industrial Congress had asked her to take charge of their display at an exhibition, "Informashow," held in connection with the convention of the National Association of Purchasing Agents from June 9 to 12, 1926. By June 8, Sharlot was installed at the Ambassador Hotel, the convention headquarters. The next four days were busy, as 2,000 purchasing agents from all over the United States inspected articles on display and asked questions. Sharlot seems to have seen more than she wanted to of fashionable young "flappers." As she told Alice, "The place seems to me a great big crude sort of Indian camp for hordes of painted savages.... In the hotel I see many lovely elderly women with long hair and simple dresses—and of course the grounds are full of the half naked painted ones." [9]

When the convention ended on Saturday afternoon, Sharlot went to see her old friend Charles Lummis at El Alisal. This occasion was her last visit with the man who had more influence on her early development as a writer than any other individual and whose Southwest Museum had inspired her own ambition to establish a similar center in Prescott. By fall of the next year, Lummis was to be told he had inoperable cancer of the brain, which ended his life on November 25, 1928. But this June evening, Lummis was his old self, delighted

Sharlot Hall in 1926

to see his little poet. Hospitable as ever, he insisted that she stay overnight. Although he was no longer able to host one of his famous "noises" for Sharlot's friends, he invited California poet Harry Knibbs and his wife over for the evening. "Bully visit," said Lummis afterward, writing in his diary. They spent the evening reading poetry, including Lummis's latest poem, "Ballad of Geronimo," based on his own experiences in the Apache War. Unfortunately, continued Lummis, Sharlot did not like the poem; as he put it, "Ballad sticks in her craw."[10] Most likely they also talked of Sharlot's long-cherished dream of building a museum to house Arizona memorabilia.

One of the first things Sharlot did when she returned to Prescott was to buy a new Star touring car to replace the worn-out Studebaker truck which she had been driving for so many years.[11] A week later, on July 25, she was granted a license to slaughter cattle, swine, sheep, and goats at Orchard Ranch and to sell the meat in Dewey.[12] In later years, Sharlot was inordinately proud of that license; in a speech made to the Prescott Business and Professional Women's Club long after she had left the ranch, she told the women: "I held the only livestock slaughtering license ever issued to a woman.... I could unload the forty-pound apple boxes a lot better after that — and haggle with road camp cooks about the price of beef...." [13]

Sharlot and the men worked steadily through the hot, dry summer. As she told Alice's husband in September that year: "I have seldom seen so hot an August, nor one when the earth dried worse and vegetation suffered more — it has been hard on 'man and beast' as the old saw goes. We are feeding all the corn fodder to the cattle as I am butchering as fast as they fatten and I can place them with the local butchers." [14] Sharlot felt the need for haste, for Carlo's departure for Italy was set for November. She drove between fifty and a hundred miles each day in the Star car, marketing her fruit, but "hardly got enough to pay for gasoline in the end," as she remarked ruefully. She was also anxious for Carlo to see something of Arizona before he left. On September 15 she drove with him to the Grand Canyon. Back at the ranch, as Carlo waited impatiently for his papers so that he could leave for Italy, everyone pitched in to harvest the fruit. By October, the peaches were off the trees and most of the apples were picked. The summer had been so dry that the apples were small, but, as Sharlot noted to Alice, at least they made good feed for the cattle.

Depressed economic conditions in Yavapai County might have been hard indeed for Sharlot had it not been for a California mining company which began to work the old placer mines on Lynx Creek that winter. "The boss man," as Sharlot told Alice, "thinks he has discovered a regular storybook heroine in my busy self...he hopes they may buy the ranch in January when their man of cash comes out—and he thinks it would be very effective and romantic to build me a studio and have me come back now and then." [15] Although Sharlot placed little credence in that idea, she was glad to have a market for Orchard Ranch beef, butter, and fruit at the new mining company.

In mid-February, to the delight of the Lynx Creek miners, it began to rain. But the rain which could have done so much good the previous summer continued to fall in a deluge. By the end of February

Sharlot reported "the biggest flood since the Walnut Grove Dam went out [in February 1890].... It scooped out the bed of the creek like a trough and chewed off some choice corners of the ranch—took fences and ditches...about a month's work added to our spring routine."[16] Despite the flooding, while Sharlot worked, she planned, envisioning herself as First Lady of the old Governor's Mansion.

When the Territory of Arizona came into being in 1863, one of the first decisions to be made was where to place the territorial capital. Tucson, the only town of any size in the new Territory, might have been a prime candidate for the honor except that, for a few months in 1862, the town had been allied with the Confederacy. At the suggestion of General James H. Carleton, Arizona's new territorial officials traveled along the Santa Fe Trail. In January 1864 the official party reached Fort Whipple, which was approximately at the geographic center of the Territory. Attracted by the abundance of wood and water in a beautiful forested basin a few miles south of Fort Whipple, Governor John N. Goodwin settled on this area as the site of the new territorial capital. By May 1864 the new town had been laid out and named Prescott, after historian William H. Prescott.

The "Governor's Mansion" at the new capital was constructed of logs cut from trees nearby; by September 1864, the eight-room building was completed sufficiently so that four of the officials—Governor Goodwin, Secretary Richard C. McCormick, Chief Justice William F. Turner, and Secretary Henry W. Fleury—moved in. A small log structure was built across Granite Creek on Gurley Street. This served as the first territorial legislature, until cold January winds whistling through the unchinked building drove the legislators to the comparative comfort of the Governor's Mansion for their deliberations.

In 1867, when the territorial capital was temporarily moved to Tucson, Henry Fleury remained in Prescott in the old log building. Sharlot met him in 1882, shortly after the Hall family arrived in Arizona. "Even then," said Sharlot, "I had a dream—that some day I might live in the big log house."[17] After Fleury's death in 1895 the property passed into private hands. Floors were laid; siding covered the sturdy log walls. The building was put to many uses, including a combined dwelling place and commercial laundry.

Though the difficult years between the death of Sharlot's mother in 1912 and that of her father in 1925 made it impossible for Sharlot to take active steps to make her dream a reality, she did not forget about the matter. Following her trip to Los Angeles for the "Informashow" in June 1926, she wrote a letter to Walter Douglas, general manager of Phelps Dodge Mining Company of Bisbee, in which she detailed her hopes for the Governor's Mansion and rather broadly hinted to Douglas that the project needed his financial backing.

My dear Mr. Douglas:

For some while I have been thinking of telling you about a dream I have for using the "Old Capitol" as it is called, in Prescott, in a way that would make it of permanent use to Arizona.

You may know that this old log building and the land surrounding it was bought by the state some years ago and turned over to the city of Prescott—to be permanently preserved and used as a local museum. However no means was taken to insure its upkeep or restoration and it has never been used as planned. . . .

I have long wished to place my collection of historic and Indian things in the old house and to make of it a very unique local museum—or rather a center of historic and other interest. . . .

I would like to surround the good-sized area on which the old house stands with a log stockade like the original Ft. Whipple (pine logs on end) and to furnish it with my old furniture which would make it somewhat as it looked when the little bride of our second governor came to live in it.

In the grounds I would like to have two old miners I know build me an old-time arastra and set up a string of sluice boxes and a rocker and a long Tom—and perhaps a "Dobe smelter." . . .

Having been a ranch-woman for forty-three years in Yavapai and taken a long (life-long) course in economy, I do not feel that elaborate plans or a small fortune are needed—nor that all the work need be done at once—but something is needed for the start. . . . [18]

Douglas was not destined to become the patron of the restoration of the Governor's Mansion, so Sharlot turned to Prescott's city officials for help. By May 1927, negotiations between Sharlot and the city fathers had progressed to the extent that she wrote a formal letter of intent to Joseph A. West, Prescott City Attorney.

> My purpose in asking the city for a life lease on this building on the very best terms which may be possible is this—for more than forty years I have been gathering in Yavapai County a collection of prehistoric relics from the Indian ruins and of things relating to the early history of the county and state....
>
> As you know the old building is neither fireproof nor in good condition—but if it is to be saved to its contemplated use as one of the historical shrines of Arizona some-one must be willing to begin very quietly and patiently to put it in order and assemble there such relics and collections as are left to us in Yavapai.
>
> This can only be done by some-one who is very familiar with the early history of Yavapai—and some-one willing and free to devote much time, thought, and hard work, to the job.
>
> I seem to be that person—and therefore, I place before you my plan—a plan to be enlarged or changed as I work and according to the necessities or possibilities of the situation.
>
> I must be free to carry out my plans without hindering—therefore I wish a life lease—with the most help and the least restriction which the honorable mayor and council may be willing to give.
>
> I wish to be sure that my personal collection will never be moved away from Prescott—either in part or in whole—and that the museum and historical library purpose will be carried on after my death.
>
> I wish absolute freedom to finance the work in whatever way may seem best as it develops. The beginning must necessarily be very modest and limited—but I hope to leave the museum an endowed institution before I die as I expect it to be my sole heir.
>
> I wish absolute freedom to develop the land around the building into the most beautiful park possible—in time—and to place upon it whatever buildings or objects may be in harmony with the original purpose and a contribution to its realization. I expect to make my home in the building for such time as that may contribute to the development of the museum plan and the care of the objects assembled.[19]

The City Council acted almost immediately. Meeting on June 6, they gave Sharlot a life lease on the Mansion and surrounding grounds, including free water, electricity, and police and fire protection. In her turn, Sharlot agreed to give her historical collection, valued at

$10,000, to be placed "in the building now on and those to be placed on" the grounds of the Governor's Mansion. In addition, "said Sharlot M. Hall will make said property her home and will spend the remainder of her life, improving and beautifying said property." The official instrument was drawn up, signed, and attested by all the parties concerned on June 20, 1927. Sharlot Hall was now the First Lady of the Governor's Mansion. [20]

15

Restoration of the Mansion

SHARLOT DID NOT MOVE into the Governor's Mansion immediately. After she signed the agreement giving her a lifetime lease on the property, she returned to Orchard Ranch and to the endless round of ranch work. June passed, and July wore on, hot and dry. Sharlot continued to butcher Orchard Ranch cattle, as she told Alice, "clearing up more of the leftovers from the last years of father's life, when he tried to farm with too much hired help and the drought was as savage as the present year."[1]

The hard work that summer on the ranch took its toll. A bout of spinal pain coupled with a persistent sore throat led Sharlot to seek out a doctor. He advised her to return to Boston to consult Dr. Sheehan, the specialist who had been so helpful when she had seen him in the summer of 1925. On September 10, having drawn up a handwritten will bequeathing all her possessions to the Governor's Mansion, Sharlot left for the East. She met with Dr. Sheehan and was relieved to find that he thought she was "in good condition considering the work—no serious throat troubles so far discovered—is treating the tonsils."[2]

No longer worried about her health, Sharlot began what she called "a regular royal progress." She spent a few days in New Hampshire with friends and then stayed with Mrs. Myron Westover in Vermont for a week. Later she visited the old Wayside Inn, setting for Longfellow's "Tales of a Wayside Inn." Restored by Henry Ford, the inn served as one inspiration for her own plans for the Governor's Mansion in Arizona.

I found Henry Ford doing with the Wayside Inn exactly what I have dreamed for thirty years of doing with the old house in Prescott. The old inn...has been rescued from as serious decay as the Old Governor's House now stands in, and has been furnished as it was when Longfellow met with his friends before the big fire-place. It has been filled with all the simple, homely things that were part of the daily life of the New England country people—things as homely as wooden clothes pins cut out by hand and old churns just like the one my mother brought in a covered wagon to Arizona.... It is a wonderful collection and the manager told me that he had a record of two thousand paid visitors a day all of last year.

Now without the Ford capital—without any capital but my own hands and brain and my own historical collection...I am going to try to make a sort of cross between the Wayside Inn at Sudbury and Mount Vernon, which is the nation's shrine....[3]

Although she was back in Prescott in December, Sharlot did not immediately make a start on the Governor's Mansion renovation. Winter weather seems to have kept her from moving into the drafty, unheated old house until some time in March 1928. The enormity of the task that Sharlot was undertaking at her own effort and expense might well have intimidated her. Her old friend, Judge Edmund W. Wells, was not encouraging when he remarked, after falling through the rotting steps on the front porch, "You can't do this—it's too big. You'll just spend every cent you've got and die in the poor house."[4]

Sharlot just smiled and went on with her planning. First there must be a new roof, a roof of pine "shakes" such as the original builders of the Mansion had used. Then Sharlot planned to build a stockade fence around the property. Next, as she told a club group that winter, her fingers "itched" to pull off the siding which Joseph Dougherty had nailed over the original logs when he bought the Mansion at auction after Henry Fleury's death in 1895.[5]

As soon as the weather moderated, Sharlot and her cousin Sam Boblett set into the job of cleaning the old Mansion. As she told Alice's husband:

The old house grows more interesting all the while—sometimes I think I have part of the dirt hoed out—and then I know that I have a year's job ahead. We literally load wheel-barrows full of concentrated soot and dust—refuse of fifty years or more.... There are going to be three great big rooms and some smaller ones—all rough and crude but very attractive when filled with my relics and furniture.... The two

The Governor's Mansion in 1929 with the siding still in place

front rooms have the lining of handplaned lumber put on about 1865. We have found a lot of whip-sawed lumber in the upper room — a big garret — and with it the back room is being lined on one side and partly ceiled — having the original logs on two sides. . . . [6]

Early in April, Joseph Dougherty, first private owner of the Mansion after Henry Fleury's death, went through the building with her and told her of the modifications and repairs which he had made. These included installation of planed floors over the dirt floors, lining of the walls with wallpaper, and covering the outside logs with siding to make a two-family private home of the building. In addition, Dougherty had added a long porch on the west side of the building and had glassed in an open porch on the east side.

The next week Sharlot traveled to Phoenix to attend the annual reunion of the Arizona Pioneers Association — all Arizona residents who had come to Arizona before 1890. Sharlot had been elected vice-president of the group at the April 1925 meeting which she had attended with her father after Coolidge's inauguration. Sponsored by Dwight Heard, owner of the *Arizona Republican,* the Pioneers Association reunions held each spring in Phoenix were to form an increasingly important part of Sharlot's activities. She played an active role in the organization either as vice-president or as president until her death in 1943. Now, as the reelected vice-president of the Association, she shared her plans for the restoration of the Governor's Mansion as principal speaker at the morning meeting, held April 17, 1928.

Once back from Phoenix, Sharlot began to work in earnest. She brought most of her furniture from the ranch to Prescott and installed it in the Mansion. By mid-June she had established herself in a bedroom-workroom in the big garret upstairs where she intended to do her writing. A room at the back had been modernized by previous tenants as a kitchen; with this and a water heater for her bathtub Sharlot felt herself well off.

Although many people had stopped informally at the Governor's Mansion to see what was going on, June 28 seems to have been the first day that the building was officially open to visitors. George Kelly, Arizona State Historian, was the first visitor to sign the new register at the Mansion.[7]

The rest of the summer was not a good one for Sharlot. Overexertion seems to have brought on a siege of heart trouble, with "a fool doctor forbidding even letter writing" for several weeks.[8] News

The Governor's Mansion in the 1930s with its new stockade fence

of the death of her old friend Matt Riordan on July 12, 1928, could hardly have helped her spirits. By mid-August, however, she was back at work again, making arrangements for pine shakes for the Mansion roof and fighting conservative Prescott citizens who considered the stockade fence she was erecting around the entire block a real eyesore. Some "cheerful bootleggers" who had been in the habit of making their deliveries over her property brought the matter to the Prescott City Council, with demands that she be "abated." As Sharlot told Matt's brother Timothy Riordan with considerable glee, "They were told by the city attorney that I had both an iron-clad lease and an iron will and was a nice lady to let alone."[9]

The sudden death of Sharlot's brother Ted on September 26 sent Sharlot on a brief and extremely difficult trip to Tucson. Sharlot had written her brother off as one who was dead after his marriage in 1908 to Petra Acosta of Sinaloa, Mexico. Although her brother and his family had lived in Tucson since 1912, she had never contacted them; as a matter of fact, even as close a friend as Grace Sparkes had no idea that Sharlot had a brother. It must have been a difficult meeting for Ted's widow as well as for Sharlot, who never referred to the matter again once she returned to Prescott.[10] That November Sharlot received word that her friend and mentor Charles Lummis had died of brain cancer.

Putting sadness behind her, Sharlot plunged once again into her all-consuming task. The two front rooms of the Mansion were now full of relics, everything from an old Mexican plow contributed by a miner who had found it by the side of the road to a century-old wax doll from France brought in by a woman's-club friend. The women of the Monday Club rallied behind her efforts, designating December 17 as "Sharlot Hall Day." She was also given a "Sharlot Hall Christmas Tree" loaded with money and artifacts for the Mansion.

Winter settled in, one of the severest in years. The old house with its cracks and holes was scarcely habitable. Sharlot's cousin Sam Boblett worked about four hours each day putting pine shakes on the roof; it was too cold to do more. Sharlot slept in her garret bedroom under a mountain of covers, with a hot flatiron and a hot-water bottle to warm the bed; in the morning her breath made steam both in the bedroom and downstairs. By Christmas the water pipes had frozen.

Sharlot Hall in the Governor's Mansion

Sharlot gave up the struggle and thankfully accepted Maymie Duke's offer of a free, warm room with hot and cold running water at the downtown St. Michael's Hotel.

The inclement weather, which kept Sharlot at her hotel retreat through the month of February, 1929, spurred her and Sam on in their efforts to insulate at least one small room at the Governor's Mansion. This room, under the dormer on the east side of the building, they padded with celotex and building paper in hopes that this would be the last winter that Sharlot's hospitable friends would have to come to her rescue.

Meanwhile, Alice's husband, L. E. Hewins, was prodding some of the members of the state legislature to introduce a bill for an appropriation to assist Sharlot in the restoration of the Governor's

Mansion. Despite the efforts of some of the legislators, House Bill 179, "Providing for the Preservation of the Old Governor's House at Prescott, Arizona, and the Historical Relics preserved therein, and making an appropriation therefor," failed to pass. It was indefinitely postponed on March 13.[11]

Sharlot's friends in the legislature, particularly Senator Alpheus Favour from Prescott, did not intend to let the matter drop, however. By the end of March Sharlot was able to tell Alice that Favour had managed to insert in the General Appropriation Bill a provision for a two-year annual appropriation of $1,000 for the operations of the Historical Society of Prescott, which he proposed to start for the benefit of the restoration of the Governor's Mansion.[12]

Although freezing weather continued in northern Arizona, Sharlot found a bright side to the matter. As she told Alice, "the continued cold up here is probably an insurance of fruit this year, and if there is more snow the range should be encouraging. I look for some movement of land by midsummer and hope to let the old place [Orchard Ranch] go."[13] Meanwhile, Sharlot and her cousin Sam forged ahead as fast as they could with work on the Mansion. By mid-March, Sharlot could report that "after a lot of work and much expense which I was not eager to incur I have a funny little bedroom which reminds me of a stope in a mine . . . but it can be kept warm, is light and sunny, and not only comfortable but quite attractive. . . . The log walls . . . are now chinked with lime plaster. . . . This with the new roof all done is a real advance. . . . "[14]

At the Arizona Pioneers' annual meeting in April 1929 Sharlot spoke about the restoration of the Governor's Mansion and her latest project, the reinterment of the remains of the granddaddy of all Arizona pioneers, Pauline Weaver, on the grounds of the old capitol. Sharlot's interest in the fate of Indian scout and trapper Pauline Weaver (1800–1867) had been piqued two years previously when her old friend Judge Edmund Wells of Prescott had completed his book, *Argonaut Tales: Stories of the Gold Seekers and the Indian Scouts of Early Arizona*.[15] One of the "Tales" concerned Weaver, who had died near Camp Verde east of Prescott and had been buried in the old Fort Lincoln cemetery there in 1867. When the Camp was abandoned as an active arm of the United States military, all of the remains in the cemetery were removed to the national cemetery near San Francisco.

After reading Wells's account of the old scout's life, Sharlot decided to do something about returning Weaver's bones to Arizona. Although the state legislature had not looked favorably on a separate appropriation for the Governor's Mansion, they were willing to vote the money for the casting of a bronze tablet to mark Weaver's new resting place, if Sharlot and Senator Alpheus Favour would make the arrangements for the reinterment.[16] By March 31, 1929, Sharlot and Favour had gotten permission from the United States Secretary of War for the exhumation. The grave was opened; the remains were placed in a three-foot-long bone box and shipped to Prescott. For some reason, perhaps the necessity of fund-raising, the planned final interment did not take place for more than half a year. On October 27, 1929, more than a thousand people paraded to the Governor's Mansion, where the old trapper's remains were buried beneath a gigantic granite boulder to which a handsome bronze plate had been affixed telling of Weaver's life and achievements.

On May 14, 1929, eight Prescott citizens met at the Governor's Mansion to officially form the Historical Society of Prescott, the object of which was "to preserve, maintain and perpetuate the gubernatorial mansion in Prescott, Arizona; to conduct and carry on a historical and educational society; to conduct and carry on investigations and expeditions into the geological and anthropological life of this section; to publish pamphlets and reports; to conduct a library; and to collect museum specimens at the headquarters of the Society." The articles of incorporation were signed by Sharlot M. Hall and seven others, including Norah Hartzell, Alpheus H. Favour, and Sharlot's cousin Edward J. Boblett.

Later in May a group of Prescott citizens, including Sharlot and Grace Sparkes, drove to Flagstaff, where they joined a bus tour from Phoenix to the recently opened bridge over the Marble Canyon gorge of the Colorado River. This bridge, a marvel of steel-girded construction, replaced the dangerous dugway and ferry-boat crossing at Lees Ferry upriver eleven miles. How well Sharlot remembered her own experience on the 1911 trip to the Arizona Strip, when she crossed the brown, roiling Colorado at Lees Ferry. It was with more than passing interest, therefore, that she joined the group on the big, comfortable bus.

Although the bridge was completed, the road from Flagstaff to the bridge was neither graded nor paved. As Sharlot put it, the "crooks and turns of that road would break the back of a Smoki bull snake." The bus itself, however, was sheer luxury, featuring cushioned wicker armchairs and a special dining section. The party stopped for lunch near a spot where years ago Sharlot had cooked on a greasewood campfire and had crawled under the wagon, the only available shady spot, to write her notes. "Now," said Sharlot, "we ate a hot meal served with table and table cloth, sat in wicker chairs and listened to a Brunswick 'portable' sing the old cowboy songs, and were so comfortable I thought it was all a dream." [17]

Back in Prescott, friends continued to contribute time, money, and historical artifacts to the Governor's Mansion. The dean of Arizona pioneers, Morris Goldwater, brought in the telegraph instruments which he himself had used in 1873 when Prescott and Tucson had first been linked with the rest of the world by telegraph lines. Meanwhile, Sharlot had decided that the time had come to sell the ranch so she would have more leisure to write and work on the Mansion:

> Two things [that I want to do] stood out beyond all else — to finish, if I might, the work on the old Governor's Mansion so that it would be a pride and inspiration to every Arizonan — and to set down a record of the pioneer life as I had lived it from a 'dug out' home in the Kansas of Sioux raids and blizzards and grass-hoppers to the Arizona of placer mining and early cattle ranches. Those are the two things which I feel will be my best contribution to my state and people. [18]

The 320 acres homesteaded under her name and J. K. Hall's were sold on December 9, 1929, to Edward G. Applegate. [19] The Orchard Ranch days were over.

16

The House
of a
Thousand
Hands

THE SALE OF ORCHARD RANCH FREED SHARLOT from the last tie to her past. Lifted by a great spurt of energy, she immediately began even more industrious efforts to collect relics of Yavapai County's heritage. With her cousins Ed and Sam Boblett she went out on a December Sunday to the site of a Spanish camp on Lynx Creek, where the three of them found stones from old arastras (primitive devices for crushing ore) and a slab of rock decorated with a pre-historic pictograph. With the aid of a wheelbarrow, they loaded the stones onto the truck and carted them back to the Governor's Mansion. Sam and Ed were forthwith commissioned to reproduce an old-time working arastra on the Mansion grounds.

In March 1930 members of the Monday Club announced that they would sponsor a benefit dinner for the Governor's Mansion restoration project. The dinner was also to be part of the "Trade at Home, Use Arizona Products Week" being sponsored by the Yavapai Chamber of Commerce. Three hundred guests crowded into the St. Michael's Hotel dining room on March 18 to eat a dinner of Arizona products. At the conclusion of the meal Sharlot, resplendent in her copper gown, was presented with a hammered copper bowl filled with $550, net proceeds from the dinner.

Sharlot used the funds from the Monday Club dinner for curtains, shades, screens, and electric lights for the Mansion. By April the last of the interior work on the building was finished. Sam Boblett began making cases to hold the artifacts, using old lumber removed from various parts of the building, particularly the siding with which Dougherty had covered the original logs.

Meanwhile, out in the world beyond the cool pines of Prescott, things were looking bleak. Arizona newspapers began alluding to the great "Depression" which by now was seriously affecting the nation. By May the aftershock of the stock-market collapse of the previous November had reached Arizona's copper industry, and most of the copper-mining companies announced a five-percent cut in wages.

In October Sharlot hosted a group of Kiwanis wives from northern Arizona. The *Prescott Courier* described what the ladies were to see on their visit to the Governor's Mansion:

> In approaching the site of the museum they will see a fence of peeled posts, similar to the fences the early settlers of the territory used. And, in the enclosure they will see a squatty log building—the original logs that were cut and hewn in the Groom Creek district and hauled to the village under escort of armed men for protection against Indians. . . .
>
> Inside the old dwelling they will find two great front rooms, each with a fire place, and in them priceless articles on display. Miss Hall lives in the back rooms of the historic structure. Upstairs in the attic, if the women are conducted thence, they will see where some of the noted characters in early Arizona history bunked for the night when in town.
>
> One of the big front rooms contains early day household articles, each item saturated with history. In the other front room are cases of prehistoric pottery and trinkets, and last remains. . . . [1]

The "last remains" seem to have consisted of nineteen skulls donated by J. W. Simmons of Prescott. These were augmented by corn cobs, double-bitted axes, stone hammers, and a bone flute.

Sharlot, who by this time was something of a public institution, was often called upon to speak for local club programs. She also started a garden club at the Mansion. In June 1931 she entertained the girls at the Girl Reserve camp at Granite Dells, telling them pioneer stories and reading her Arizona poems. One of the girls recalled: "We thought that she was oddly old-fashioned in dress with her heavy dark clothes, long skirts, high collars, and *always* a black, round, crinkled, homemade-looking hat. She looked old to us. . . but her manner was cheerful and humorous and she soon dispelled notions that she wasn't living in our same age or wasn't 'with it.'"[2]

Sharlot continued to write poetry. "Paw an' Me (Ranchman Junior)," published in June 1931, is an example of her use of cowboy dialect.

Paw an' me, we're men, you bet;
We kin cuss an' chew, an' spit.
I kin spit as fur as Paw,
Roll a wad 'round in my jaw
Till ye'd think 'twas mumps I had.
    (Year fore las' I had 'em bad
    On both sides, an' couldn't spit
    Ner chaw—well, hardly not a bit).
Got an outfit jis' like Paw's,
Spanish bit kin break th' jaws
Of any bronk gits fresh with me.
An' yer eyes would bug to see
My new chaps—Angorry hair
All fixed up to look like bear.
Silver spurs 'at long ago
Paw, he brung from Mexico
With little bells an' jinglin' chains.
An' my bridle, it's got reins
Wove of hair by Chappo when
He done time down in th' Pen.
Fancy headstall—Gee! Now, son
It's finest Chappo ever done.
Silver conchos in a row
Carved by some old Navajo
Fer his war-belt. Paw says: "Now
That buck don't need 'em anyhow."

An' th' saddle that I ride,
That was Seenyor Calles' pride.
Calles, th' jim-dandy best
Saddle-maker, East or West.
Skirts all carved with ballin' steers,
An' bronks a-buckin' on their ears;
An' our brand, Paw's brand an' mine
On th' cantle...J-bar-nine
Tapideros sweep th' groun'
When I go sash-shayin' 'roun'.

. . . .

> Maw, sometimes she'll r'ar an' pitch,
> Talkin' about school, .. an' sich,
> Waste o' time fer men like us.
> Paw, he always lets her fuss
> Some.. 'n' then ca'm her, like he can.
>
> Gee! I'm glad 'at I'm a man!
> Wimmin folks 'll do fer maws,
> But it takes us men fer paws. [3]

The fact that Sharlot carried out a continued round of activities during the spring and summer of 1931 would seem to indicate that her health was excellent. Yet a letter written August 14, 1931, says otherwise. Evidently in an apology to her correspondent for neglecting to write, she said:

> This has not been a forgetting of the heart in the spiritual sense but bad behavior of the physical heart over quite a long time.
>
> When it is very bad I am like the old lady who said on her good days she would "Set in the sun and think— and on the bad days she *just set.*" I have "just set" for a good many months until about a week ago when like the click of a camera the good days came in and I am taking stock of all the things I want to do and beginning to do some of them.... [4]

Sharlot continued her social and civic activities in 1932, including attending the Arizona Pioneers' picnic in April. But her pleasure in this reunion was marred by the death of her favorite cousin, the gentle, crippled Ed Boblett. Never an ambitious man, Ed had spent much time with Sharlot and her father at Orchard Ranch when he was not working the placer mines at Lynx Creek and elsewhere. He had also given her his constant help and encouragement in the Governor's Mansion restoration project. He and his partner had been out on Lynx Creek on April 19, working the gravel for gold, when suddenly he had leaned against a large cottonwood tree and dropped dead.

In July 1932 the Federal Reconstruction Finance Corporation Act (RFC) for financial aid for work relief came into being. Arizona's initial share in the appropriation was a quarter of a million dollars. Of this sum, Prescott was allocated $50,000. Several projects were hastily started to put as many unemployed men to work as possible.

Among these early RFC-funded projects were two which were placed under Sharlot's control: the clearing of the grounds of the Governor's Mansion and the cleaning, ditching, and repair of the Pioneer Cemetery in Miller Valley.[5]

As the news of the Reconstruction Finance Corporation Act traveled to Arizona, a great deal of local interest was focused on battles for the primary elections to be held in September. Ever since her 1925 trip to Washington as presidential elector for Calvin Coolidge, Sharlot had taken more than a passing interest in the political scene, though she had never actively campaigned for any candidate. That fall she certainly was more interested in her own projects, the cleaning up of the cemetery and Governor's Mansion grounds and the constant search for more relics, than in any political campaign. So when her friend Grace Chapman, Yavapai County Recorder (and just incidentally running for reelection on the Democratic ticket), invited Sharlot to accompany her on a short trip to a region of old-time ranches that Sharlot had been longing to scour for such items as old spurs, bridle bits, and early farm tools, Sharlot jumped at the chance.

One evening a little later in October, as Sharlot peacefully dried dishes at the Governor's Mansion, she was surprised to find a representative from the Prescott Republican Party headquarters on her doorstep. It seemed, as Sharlot related the story later, that

> my conduct of late had been such as to call for a reprimand. Hastily I searched my mind for some misdeed—I had stayed at home nights; I had faithfully cared for the relics— I had met all visitors in as nearly the manner of a lady as is natural for me—wherein was I at fault?
>
> Soon it was made clear—I had been seen in public with a lady who now holds office in Yavapai county—a lady elected by the opposing party—and thereby I had given some Republican voters the anxious fear that I might be supporting her instead of the party nominee.
>
> Party loyalty, it seems, demanded more circumspect conduct from me than from some others because in 1924 I had been selected as one of the presidential electors of Arizona and had later had an interesting trip to Washington—for which it was now up to me to pay by so behaving myself in public that I would stir up no doubts in the minds of possible voters as to whether I might not think some candidate of the other party better fitted to hold certain offices.

Still puzzled by her visitor's accusations, Sharlot went to the local Republican headquarters the next day. Said Sharlot, "I went up those stairs (after hunting around to find where the headquarters was) still a gentle lady, as I thought. I came down those stairs a red hot independent—with the branding iron of insurgency in me for life."[6]

Sharlot was not finished. She celebrated her sixty-second birthday on October 27, a birthday which, as she proudly pointed out, she shared with former president Theodore Roosevelt—by declaring her political choices for the coming election. Republican Sharlot intended to support not only her Democratic friend, incumbent county recorder Grace Chapman, but also Democratic Senator Carl Hayden and Democratic Representative Lewis W. Douglas. Since Sharlot's personal friend Ralph Cameron, with whom she had stayed when she was in Washington in 1925, was running against Hayden in this campaign, her forthright refusal to support him, on grounds that he had "been too long away from Arizona," took considerable courage.[7]

Recalling the day nearly thirty years previous when she had stood up to President Roosevelt over the issue of separate statehood for Arizona, she said:

> It's good to remember what a fighter Teddy Roosevelt was—how he challenged the schemes of evil interests that did not dare to come out into the light... good to recall his love of all of us common folk—even my scrappy self with whom he soon made a truce.... Doubtless I have not so many more birthdays to celebrate with Theodore Roosevelt —but when I "Go West" he will not be able to say to me: "You sure got too peaceful in your old days." Instead I want to hear him say: "Comrade, you sure put up a good lone fight for the things you thought worth while."[8]

On November 8 a Democratic landslide swept Chapman, Hayden, and Douglas into office along with Franklin Delano Roosevelt. Sharlot's political rebellion probably had little if anything to do with the outcome, but it established her once again as an outspoken lady who knew her own mind and was not afraid to tell the world where she stood.

Early in 1933 Sharlot's friend Grace Sparkes, long-time secretary of the Yavapai County Chamber of Commerce, was named local chairman in charge of Federal Reconstruction Finance Corporation relief projects. With Grace Sparkes in charge, projects were quickly coordinated. Unemployed local men were put to work washing the walls at the Yavapai County courthouse, repainting the names of the county officials on their office doors, and doing sundry other tasks including road work, sewer-ditching, and cemetery cleanup— the last under Sharlot Hall's direction.

On Thursday, March 2, 1933, Governor B. B. Moeur called for a three-day closing of all Arizona banks. By March 4 the governor had extended the moratorium to March 13. Conditions in Prescott reflected those all over the country; cash was in short supply, and men working for Sharlot on her RFC project were paid in store orders, as was Sharlot herself for her supervision of the workmen.

In an easing of prohibition laws, beer was legally sold across the United States beginning April 7, 1933. For Arizona, this was the first legal liquor since December 31, 1914. The long-awaited day was considerably less than amusing as far as Sharlot Hall, a rigid teetotaler, was concerned, though she chuckled to Alice over some of the brouhahas that occurred as the first truckloads of beer arrived at the local saloons. "A bottle of beer seemed to call for a bottle of bootleg and it didn't mix so well," observed Sharlot. "I expect we will have the jail full until the novelty wears off." Far less amusing, as far as Sharlot was concerned, was "a noisy lunch stand with a bawling radio right across the street to the north of me...my big porch catches every sound—also my upstairs bedroom echoes to crooners and cowboys till midnight. I am sleeping downstairs and wondering what the full blast of summer activity will bring."9 But summer lingered in the wings as five inches of snow fell on Prescott on May 11. By the end of May, federal RFC funds were exhausted all over the state. With considerable regret, Sharlot saw the three men who had been assigned to help her at the Governor's Mansion that month leave.

On November 18, 1933, the *Courier* carried news of the most ambitious effort to date of the federal government to provide relief work for the unemployed: the Civil Works Administration (CWA). This short-lived (November 1933–March 1934) and hastily implemented program provided materials and laborers for locally sponsored construction projects.10 Grace Sparkes was appointed chairman of the Yavapai County CWA.

Faced with a deadline of December 1 for the start of all CWA funded projects, Grace leaped into action. In the next two days she met nearly around the clock with state CWA leaders, surfacing on November 23, "physically and mentally weary...but pleased." Well might she have felt satisfaction; she obtained CWA funding for nine Prescott District construction projects, among them the construction to the west of the Governor's Mansion of "a permanent building for the preservation of valuable early-day Arizona relics," to be known eventually as the Sharlot Hall Museum. [11]

So the House of a Thousand Hands was begun. An optimistic article in the *Courier* less than two months later reported progress on the museum building:

> Rapidly taking shape just to the rear of the Old Governor's Mansion...is a long, squat rough stone building, near fireproof in construction intended to house many early-day Arizona relics....It... now stands approximately seventy percent complete, in the opinion of...the foreman in charge of the project. By the end of another five weeks he expects the building to be ready for use.
>
> It has a total length of nearly eighty feet, counting an offset on the north end, connecting with a great room fifty feet wide and about that long, and an apartment on the other end having inside dimensions of 22½ x 24½ feet. Underneath the apartment will be a basement.
>
> It is a building somewhat larger than Miss Hall had in mind but will be used by her to store many articles that might not be safe should the Old Governor's Mansion catch fire. For particularly valuable relics there is being built into the new structure a vault 8½ x 10 feet in dimensions, with rock walls and concrete floor and ceiling, located in the southwest corner of the main room. She also will put into the building many Indian relics, saving the "white man's" keepsakes for the old mansion.
>
> ...[The workmen] are erecting a building that will defy time and perhaps will be standing long after the old mansion's heavy timbers have decayed.... [12]

The Civil Works Administration was replaced on April 2, 1934, by the Federal Emergency Relief Administration (FERA). But FERA funding was not as liberal as that granted under CWA. Work on the museum building slowed to a halt.

Sharlot, although she was concerned about finishing the museum building, was glad for a break in her supervisory responsibilities. The Arizona Pioneers reunion, cancelled the year previous because of the nationwide financial crisis, was once again on the docket. Sharlot traveled to Phoenix on April 9, staying with a close friend, Mrs. Holland Merryman. Sharlot felt that she could no longer stay with Alice; the Hewins family had fallen on hard times financially, and Ned Hewins was very ill.

Once back in Prescott, Sharlot kept busy at the Governor's Mansion, supervising the dwindling FERA work, adding Arizona artifacts to her collection, and assisting Grace Sparkes with Frontier Days promotion over the Fourth of July. Although the annual Prescott Rodeo broke all attendance records, the Yavapai County economic picture continued bleak.

Sharlot's overriding concern in 1934 and 1935, naturally, was the slow and sometimes erratic progress of the museum construction project. In May 1935 she wrote a lyrical tribute to the hundreds of relief workers who had helped raise the walls of the museum building, or "The House of a Thousand Hands," as she called it. A thousand hands? mused Sharlot,

perhaps half again that number; only the time keeper could give a better guess than I—together we have watched the workmen come and go. . . .

The men who worked here did not think much about [history] . . . they were concerned with earning a grub stake and their periods of work have often been short—and the big stone house [the museum building] reflects the many moods of many minds—the varying skill of many, many hands—rather than the courage and good cheer and high hopes of those who swung adze and broad axe on the Old Governor's Mansion.

The "Days of Gold" with their boundless dreams and visions, live in every log of the old house [the Governor's Mansion]. . . . The big stone house is of another day—it grew out of keen human need that could not dream. Men must eat and be sheltered—and many, many men must work, even for only a few days each. So this new "House of a Thousand Hands" is a house of service—a house of human needs. . . . Every stone in the walls was brought here because some man needed a pay check—laid that some family might be warm and sheltered and fed. It could not be like other houses—and at least while I live in it, it could not have careless uses—it must be a house of service, a house of help and inspiration.... [13]

On November 1 work began again on the museum, this time under the new Works Progress Administration. A list of WPA-funded projects approved by the federal government included "inside structural improvements in the new Sharlot Hall Museum, cataloging old newspaper files, and carrying on various jobs similar in character." [14]

As Sharlot once again took up the supervision of the constant trickle of unemployed men and women sent to the museum, her long-time friend Alice Hewins had also found employment under the WPA program; she was working on the Arizona Historical Memorials project, assisting with the gathering of historical records in Phoenix. Alice's husband, Ned, had been suffering with chronic heart failure for some years. On January 10, 1935, Alice wrote Sharlot that Ned, who had suffered a stroke, was "just alive and that is all." Would Sharlot write his obituary? Alice did not ask Sharlot to come to her, but a mutual friend, Holland Merryman, seeing Alice's great need, drove up to Prescott, got Sharlot, and brought her to Phoenix. Sharlot was there when Ned died, Sunday night, January 12.

Sharlot remained with Alice in Phoenix until January 25. It was a difficult visit; Alice was on the point of collapse from the strain of caring for Ned in his final illness and from grief. Both women sensed that Ned's passing closed a door on the long years of their intimate relationship; they were to see each other from that time only in passing, chiefly when Sharlot came to Phoenix on business and took the time to visit Alice at the capitol, where she continued to work.

Meanwhile, The WPA-sponsored project at the museum continued. Several local women worked under Sharlot's direction, classifying and arranging archival material and making a detailed index of the early Prescott newspapers which had recently been transferred from the Governor's Mansion to the new stone museum building. [15] That June saw the completion of a small WPA-funded project which had been aborted by the demise of the Federal Emergency Relief Administration program in March 1934: the transfer of "Old Fort Misery" to the grounds of the Governor's Mansion. This little log building, former office of an early Prescott lawyer, Judge Howard, who had dispensed his particular brand of misery from the premises to violators of the law, had served as a storage shed for some years at the back of a lot on South Montezuma Street. Workers dismantled and carefully reassembled it, log by log, at the northwest corner of the Mansion grounds.

That fall Sharlot was thrilled to meet a California woman who had been born near the old site of Fort Misery. "When spankings were imminent (during her childhood) she fled to her friend Judge Howard." The woman remembered where each piece of furniture had stood in the little log cabin. Said Sharlot of the visit:

> ... That sweet old lady who had played in the old house as a child — she can never know how her eager remembering made the whole scene come alive to us — and speeded up our determination to make it look as if Judge Howard had just gone down the street to share one of Judge Fleury's Sunday dinners."

> ... Our work here has been done mostly by the grace of God — after I had spent everything out of the sale of the old ranch and the cattle left when father died, the Federal work projects came along like Aladdin's lamp. They gave us the big stone building and set in place Fort Misery and have allotted us workmen for the log ranch house — and if we can still have workmen we will show the world what used to be in Yavapai County. [16]

The WPA also sponsored the building of a facsimile of a typical, early-day Yavapai County log ranch house on the museum grounds. Here Sharlot planned to house her branding-iron collection, her saddle collection, and some furniture and equipment from old Yavapai County ranch houses.

In November 1936 the museum building and the Fort Misery reconstruction projects were declared completed. The total cost of the project was $7,042, of which the federal government paid $6,666; the difference of $376 presumably was paid by Sharlot herself. [17] Except for the finishing off of the little peeled log ranch house, this project was the last of Sharlot's direct involvement with work-relief construction.

17

"Sunset –
and the
End of the Trail"

INSTALLED IN HER NEW APARTMENT in the stone museum building, Sharlot weathered the cold January of 1937 in comfort. Twenty-two inches of snow had fallen by January 8; on January 22 the temperature dropped to twenty-one degrees below zero. The apartment in the museum gave Sharlot the space and sense of permanence to begin unpacking all the belongings she had put away in 1912 when she had planned to move to Phoenix with her father. During 1938 she used odd moments of free time to unpack the boxes which had remained unopened for twenty-six years.

Sharlot's perennial plea for artifacts bore strange fruit in April 1938. Just as she was showing fifty schoolchildren around the building, "a kindly person arrived with a truck in which was the platform and trap door used in several executions in the past of Prescott." Sharlot described the ensuing scene to Alice:

> You could not have kept from laughing as these young citizens fell upon the latest display. The boys tugged to help the men unloading— and wanted to set up the thing and try it out at once. Even the nice young teacher had to laugh at last—though it was evident she did not approve of this kind of history—but I have been laughing ever since—those little rascals were so blood thirsty—struck the pose of sheriff and guards, even willing to be prisoner. [1]

During the first week in September Dr. Frank C. Lockwood, professor of English at the University of Arizona, came to Prescott to visit

Sharlot. Lockwood had long been Sharlot's admirer; more than ten years before, he had unsuccessfully prodded her for autobiographical material to include in his book, *Arizona Characters*. Lockwood stayed an entire week; his admiration for this woman, six years his junior, is evident from the long, adulatory biographical sketch which he wrote after he returned to Tucson.[2] As for Sharlot, once she discovered that Lockwood had grown up on the Kansas prairie only a few miles north of the Halls' third Kansas homestead, she relished every moment of the visit.

Because Lockwood wanted to see Orchard Ranch, Sharlot drove out with him. She found the journey depressing; as she told Alice, "The orchard is all dead but a few trees and the surface of the fields are washed and scarred. The house is breaking as to windows and doors and soon an accidental fire will likely come along and wipe out all but a handful of ashes."[3] Lockwood obviously thought otherwise; he wrote of the house, "It is beginning to be a place of historic interest; and will no doubt in the future become an Arizona shrine."[4] As it happened, neither Lockwood's nor Sharlot's prediction concerning the house at Orchard Ranch came to pass. Neglected and run down, the house was occasionally rented until it was declared unfit for habitation and razed.[5]

Late that fall Sharlot wrote a summary of work done in the past two years at the old Governor's Mansion. Highlights of the year 1937 had been the completion of the little ranch house on the Mansion grounds and the gathering of appropriate objects for display in it. In addition, "the old well, dug in the time of the first governor, was completely restored and a small stone water tank was built beside it. This well," said Sharlot, "can now be used and the water is as cold and fine as in early days when it was called the best in Prescott."

"1938," continued Sharlot,

saw many things completed, including some very attractive stone walks about the yard. Both large buildings were kept in the best possible condition; the roofs have been oiled for preservation and the log walls of the Old Governor's house have had three such treatments at intervals because the preservative value is very evident. After standing since 1864 the logs are in almost as good a condition as when laid. . . .

The yard has had special care because I have desired to protect an area of old-time range grasses which Dr. Thornber told me were rare now, though once typical of this mountain region. They are very beautiful and attract much attention.[6]

Grace Sparkes had long considered Sharlot and the Governor's Mansion project to be high on the Yavapai County Chamber of Commerce's promotion list. What was good for Sharlot and the Governor's Mansion was good for the county. In addition, there is no doubt of Grace's real fondness for the Lady of the Governor's Mansion. And Sharlot needed help. As Alice Hewins put it, "Sharlot's bump of orderliness had never been strong."[7] As Sharlot grew older, though she remained a charming and knowledgeable tour guide, conversationalist, and speaker, she was increasingly unable or unwilling to handle her business affairs. So Grace added these matters to the long list of her activities. She balanced Sharlot's books; she served as go-between with the Board of Directors of State Institutions at the state capital; she made sure that Sharlot received her modest monthly salary from the Board of Directors; she made patient (and unsuccessful) efforts to prod responses out of Sharlot to occasional fan mail.

Perhaps Sharlot's increasing dislike of bothering with business affairs made her neglect the duties which must have gone along with her year as president of the Arizona Pioneers Association. If she carried on any correspondence regarding Association matters during her tenure as president, these letters have not surfaced. She did go to Phoenix, as was her custom, for the two-day reunion. However, though she was photographed several times, there is no indication that she did more than greet the group informally and chair the business meeting. On April 12, 1939, at this meeting, Lin B. Orme, incumbent vice-president of the Association, was elected president. Sharlot returned to her long-time position as vice-president.

Sometime that summer Southwestern writer Erna Fergusson visited Prescott as part of her fieldwork for a coming book, to be titled *Our Southwest*.[8] While she was in the city she met Prescott's two best-known residents: Grace Sparkes and Sharlot Hall. She was so overwhelmed by the one and charmed by the other that she devoted an entire chapter of her book to the two of them. Grace emerges as the archetypical Chamber of Commerce secretary. According to

Grace, as reported by Miss Fergusson, Prescott was the center of the cattle business, the center of the sheep business, the center of the mining region, and the center of the guest-ranch business. But even this stunning centrality palled beside Grace's next claim: as she told her visitor, "This is the one spot in the great Southwest where we have four distinct seasons, spring, summer, fall and winter."

"I bow to the Yavapai Chamber of Commerce," said Fergusson. "Weeks of travel had accustomed me to centers, but pre-empting the seasons was 'tops' in my experience."[9]

Following her encounter with Grace, Miss Fergusson made her way up Gurley Street to the old Governor's Mansion, rather dubious as to what might await her there. Within moments, however, she was completely captivated by Sharlot:

> Her room was not in order; my visit was too early. But Sharlot Hall does not apologize, any more than she makes unnecessary gestures with her worn and shapely hands. She stood firmly on adequate feet, and so erectly that a body no longer young rose like a fine tower to a heavy twist of hair still brown above the graying temple growth. Manner, voice, and enunciation were of a correctness not often met, but without pedantry. When she needed a racy word or provincial expression, she used it with the finality of a Dr. Johnson admitting it to the English language.
>
> "Yes, the pioneers stuck together all right. They knew they'd better, or they'd be planted." . . .
>
> Scorn is closer to Miss Hall's speech than humor. "Competency is no longer valued by a generation that expects a living without working for it. I offered a job to a high-school boy, and he said no, he'd get a government job at eighty-five dollars a month. I said: 'What can you do that would be worth eighty-five dollars to anybody?'"[10]

"To me," concluded Miss Fergusson,

> Sharlot Hall was an infinitely more important experience than any quantity of old furniture, branding irons, prints, and even books. For no more Sharlot Halls are being produced, and no book will ever convey the living feeling or the true importance of this one. . . . I decided not to return to the Chamber of Commerce. My mood was spoiled for more assurances of the priority and centrality of Prescott. . . . I wanted to leave Prescott remembering most sharply

a woman who is in herself as worthy a monument to the old Southwest as the bronze Bucky O'Neill in the plaza. Spectacular as he is,
he is not a shade more gallant. [11]

After Erna Fergusson's visit Sharlot settled back into her pleasant
routine, speaking to groups of schoolchildren either at the public
school or at the museum, addressing civic groups and clubs, and
writing historical pieces and obituaries for the *Courier*. The
obituaries were sad reminders of Sharlot's dwindling circle of older
friends. The death of Sharlot's cousin Sam Boblett on June 29, 1942,
was a blow to Sharlot. Sam had been a part of her life since her
childhood; his father, John Boblett, had come to Lynx Creek from
Kansas in 1877. In 1882, when the Hall family arrived in Arizona,
they camped first on the Boblett spread while James Hall located
a claim.

   At the end of 1942, as Sharlot's step seemed to grow slower
and age and a failing heart etched the lines more deeply in her face,
her friend Charles Franklin Parker, Prescott Congregational Church
minister, urged her to tell him of her early life. The resulting biographical sketch, along with Parker's personal appraisal of her
poetry, appeared in the January 1943 issue of *Arizona Highways*
under the title "Out of the West of Long Ago." In a warmly appre-
ciative tribute to Prescott's most revered citizen, Parker praised
Sharlot as "a historian, a gatherer, recorder, and interpreter of
fact, of people, and times." [12]

   Holland Merryman had written to invite Sharlot to stay at her
house when she came to Phoenix for the annual pioneer reunion in
April 1943. But Sharlot was not to be present at the reunion. On
April 2 she had a heart attack. Dr. R. N. Looney and Grace Sparkes
were both called; they agreed that Sharlot must go to the hospital.
There were two alternatives: the new Prescott Community Hospital,
dedicated and opened just two weeks previously, or the hospital attached to the Arizona Pioneers' Home. This facility was reserved for
persons eligible for residence in the Home, the criteria being at least
thirty-five years of continuous residence in Arizona, age of sixty years
or older, only moderate use of alcohol or drugs, good character and
activity in the development of Arizona, and the inability "to properly
provide himself (herself) with the necessary and ordinary comforts

of life."[13] Certainly Sharlot filled the first four of the criteria; as for her financial circumstances, to Grace's knowledge, Sharlot had never had much money. If she were hospitalized in the new community hospital, who would pay the bills?[14]

Sharlot, at any rate, was too sick to protest. The ambulance was called, and she was taken to the Pioneers' Home hospital on the hill. Since Sharlot was too ill to make out the papers for admission—and might have rebelled at doing so, had she been well enough to take any part in the procedure—Grace signed a "Friend's Certificate" attesting to Sharlot's eligibility for admission.[15] On April 6 the official application for admission to the Home was duly approved by Richard Lamson, Judge of the Superior Court,[16] and sent on to Phoenix for Governor Sidney P. Osborn's approval. Osborn acted quickly; in a letter dated April 8 he told Sharlot:

> While I regret that it is necessary for you finally to accept the opportunity to enter the Home, because of advancing age and attendant infirmities, I am very glad that our state is in a position to offer the comforts and hospitality of the Pioneers' Home to a fine citizen such as you. You have well earned this consideration by the State of Arizona through a lifetime of able and patriotic service to your state. I wish you much happiness and contentment.[17]

Sharlot never read the letter. At 6:30 A.M. on Friday, April 9, she came to the end of the trail that she had walked for so many years with other Arizona pioneers.

> Sunset—and the end of the Trail!
> Here the last faint footsteps fail
> And I go on alone
> Into the untracked ways;
> I who in other days
> Blazed many a road straight up
> To the peaks that touch the sun—
> But now the climbing is done....
>
> Life, I have loved you well;
> Forget the rest when you tell—
> This soul did not falter nor quail—
> Nor shrink from the End of the Trail.[18]

Ten years earlier Sharlot had written to Lester Ruffner, director of the local funeral home and a long-time personal friend, to request extreme simplicity in her burial service:

> I do not wish a service of any sort—nor do I wish anyone beside the necessary care-takers to see my body—just wrap it in a sheet and place it in the coffin.
>
> Bury me in the plot beside my parents—if it is not too much trouble, take me out before sunrise—and I do not wish my friends to go with me—or to feel that I am gone from among them.
>
> This is not because I do not treasure the regard of my friends—or respect every form of service for the dead—but when I think of the prehistoric people of this immediate region who laid their dead away so lovingly—only to have them become objects of curiosity—I feel the futility of all customs and services.
>
> I know that you will find it hard to yield to this wish of mine for complete privacy—but you have been too good a friend not to be able to humor my last wish. . . . [19]

Sharlot's request was not carried out, for her funeral was a splendid affair at the museum with the governor himself there to give the principal address.

Sharlot had seen clearly long ago that for her and the old Governor's Mansion which had become her whole life there was in actuality no "end of the trail." As she said when she first signed the lease at the beginning of her last and greatest adventure, "The old house and the Prescott of yesterday and today and tomorrow and the woman who dreamed are going out on new trails together— but no one sees the end of the trail."[20]

Supplementary
Material

ABBREVIATIONS

AH   Alice Hewins

AHS   Arizona Historical Society,
Tucson

ASU   Arizona State University,
Tempe

CFL   Charles Fletcher Lummis

NAU   Northern Arizona University,
Flagstaff

SH   Sharlott Hall

SHM   Sharlot Hall Museum,
Prescott, Arizona

SWM   Southwest Museum,
Los Angeles

Notes to the Chapters

NOTES TO CHAPTER 1

1. Fragment, SHM. Quotations and information without citations are from otherwise unidentified fragments written by Sharlot Hall and preserved in SHM. They have been reprinted by permission of the Sharlot Hall Historical Society.

2. Fragment of novel, "Martin Hains," SHM.

3. Military service record files, National Archives of the United States, do not list his name as a veteran.

4. Coleman letter, SHM.

5. Ibid.

6. Ibid.

7. Frank C. Lockwood, unpublished manuscript biography of SH, AHS.

8. Coleman letter, SHM.

9. Sharlot Hall, "Courier Editorial Revives Memory of Early Day Kansas Indian Kidnap," *Prescott Courier,* 26 May 1939.

10. Alice Hewins, "Memories of Sharlot Hall," unpublished biography of Sharlot Hall, p. 2. Arizona State Library.

11. Table from Report of 10th Census of the U.S., v.4, *Transportation,* reproduced in O. C. Hull, "Railroads in Kansas," Kansas State Historical Collection, v.12, 1911–1912, p. 45.

12. Kansas State Board of Agriculture, 5th Annual Report, 1875, p. 222.

13. Several of these old scrapbooks are preserved in the Sharlot Hall Museum.

NOTES TO CHAPTER 2

1. Sharlot Hall, "A Memory of Old Gentlemen," *Atlantic Monthly,* January 1903, p. 116.

2. Ann E. Bingam, "The Grasshopper Plague," in Everett Rich, ed., *The Heritage of Kansas* (Lawrence: University of Kansas Press, 1960), p. 149.

3. Coleman letter, quoted in James J. Weston, "Sharlot Hall: Arizona's Pioneer Lady of Literature," *Journal of the West,* October 1965, p. 540.

4. Sharlot Hall, "A Christmas at the Grand Canyon," *Out West,* 26 (January 1907), pp. 10–11.

5. Kansas, Census records, 1875, Schedule 2, p. 1.

6. Hall, "Memory of Old Gentlemen," p. 116.

7. Ibid., p. 117.

8. "Of the Desert Does She Sing," *Los Angeles Times,* 18 June 1905.

9. Sharlot Hall, "Work at the Rodeo is Like the Circus," *Prescott Courier-Journal,* 29 June 1937, p. 3.

10. Ibid.

11. SH to D. M. Riordan, 15 April 1913, SHM.

12. SH to D. M. Riordan, 15 April 1913, SHM.

13. Sharlot Hall, quoted by Claudette Simpson, "Sharlot Hall on Men," *Prescott Courier, Westward Magazine,* 26 June 1974.

14. Sharlot Hall, fragment of unpublished manuscript, "Anne of the Old Frontier," SHM.

15. Adriane Edwards, "Pioneer Rodeo Rider Copped Honors," *Arizona Republic,* 13 February 1955.

NOTES TO CHAPTER 3

1. Sharlot Hall, "The Santa Fe Trail," in her *Cactus and Pine,* 2nd ed. (Phoenix: Arizona Republican Print Shop, 1924), p. 14.

2. SH to CFL, 20 May 1903, SWM.

3. Erna Fergusson, *Our Southwest* (New York: Knopf, 1940), p. 187.

4. Sharlot Hall, "From the Old Governor's Site," 10 December 1929.

5. SH to CFL, April 1901, SWM.

6. It is obvious from Sharlot's recollections of the trip that the Hall-Boblett party followed the same trail taken six years earlier from Kansas to Prescott, Arizona, by Lydia E. English and her husband. The diary which Lydia kept of their journey has been used for some of the descriptive details of the Hall trek. It has been printed in the *Kansas Historical Quarterly,* 36 (Winter 1970), pp. 369–89.

7. SH to D. M. Riordan, 10 April 1913, SHM.

8. *The Weekly Arizona Miner,* 18 March 1882.

9. *Miner,* 2 June 1882.

10. Sharlot Hall's journal, 1915, notes, SHM.

11. *Miner,* 10 March 1882.

12. "Gets Building for Life Time," *Arizona Republican,* 28 June 1927.

13. Sharlot Hall's notebook, 1897–1899, "phrases, hints and odds and ends of thought," SHM.

14. "A Valley of Degeneration," unpublished manuscript, SHM.

15. Mercy Hospital, Prescott, Arizona, records, SHM.

16. SH to CFL, 5 December 1910, Colorado State University Library.

17. Undated suffrage letter, written between 1912 and 1914, SHM. Probably written to Myron Westover.

18. Sharlot Hall, "Wild Morning Glories," *Poems of a Ranch Woman* (Prescott: Sharlott Hall Historical Society, 1953), p. 42.

19. Sharlot Hall, "Education in Arizona," *Arizona Republican,* 10 November 1911.

20. "Interesting Interview with Sharlot M. Hall," *Yavapai Magazine,* 12 (October 1924), p. 16.

21. Yavapai County School records.

22. Carrie Johnson Aitken to SH, from Portland, Oregon, SHM.

23. Ida Williams Davisson, "My Memories of Sharlot Hall," typescript, AHS.

24. "Gets Building for Life Time," *Arizona Republican,* 28 June 1927.

25. Sharlot Hall, "Old Range Days in Yavapai," *Yavapai Magazine,* 21 (June 1931), p. 31.

26. Yavapai County Mining Records, v.22, p. 504, Mustang Mine. On New Year's Day 1887 James Hall had claimed another mine, located in the Black Hills 2,000 feet south of Grapevine Gulch in the Lynx Creek district ("Grubstake Mine," Yavapai County Mining Records, v.23, p. 41; "½ mile east from Cor. x T14 NRIE").

27. SH to CFL, April 1901, SWM.

NOTES TO CHAPTER 4

1. Sharlot Hall, "Yavapai County's Apples Earn Her the Title Ozark of the West," *Journal-Miner,* 29 October 1919.

2. Sharlot M. Hall, "The Genesis of the Earth and the Moon, a Moqui Folk Tale," *Wide Awake,* 33 (October 1891), pp. 460–61.

3. D. Lothrop Co. to SH, 9 November 1891, SHM.

4. Sharlot Hall, "The Cliff Dwellings of the Lower Verde Valley, Northern Arizona," *The Archaeologist,* 3 (April 1893), pp. 119–20.

5. Sharlot Hall, "Sharlot Hall Sounds Clarion Call to Save Arizona's Prehistoric Monuments From Wanton Destruction," *Tucson Citizen,* 20 May 1929.

6. *Journal-Miner,* 13 January 1892: "Hall of Lynx Creek was in town being his first visit since his sickness." Sharlot says her father had an illness that kept him in bed for three months—beginning in March when her brother was sixteen. Edward Hall was born March 11, 1874, which would make him seventeen at the time, but a year earlier seems extremely unlikely, since according to a fragment in SHM the Halls were still on the placer mining claim at that time.

7. Adeline Hall Bracamonte, Edward Hall's daughter, stated to Margaret F. Maxwell that her father attended college in Colorado or Kansas. A check of colleges now existing in those states show no record of Edward Vermond Hall's attendance.

8. Sharlot Hall, "The Log Book of the Mountain Schooner," two unpublished versions in manuscript, SHM.

9. Quoted from Watt's speech at Free Thought Conference, Chicago, 13 November 1896, "Find Death Together," *Chicago Tribune,* 13 December 1896, p. 3.

10. Samuel P. Putnam, *400 Years of Freethought* (New York: Truth Seeker Co., 1929), v.1, p. 295.

11. 23 February 1895, p. 120.

12. George E. Macdonald, *Fifty Years of Freethought* (New York: Truth Seeker Co., 1929), p. 576.

13. Sharlot Hall's personal copy, SHM.

14. *Truth Seeker,* 2 February 1895, p. 72.

15. *Truth Seeker,* 9 February 1895.

16. *Truth Seeker,* 16 February 1895, p. 104.

17. *Daily Journal* (Lawrence, Kansas), 9 September 1879.

18. Information about this aspect of the Freethought movement is to be found in Hal D. Sears, *The Sex Radicals: Free Love in High Victorian America* (Lawrence: Regents Press of Kansas, 1977), particularly chapter 3, pp. 34–52. See also James C. Malin, *A Concern About Humanity: Notes on Reform, 1872–1912 at the National and Kansas Levels of Thought* (Lawrence, Kansas: the author, 1964), particularly pp. 60–77.

19. Quoted in Sears, *The Sex Radicals,* p. 45.

20. Ibid.

21. Sharlot Hall, "The Best Freethought Novel," *Truth Seeker,* 10 February 1901, pp. 90–91.

22. Samuel P. Putnam, *The Golden Throne* (Boston: G. Chainey, n.d.), pp. 142–45.

23. *Truth Seeker,* 2 March 1895, p. 136.

24. Sharlot Hall, *Poems of a Ranch Woman* (Prescott: Sharlot Hall Historical Society, 1953), p. 135.

NOTES TO CHAPTER 5

1. Robert G. Ingersoll, "The Gods," in *Complete Lectures* (Chicago: Donohue, n.d.,), p. 244.

2. Robert G. Ingersoll, "Intellectual Development," *Complete Lectures,* p. 106.

3. 1895 Calendar, annotated by SH, SHM.

4. *Prescott Journal-Miner,* 22 and 29 May 1895.

5. Putnam to SH, 8 June 1895, SHM. (This is the only Putnam material in SHM.)

6. SH's Calendar for 1895.

7. Yale T. Richardson, Jr., to Margaret F. Maxwell, 13 September 1977.

8. SH's Calendar for 1895.

9. Sharlot Hall, *Cactus and Pine* (Phoenix: Arizona Republican Print Shop, 1924), p. 41.

10. SH's Calendar for 1895.

11. Charles F. Lummis, "The Lion's Den," *Land of Sunshine,* December 1895, p. 45.

12. "Sharlot M. Hall, Prescott. R. Ventura. Try A. 200," Lummis's business accounts, December 1, 1895–March 29, 1897, University of Arizona Library. The cryptic record may be translated to indicate that Lummis received "Ventura" from SH and that he returned it with a 200-word letter suggesting that she try again.

13. Lummis's notebook, September 3, 1896, and December 14, 1896. University of Arizona, Library Special Collections.

14. *Land of Sunshine,* 6 (December 1896), p. 27.

15. New York, G. P. Putnam's Sons, 1877. Notes in the books in Sharlot's hand indicate that they were gifts from Putnam in 1896, SHM.

16. "Find Death Together: S. P. Putnam and Mary L. Collins Asphyxiated in Boston," *Chicago Tribune,* 13 December 1896, p. 3.

17. George E. Macdonald, *Fifty Years of Freethought* (New York: Truth Seeker Co., 1931) p. 135.

18. Ibid., p. 134.

19. SH to Ida Williams Davisson, 30 April 1900, SHM.

20. Dated January 1897 in Sharlot Hall's manuscript book of poetry, 1897–1900; SHM. An expanded and revised version was published under the title "Wine of Dreams" in her *Cactus and Pine* (1924), pp. 187–88.

21. *Prescott Journal-Miner,* 17 February 1897. Her prize-winning poem was "The Singing of the Pines," *Midland Monthly,* 7 (March 1897), p. 234.

22. *Journal-Miner,* 29 January 1896.

23. *Land of Sunshine,* 7 (September 1897), p. 147.

24. "How I Saw the Grand Canon of the Colorado at Midnight," *Travel,* 11 (September 1897).

25. Sharlot Hall, *Cactus and Pine* (Phoenix: Arizona Republican Print Shop, 1924), p. 169.

26. *Truth Seeker,* 11 December 1897, p. 789.

27. Hall, *Cactus and Pine,* pp. 36–37.

28. Yavapai County Deeds, v.43, pp. 281, 286.

29. Sharlot Hall, manuscript poetry book, 1897–1899, SHM.

30. Hall, *Cactus and Pine,* pp. 174–76.

31. *Truth Seeker,* 25 (10 December 1898), p. 789.

32. Note at bottom of manuscript copy of poem.

33. Sharlot Hall, unpublished manuscript book dated April 19, 1898, SHM.

34. Sharlot Hall, unpublished manuscript poetry, 1897–1899, SHM.

NOTES TO CHAPTER 6

1. Although "The Range Rider" had to wait for *Cactus and Pine* (Phoenix: Arizona Republican Print Shop, 1924, pp. 102–3) before it saw publication, it was popular enough to be included in Robert Frothingham's anthology, *Songs of Horses* ([Boston]: Houghton Mifflin Co., 1920).

2. *Land of Sunshine,* 10 (January 1898), pp. 4–11.

3. Sharlot Hall, undated manuscript fragment, SHM. Later version is "Dry Bones," in *Poems of a Ranch Woman* (Prescott: Sharlot Hall Historical Society, 1953), p. 55.

4. Maynard Dixon, unpublished manuscript chronology, in possession of Edith Dixon Hamlin, San Francisco.

5. Maynard Dixon, "A Visit to Miss Hall," *San Francisco Examiner,* 16 February 1902, p. [10].

6. Dixon to CFL, 5 August 1900, SWM.

7. SH to CFL, 18 November 1900, SWM.

8. Sharlot Hall, "The Lost Queen of the Papagos," *The Designer,* 14 (May 1901), pp. 69–71, second-prize story.

9. SH to CFL, 23 November 1900, SWM.

10. SH to CFL, 16 April 1901, SWM.

11. *Land of Sunshine* (February 1901); *Cactus and Pine* (Phoenix: Arizona Republican Print Shop, 1924), p. 45.

12. Sharlot Hall, "The Price of the Star," *Everybody's Magazine,* 5 (September 1901), pp. 335–39.

13. Kevin Starr, *Americans and the California Dream, 1850–1915* (New York: Oxford University Press, 1973), p. 388.

14. Hall, *Cactus and Pine,* p. 9.

15. CFL Diary, 25 November 1901, SWM.
16. Hall, *Cactus and Pine,* p. 9.
17. Charles F. Lummis, "From the Lion's Den," *Out West,* 15 (January 1902), p. 67.
18. *Out West,* 15 (January 1902), pp. 101–15.

NOTES TO CHAPTER 7

1. Undated clipping. SHM.
2. *Prescott Journal-Miner,* 9 March 1902.
3. *Out West* (August 1908) pp. 140–41; Hall, *Cactus and Pine,* pp. 113–15.
4. *Phoenix Republican,* 25 June 1902.
5. *Tucson Citizen,* 26 June 1902.
6. Hall, *Cactus and Pine,* pp. 165–66.
7. *Journal-Miner,* 16 September 1903.
8. SH to CFL, 4 November 1903, SWM.
9. CFL to SH, 13 November 1903, SWM.
10. SH to CFL, 4 February 1904, Colorado State University Library.
11. CFL to SH, 17 June 1904, Colorado State University Library.
12. SH to CFL, 4 September 1904, Colorado State University Library.
13. Grace Sparkes biography, Grace Sparkes Collection, AHS.
14. SH to CFL, 12 October 1904, Colorado State University Library.

NOTES TO CHAPTER 8

1. Yavapai County Deeds, v. 71, p. 481; SW ¼ Section 22, T14N.
2. Sharlot Hall, *Cactus and Pine* (Phoenix: Arizona Republican Print Shop, 1924), p. 154.
3. Sharlot Hall, Journal, November 1900–, SHM.
4. *Out West,* 23 (July 1905), pp. 3–4. Reprinted in *Cactus and Pine,* pp. 38–40, under the title, "The Mercy of Na-chis."
5. *Out West,* 26 (June 1905), pp. 362–78.
6. "The Love That Endures," *Ladies' Home Journal,* 22 (June 1905), p. 11.
7. Hall, *Cactus and Pine,* pp. 87–88.
8. *Out West,* 23 (August 1905), pp. 142–51.
9. CFL to John Muir, 15 June 1905, SWM.
10. For the full story see Margaret F. Maxwell, "The Lion and the Lady," *American Libraries,* 9 (May 1978), pp. 268–72.
11. Sharlot Hall, Journal, June 1905, SHM.
12. William O'Neill, *Everyone Was Brave, The Rise and Fall of Feminism in America* (Chicago: Quadrangle Books, 1969), p. 41.
13. Sharlot Hall, Journal, July 1905, SHM.
14. Hall, *Cactus and Pine,* pp. 142–43. Manuscript of poem says it was begun in spring 1905, finished in Los Angeles, July 1905.
15. Sharlot Hall, Journal, August 1905, SHM.
16. CFL's Diary, 2 October 1905, SWM.
17. Sharlot Hall, Journal, June–October 1905, SHM.
18. *Out West,* 18 (February 1903), p. 219.
19. Moody, "Joint Statehood or Justice?" *Out West,* 24 (January 1906), p. 137.

20. "Arizona," *Cactus and Pine,* pp. 106–10.

21. Undated clipping. SHM.

NOTES TO CHAPTER 9

1. From an untitled speech by SH in SHM archives.

2. "Hassayamper's Evening," *Journal-Miner,* 20 and 23 January 1907.

3. *Journal-Miner,* 23 January 1907, p. 4.

4. "The Sequoia League," *Out West,* 18 (January 1903), p. 83.

5. SHM.

6. Arthur Upson to SH, 10 June 1908, SHM.

7. Unfinished pencil fragment, undated, SHM.

8. SH's diary, 13 July 1908, SHM.

9. Sharlot Hall, "Every Day Was Frontier Day in Early Years in Prescott," *Prescott Courier,* 29 June 1946, Sec. 2, p. 8.

10. Sharlot Hall, Notebook #6, 23 August–10 September 1908, SHM.

11. D. M. Riordan to CFL, 8 September 1908, SWM.

12. SH to CFL, 13 October 1909, SWM.

NOTES TO CHAPTER 10

1. "A Historian of Arizona," *Arizona Republican,* 3 January 1909, p. 2.

2. *Phoenix Gazette,* 14 January 1909, p. 2.

3. Sharlot Hall, "Year's Delay Means Much," *Arizona Republican,* 18 February 1909, p. 3.

4. "Phoenix Bill to Governor," *Arizona Republican,* 9 March 1909, p. 1.

5. Philip M. Burnett, "The Development of State Libraries and Library Extension Service in Arizona and New Mexico," *Library Quarterly,* 35 (Jan. 1965), 44.

6. "The Woman's Club Files a Protest," *Arizona Republican,* 17 March 1909, p. 6.

7. "Historian of Arizona," *Arizona Republican,* 18 March 1909, p. 1.

8. Ibid.

9. "New Offices Will Open," *Arizona Gazette,* 30 March, 1909, p. 14.

10. "Historian Obtains Valuable Data," *Arizona Gazette,* 25 May 1909, p. 3.

11. H. B. Wilkinson of Phoenix, 12 November 1931, Historical Card File, Arizona Historical Society.

12. Proposition 21, Sections 2 and 7, Arizona Territorial Constitutional Convention, October 1910.

13. Rudd to Sloan, 22 November 1909, Arizona State Library.

14. SH to D. M. Riordan, 20 July 1910, SHM.

15. J. Walter Fewkes, "Navaho National Monument, Arizona," *Smithsonian Institution, Bureau of American Ethnology, Bulletin 50* (Washington, 1911), p. 7.

16. SH to D. M. Riordan, 31 July 1910, SHM.

17. Hall, *Cactus and Pine,* p. 1.

18. Joseph Fish, *The Life and Times of Joseph Fish* (Danville, Ill.: Interstate Printers and Publishers, 1970), p. 474.

19. SH to D. M. Riordan, 13 August 1910, SHM.

20. Richard F. Sloan to SH, 17 August 1910, SHM.

21. Fish, *The Life and Times of Joseph Fish,* pp. 474–75, and Alice B. Good, Arizona State Librarian, to Fleming Bennett, University of Arizona Librarian,

3 December 1958. The State Library has a copy of Fish's manuscript, evidently re-typed by Thomas Farish, first state historian (1912–1919). Another copy of the manuscript is in Special Collections, University of Arizona Library.

22. SH to D. M. Riordan, 13 August 1910, SHM.

23. SH to D. M. Riordan, 29 August 1910, SHM.

24. Leo Crane, *Indians of the Enchanted Desert* (Boston: Little, Brown, 1929), pp. 91–92.

25. "What Miss Hall Saw in Northern Arizona," *Arizona Republican,* 23 October 1910.

26. SH to D. M. Riordan, 10 September 1910, SHM.

27. Copyright Office to Mrs. Albert Mackenzie, 15 September 1949, copyright record no. A278156, SHM.

28. SH to CFL, 31 January 1911, Colorado State University Library.

29. This interesting "Report of the Arizona Historian" (32 pages) was pub-lished separately from other official documents submitted by Governor Richard E. Sloan to the Legislature at the close of his incumbency in 1912. Phoenix, 1912.

30. Sharlot's report of her trip appeared as "Diary of a Journey Through Northern Arizona and the Arizona Strip," in *Arizona Magazine* between December 1911 and April 1913. In 1975 Sharlot's "Diary" was edited by C. Gregory Crampton and published under the title *Sharlot Hall on the Arizona Strip* by Northland Press. The reader interested in detailed information on Sharlot's summer in northern Arizona is referred particularly to the Northland Press edition.

A shorter version of Sharlot's summer's travels appeared in the *Arizona Gazette,* shortly before Arizona became a state, on 29 January 1912, but possibly more interesting was a reminiscent article, written at the time of the comple-tion of the great Marble Canyon Bridge across the Colorado below Lees Ferry, more than two decades after her daring journey of 1911. It was entitled "Tells of Early Mormon Trails," *Prescott Courier,* 10 October 1935, p. 8.

31. "The Arizona Strip Coveted by Utah," *Arizona Republican,* 21 De-cember 1905, p. 8.

32. C. G. Crampton, ed., *Sharlot Hall on the Arizona Strip* (Flagstaff, Ariz.: Northland Press, 1975), p. 14.

33. Sharlot Hall, "Tells of Early Mormon Trails," *Prescott Courier,* 10 Oc-tober 1935, p. 8.

34. A. M. McOmie, C. C. Jacobs, and O. C. Bartlett, *The Arizona Strip: Report of a Reconnaissance of the Country North of the Grand Canyon* (Phoenix: Arizona State Board of Control, 1915), p. 21.

35. Contract dated 28 July 1911 and addressed to SH in Phoenix; SHM.

36. Quoted in John S. Goff, *George W. P. Hunt and His Arizona* (Pasadena, Calif.: Socio Technical Publications, 1973), p. 47.

37. *Arizona,* 2 (January 1912): 1.

38. Senate Bill 1, passed by the Senate, 8 June 1912, indefinitely postponed by the House, 13 June 1912. *Journals of the First Legislative Assembly of the State of Arizona, Extra Session,* pp. 239, 315.

39. "Winsor Holds Public Teat Record," 20 May 1912, clipping in Hunt scrapbook, University of Arizona, Special Collections.

40. "Some Facts by Miss Hall; Letter to Members of the Legislature Conveying Information Regarding the Proposed Office of State Historian," *Arizona Republican,* 31 May 1912.

41. Hunt to SH, 3 June 1912, SHM.

NOTES TO CHAPTER 11

1. Copy of contract, dated 8 May 1912, entered as part of evidence in *S. J. Clarke Pub. Co.* v. *Sharlot M. Hall*, filed 2 March 1914 in United States District Court; records in Los Angeles Federal Archives.

2. Information from U.S. District Court records, 2 March 1914, *S. J. Clarke Pub. Co.* v. *Sharlot M. Hall*, "Answer," p. 5.

3. J. A. Munk, *Southwest Sketches* (New York: Putnam's Sons, 1920), pp. 41–42. Sharlot's own notes of the journey corroborate Munk's account, although Munk says nothing of having a female traveling companion.

4. Munk, *Southwest Sketches*, p. 42.

5. Ibid., p. 45.

6. Alice Hewins, "Memories of Sharlot Hall," unpublished typescript, 1945, Arizona State Library.

7. SH to AH, 8 September 1912, Arizona State Library. Excerpts from Sharlot's letters to Alice Hewins have been reprinted by permission of the Arizona Department of Library, Archives and Public Records.

8. SH to AH, 8 August 1925, Arizona State Library.

9. Fragment in Sharlot Hall's handwriting, SHM.

10. DeLong to SH, 17 December 1912, SHM.

11. Contract as quoted in lawsuit, p. 3.

12. SH to AH, 20 February 1913, Arizona State Library.

13. *Arizona Gazette*, 5 March 1913, p. 4.

14. SH to AH, 27 October 1913, Arizona State Library.

15. SH to AH, January 1914, Arizona State Library.

16. Ibid.

17. SH to AH, 13 February 1914, Arizona State Library.

18. SH to AH, 13 March 1914, Arizona State Library.

19. Court records, Docket, U.S. District Court.

20. SH to AH, 3 August 1914, Arizona State Library.

21. Clerk of Court to Sloan and Westervelt, 14 September 1914, U.S. District Court records.

NOTES TO CHAPTER 12

1. SH to AH, January 1915, Arizona State Library.

2. Ibid.

3. SH to AH, 27 February 1915, Arizona State Library.

4. SH to AH, 23 September 1915, Arizona State Library.

5. SH to AH, 2 January 1916, Arizona State Library.

6. SH to CFL, 26 January 1916, SWM.

7. SH to CFL, 22 July 1916, SWM.

8. Henry James, quoted in *The Diary of Alice James*, edited by Leon Edel (New York: Dodd, Mead, 1964), p. 8.

9. Barbara Ehrenreich and Deirdre English, *For Her Own Good: 150 Years of the Experts' Advice to Women* (New York: Doubleday, 1978), p. 97.

10. SH to CFL, 18 February 1920, Colorado State University Library.

11. Mary Edenia Richardson Wingerter to Margaret F. Maxwell, Fall 1976.

12. CFL to Mrs. Edward E. Ayer, 1 March 1917, SWM.

13. Arizona Legislature, Acts, Resolutions and Memorials of the Regular Session, 3rd Legislature (Phoenix, 1917), p. 41.

14. Mortgage paper, dated 5 March 1918, SHM.

15. SH to AH, 16 December 1918, Arizona State Library.

16. SH to AH, 5 February 1919, Arizona State Library.

17. *Atlantic Classics,* 2d ser. (Boston: Atlantic Monthly Press, 1918), pp. 227–34.

18. SH to CFL, 18 February 1920, SWM.

19. SH to AH, 14 February 1920, Arizona State Library.

NOTES TO CHAPTER 13

1. Samuel P. Putnam, *Four Hundred Years of Freethought* (New York: Truth Seeker Co., 1894), p. 13.

2. SH to AH, 9 February 1921, Arizona State Library.

3. SH to AH, "Easter Sunday Afternoon, 1921," Arizona State Library.

4. Ibid.

5. SH to CFL, 11 July 1921, Colorado State University Library.

6. SH to AH, 29 August 1921, Arizona State Library.

7. SH to AH, Good Friday [April 14] 1922, Arizona State Library.

8. Ibid.

9. SH to AH, May 1922, Arizona State Library.

10. Ibid.

11. Copyright date 9 June 1922; correspondence Mrs. A. McKenzie to Library of Congress, Copyright Office, 15 September 1949.

12. SH to AH, 16 April 1923, Arizona State Library.

13. SH to AH, end of April 1923, Arizona State Library.

14. Margaret Wheeler Ross, *History of the Arizona Federation of Women's Clubs and Its Forerunners* (Arizona? 1944?), p. 113.

15. CFL, Journal, 4 June 1924, SWM.

16. CFL, Journal, 11 June 1924, SWM.

17. SH to AH, July 1924, Arizona State Library.

18. Sharlot Hall, *Poems of a Ranch Woman* (Prescott: Sharlot Hall Historical Society, 1953), pp. 71–72. Reprinted by permission of the Sharlot Hall Historical Society.

19. "Miss Sharlot M. Hall Will Deliver Electoral Vote of State to National Capitol," *Arizona Republican,* 13 January 1925, p. 1.

20. "The President Kind, Not Cold...Sharlot Hall Finds," *Tucson Citizen,* 6 February 1925.

21. Ibid.

22. Her research resulted in *The Arizona Rough Rider Monument and Captain W. O. O'Neill* (Prescott: Prescott Evening Courier, 1929).

23. "Washington Observations," *Arizona Republican,* 28 February 1925, Hewins Papers, Arizona State Library.

24. SH to AH, 25 February 1925, Arizona State Library.

25. SH, typed paper, undated, to be read to the Monday Club, Prescott, March 1925, SHM.

26. SH to AH, from Schenectady, 31 March 1925, Arizona State Library.

27. N. Hartzell to AH, 8 April 1925, SHM.

28. SH to AH, 15 April 1925, Arizona State Library.

NOTES TO CHAPTER 14

1. SH to AH, 15 April 1925, Arizona State Library.

2. SH to AH, 8 August 1925, Arizona State Library.

3. SH to AH, 8 September 1925, Arizona State Library.

4. SH to AH, 17 October 1925, Arizona State Library.

5. Richard E. Sloan, *History of Arizona, Biographical,* v.4 (Phoenix: Record Pub. Co., 1930), p. 423.

6. Interview with Evelyn Carnapas, 15 June 1977.

7. *Out West,* 25 (November 1906), pp. 385–412.

8. SH to AH, 18 May 1926, Arizona State Library.

9. SH to AH, 11 June 1926, Arizona State Library.

10. CFL, Diary, Saturday, 12 June and 13 June 1926, SWM.

11. Sales contract for the Star automobile is in SHM; total cost was $737.00.

12. License, SHM.

13. "Sharlot Hall and the BPW," *The Paper,* Thursday, 18 December 1975, p. 21.

14. SH to L. E. Hewins, 6 September 1926, Arizona State Library.

15. SH to AH, 9 October 1926, Arizona State Library.

16. SH to AH, 27 February 1927; *Prescott Courier,* 15 May 1964, states that Yavapai County received a record-breaking 33.97 inches of rain during the year 1927.

17. "Miss Sharlot Hall Writes Interestingly of Her Plans to Rescue Old Capitol Home," *Arizona Gazette,* 2 July 1927, p. 5. According to R. T. Mikulewicz, the Governor's Mansion was acquired by Henry Fleury "by patent," 2 May 1876, with a mortgage being held by Chief Justice C. G. W. French. Justice French willed the property to the Congregational Church of Prescott; after his death it was sold to Joseph Dougherty, 9 February 1899 (Mikulewicz, "Sharlot Hall Played Large Part in Preserving History of Arizona," *Arizona Republic,* 27 October 1960).

18. SH to Walter Douglas, 10 July 1926, SHM.

19. SH to Joseph Andrew West, Prescott City Attorney, 28 May 1927, SHM.

20. "Agreement Between City of Prescott and Sharlot M. Hall," 20 June 1927, SHM.

NOTES TO CHAPTER 15

1. SH to AH, 20 July 1927, Arizona State Library.

2. SH to AH, 1 October 1927, Arizona State Library.

3. Typed manuscript, about January 1928, SHM.

4. Sharlot M. Hall, "Big Visitor List at Old Mansion," *Prescott Courier,* 30 October 1936.

5. Sharlot M. Hall, untitled typed manuscript, about January 1928, SHM.

6. SH to L. E. Hewins, 2 April 1928, Arizona State Library.

7. Sharlot M. Hall, "Gets Souvenir of Battleship," *Prescott Courier,* 7 August 1930, pp. 1, 7. Unfortunately, as of 1981 early guest registers for the Governor's Mansion had not been located at SHM.

8. SH to T. A. Riordan, Flagstaff Lumber Co., 3 September 1928, NAU, Riordan Collection.

9. SH to T. A. Riordan, 3 September 1928, NAU, Riordan Collection.

10. Mortuary receipt for Edward Hall's funeral expenses in SHM; also see SH to T. A. Riordan, 4 October 1928, NAU, Riordan Collection.

11. Arizona, Legislature, *House Journal,* 9th Legislature, Jan. 14–March 14, 1929, Phoenix, 1929, p. 589.

12. SH to AH, 30 March 1929, Arizona State Library (this is the first mention of the society, later called the Sharlot Hall Historical Society); Arizona, Legislature, Acts, Resolutions, and Memorials of the Regular Session, 9th Legislature, Jan. 14–March 14, 1929. Phoenix, 1929, p. 389; also Arizona, Legislature, *House and Senate Journals,* Phoenix, 1929, pp. 503, 576.

13. SH to AH, 26 February 1929, Arizona State Library.

14. SH to L. E. Hewins, 15 March 1929, Arizona State Library.

15. New York: F. Hitchcock, 1927.

16. Arizona, Legislature, *Senate Journal,* 9th Legislature, Jan. 14–March 14, 1929; SB 65 signed March 12, 1929, approved by governor March 15; Index, p. 563.

17. Sharlot Hall, "Tells of Trip to New Bridge," *Prescott Courier,* 28 May 1929, pp. 1, 5.

18. Sharlot Hall, "From the Old Governor's Site," *Prescott Courier,* 15 December 1929, p. 3.

19. Yavapai (Arizona) County, Index to Deeds (indexed under Hall, Sharlot M.), Yavapai County Courthouse, Prescott, Arizona.

NOTES TO CHAPTER 16

1. "Kiwanis Ladies to See Museum," *Prescott Courier,* 10 October 1930, pp. 1, 6.

2. Judith Carlock Wilder to Margaret F. Maxwell, 8 May 1977.

3. Sharlot Hall, *Poems of a Ranch Woman* (Prescott: Sharlot Hall Historical Society, 1953), pp. 87–88. Reprinted by permission of the Sharlot Hall Historical Society.

4. SH to Mrs. Gibbs, 14 August 1931, AHS, Sparkes Collection.

5. "Gives Resume of RFC Work," *Prescott Courier,* 29 April 1933, p. 7.

6. Sharlot Hall, "Call Miss Hall to GOP Mat," *Prescott Courier,* 24 October 1932, pp. 1, 7.

7. Sharlot Hall, "Lauds Teddy Roosevelt as a Hard Scrapper," *Prescott Courier,* 27 October 1932, pp. 1, 7.

8. Ibid.

9. SH to AH, 9 April 1933, SHM.

10. Information on the CWA is to be found in Arizona Appraisal Committee, Report (Phoenix, 1938), pp. 5–6, and in Grace Adams, *Workers on Relief* (New Haven: Yale University Press, 1939), pp. 9–12.

11. "635 in Yavapai are given jobs," *Prescott Courier,* 23 November 1933, p. 1. Under the original terms of the CWA contracts, workers were to be paid a maximum of $65.00 per month at a rate of 50¢ per hour for common labor and up to $1.00 per hour for skilled carpenters. Projects were funded for a maximum of ninety days; large construction projects which could not be completed in this period were not to be undertaken. Presumably Sparkes thought that the museum annex to the Governor's Mansion could be completed in the time allotted; as it worked out, however, this and many other construction projects were continued under succeeding programs after the demise of CWA.

12. "New Museum 70 Percent Done," *Prescott Courier,* 16 January 1934, pp. 1, 2.

13. Sharlot Hall, "The House of a Thousand Hands," *Prescott Courier,* 23 May 1935, p. 10.

14. "List Prescott Work to Start," *Prescott Courier,* 31 October 1935, pp. 1, 8.

15. *Works Progress in Arizona: Official Bulletin* (Phoenix, v.1, no.1, January 1936, p. 4). The resulting newspaper index on cards is in the SHM.

16. Sharlot Hall, "Big Visitor List at Old Mansion," *Prescott Courier,* 30 October 1936, p. 15.

17. Works Progress Administration, *Monthly Narrative Report of the WPA for Arizona,* February 20, 1937 (Phoenix, 1937), p. 12.

NOTES TO CHAPTER 17

1. SH to AH, 22 April 1938, Arizona State Library.

2. Frank C. Lockwood, "Sharlot M. Hall—Arizona Poet," unpublished typescript manuscript, 36 pp.; first state, Grace Sparkes Collection, AHS; revised, Lockwood Collection, AHS; published in condensed form under title, "She Writes of the Old West," *Desert Magazine,* December 1939, pp. 3–5, 36.

3. SH to AH, 14 September 1938, Arizona State Library.

4. Lockwood, unpublished biography of Sharlot Hall, p. 12; Sparkes Collection, AHS.

5. The house was torn down in about 1966. Interview with Sue Fain, daughter of Norman Fain, owner of Orchard Ranch site, 4 July 1977.

6. Sharlot Hall, "General List of Work Done in 1937 and 1938 at the Old Governor's Mansion in Prescott, Arizona," typescript, SHM.

7. A. Hewins, unpublished biography of Sharlot Hall, Arizona State Library.

8. Erna Fergusson, *Our Southwest* (New York: Knopf, 1940).

9. Fergusson, *Our Southwest,* pp. 181–83.

10. Considering that Sharlot's own salary was $181.93 per month, one can understand her feeling. Voucher for December 1939, SHM.

11. Fergusson, *Our Southwest,* pp. 184–88.

12. Charles Franklin Parker, "Out of the West of Long Ago," *Arizona Highways* (January 1943), pp. 6–11, 35.

13. Admission papers for Sharlot M. Hall, Arizona Pioneers' Home, Prescott.

14. Grace Sparkes and Grace Chapman, administratrices of Sharlot Hall's estate, discovered among Sharlot's possessions a total of $1,883.50 in uncashed state warrants, chiefly payments of Sharlot's monthly salary of $166.66. This sum together with other personal property was appraised at $27,458.97, all of which by terms of Sharlot's will was bequeathed to the Historical Society of Prescott for the Sharlot Hall Museum. Probate file, Superior Court, Yavapai County, Inventory and Appraisal, 26 July 1943; final account dated 29 February 1944; order approving final account, 14 March 1944 (copies of documents, SHM).

15. "Friend's certificate," for Sharlot M. Hall, dated 2 April 1943, in Arizona Pioneers' Home, Prescott.

16. Admission papers for Sharlot M. Hall, 6 April 1943, Arizona Pioneers' Home.

17. Sidney P. Osborn to SH, 8 April 1943, SHM.

18. Sharlot Hall, "The End of the Trail," quoted in "Death Claims Sharlot Hall," *Prescott Courier,* 9 April 1943, pp. 1, 3.

19. SH to Lester Ruffner, 21 October and 15 November 1933, SHM.

20. Sharlot Hall, "Sharlot Hall Leases Capitol," *Prescott Courier,* 28 June 1927, p. 6.

Bibliography

UNPUBLISHED MATERIAL

Los Angeles. Southwest Museum Library. Papers of Charles Fletcher Lummis.

Phoenix. Arizona State Library. Alice B. Hewins Collection.

Phoenix. Phoenix Public Library. James H. McClintock Papers.

Prescott, Arizona. Sharlot Hall Historical Society. Papers of Sharlot Mabridth Hall.

Tucson, Arizona Historical Society. Ida Williams Davisson Papers; Grace M. Sparkes Papers.

Tucson, University of Arizona, Special Collections. G. W. P. Hunt Clipping File, 1910–1912.

NEWSPAPERS AND PERIODICALS

Arizona Gazette (Phoenix), 1904–1924

Arizona Magazine (Phoenix), 1910–1925

Arizona Republican (Phoenix), 1905–1930, and later name, *Arizona Republic*, 1930–1943

Delineator (New York), 1898

Farm and Ranch (Dallas), 1894–1929

Journal-Miner (Prescott), 1882–1932

Land of Sunshine (Los Angeles), 1896–1901, and later name, *Out West*, 1902–1909

Los Angeles Times, 1923–1926

Prescott Courier, 1928–1943

Truth Seeker (New York), 1895

Tucson Citizen, 1912–1924

Yavapai Magazine (Prescott), 1914–1932

INTERVIEWS

Andres, Emma. Interview August 18, 1977.

Baguley, Billy Jane (Mrs. Peter). Interview May 6, 1977.

Baumert, Mrs. Fred. Interview August 25, 1977.

Biles, Mrs. David H. Interview October 4, 1977.

Boblett, Fay. Interview April 8, 1977.

Bracamonte, Adeline Hall. Interview April 11, 1977.

Carnapas, Evelyn. Interview June 15, 1977.

Davis, Eleanor Winsor. Interview June 24, 1977.

Duke, Maymie. Interview August 22, 1977.

Fain, Sue. Interview July 4, 1977.

Favour, Al. Interview August 31, 1977.

Genung, Millicent. Interview September 22, 1977.

Gillmor, Frances. Interview June 12, 1977.

Hamlin, Edith. Interview November 2, 1977.

Hardesty, Elinor Pauline. Interview July 5, 1977.

Hazeltine, Mary Favour. Interview June 15, 1977.

Heap, Dora. Interview August 18, 1977.

Hicks, Taylor. Interview August 17, 1977.

Johnson, Bessie (Mrs. Bert). Interview September 1, 1977.

Ladd, Ione. Interview May 12, 1977.

Merritt, Evelyn. Interview August 25, 1977.

Miller, Clara Ritter. Interview August 29, 1977.

Miller, Joseph. Interview August 24, 1977.

Morgan, Edith. Interview August 26, 1977.

Payne, Morris. Interview July 4, 1977.

Prince, Nellie Marshall. Interview September 1, 1977.

Quinn, Charles. Interview August 17, 1977.

Reeves, Genevieve Hunt. Interview September 8, 1977.

Rider, Jane. Interview June 15, 1977.

Rigden, Margaret Hays. Interview September 1, 1977.

Sloan, Eleanor B. Interview June 15, 1977.

Webb, Harriet. Interview October 12, 1977.

Wilder, Judith C. Interview May 12, 1977.

Williams, Sally Munds. Interview August 29, 1977.

THE WORKS OF SHARLOT M. HALL

Sharlot Hall's published works include articles, short stories, and poems. Many of these, hastily written, appeared in Phoenix and Prescott newspapers as well as in most of the principal periodicals of her day. Few are indexed in such a way that they are easily retrievable. This author has located more than 500 articles, short stories, and poems, many of these reprinted more than once, appearing between 1891 and 1940 (a complete bibliography is on file at the Sharlot Hall Museum in Prescott). In addition, ten books bear Sharlot Hall's name as author. She is chiefly remembered, however, for two collections of poetry: *Cactus and Pine: Songs of the Southwest* (Boston: Sherman, French, 1910), [Second edition (Phoenix: Arizona Republican Print Shop, 1924)]; and *Poems of a Ranch Woman*, posthumously compiled by Josephine Mackenzie, with a biography by Charles Franklin Parker (Prescott: Sharlot Hall Historical Society, 1953). The diary of her 1910 journey to the Arizona Strip has been published as *Sharlot Hall on the Arizona Strip*, edited by C. Gregory Crampton (Flagstaff: Northland Press, 1975).

BIOGRAPHICAL MATERIAL ABOUT SHARLOT M. HALL

Boyer, Mary G. *Arizona in Literature*. Glendale, Calif.: A. H. Clark Co., 1935, p. 282.

Buchanan, S. E. "Poet Laureate of the Household." *Farm and Ranch*, June 13, 1914, p. 2.

Butcher, Harold. "Sharlot Hall Lives in Her Poems." *Arizona Days and Ways*, Apr. 6, 1958, pp. 26–27.

"Hall, Sharlot M." *American Women*. Los Angeles: American Publications, 1937–38.

"Hall, Sharlot M." *Who's Who in America*. Chicago: Marquis Who's Who, 1912–41.

"Hall, Sharlot Mabridth." *Who's Who in Arizona*. Phoenix: Survey Pub. Co., 1940.

"Hall, Sharlot Mabridth." *Yavapai Magazine*, 19 (April 1922), p. 21.

Lockwood, Frank C. "She Writes of the Old West." *Desert Magzine*, 3 (Dec. 1939), pp. 3–5.

Lockwood, Frank C. "Arizonans to Pay Tribute to Sharlot Hall on Official Opening of State Poetry Week." Undated clipping, probably April 1944, SHM.

Loraine, M. W. "Arizona's Best Loved Woman." *The West Coast Magazine,* Jan. 1911, pp. 293–97.

Lummis, Charles F. "In Western Letters." *Land of Sunshine,* 14 (Apr. 1901), pp. 302–5.

"Of the Desert Does She Sing." *Los Angeles Times,* June 18, 1905.

Oliver, Etta J. "A Child Visits Arizona's Garden of Memories." *Arizona Highways,* March 1952, pp. 30–37.

Parker, Charles Franklin. "Arizona's Sharlot Hall." *Arizona Days and Ways,* Apr. 11, 1954, p. 6.

Parker, Charles Franklin. "Out of the West of Long Ago." *Arizona Highways,* 19 (January 1943), pp. 6–11, 35
Reprinted in *Poems of a Ranch Woman* (Prescott: Sharlot Hall Historical Society of Arizona, 1953).

Peplow, Edward A. *History of Arizona.* New York: Lewis Hist. Pub. Co., 1958, v. 2, pp. 475–76.

Peplow, Edward A. "Women of the Old West." *Outdoor Arizona,* 45 (July 1973), pp. 23–26, 43–46.

Ranney, Diane. "Prescott's Sharlot Hall." *The Paper,* July 1, 1976.

Robinson, Edna L. "A Western Poet." *New Orleans Daily Picayune,* Feb. 9, 1902.

"Second Edition of Sharlot M. Hall's Cactus and Pine Comes From the Press." *Arizona Republican,* December 7, 1924.

"Sharlot M. Hall Dies in Prescott." *Arizona Republic,* April 10, 1943, p. 1.

Upson, Arthur. "Sharlot Hall: A Note on the Life and Work of the Arizona Author." *The Bellman,* Apr. 27, 1907, pp. 508–9.

Weston, James J. "Sharlot Hall: Arizona's Pioneer Lady of Literature." *Journal of the West,* 4 (Oct. 1965), pp. 539–52.

Willson, Roscoe G. "Arizona Will Remember a Fighting Poet." *Arizona Days and Ways,* Feb. 11, 1962, pp. 104–7.

"Writers of the Day: Sharlot M. Hall." *The Writer,* 14 (July 1901), p. 16.

Hodge, Hiram C. *Arizona As It Is: Or, The Coming Country.* Boston, 1877. (Reprinted in 1962 under title: *Arizona As It Was, 1877.*)

Howe, Henry. *The Great West* . . . Enlarged ed. New York: G. F. Tuttle, 1859.
"Exactly like the places where we lived from my babyhood on," Sharlot wrote.

Hubbard, Howard A. "Arizona's Struggle Against Joint Statehood, 1904–1906." *Pacific Historical Review,* 11 (Dec. 1942), pp. 415–24.

Ise, John. *Sod and Stubble: The Story of a Kansas Homestead.* Lincoln: University of Nebraska Press, 1936.

Kansas. State Board of Agriculture. *Fifth Annual Report.* Topeka, 1876.

Kelly, George H. *Legislative History of Arizona, 1864–1912.* Phoenix, 1926.

McGinnis, Tru Anthony. "The Influence of Organized Labor on the Making of the Arizona Constitution." Master's thesis, University of Arizona, 1930.

Miller, Myle H. *Kansas: A Pictorial History.* Topeka: Kansas Centennial Commission and the State Historical Society, 1961.

Excellent illustrations and historical maps.

Nye, Russel B. *Midwestern Progressive Politics: A Historical Study of Its Origin and Development, 1870–1950.* Lansing: Michigan State College Press, 1951.

Good background for Kansas period.

Perceval, Don. *Maynard Dixon Sketch Book.* Flagstaff: Northland Press, 1967.

Potter, Alvina N. *The Many Lives of the Lynx.* Flagstaff: Northland Press, 1964.

History of the Lynx Creek mining area.

"Prescott, Arizona." *Arizona Graphic,* 1 (Nov. 25, 1899), pp. 1–3.

Panoramic photographs of nineteenth-century Prescott before the fire of 1900.

Rusho, W. L. *Desert River Crossing: Historic Lee's Ferry on the Colorado River.* Salt Lake City: Peregrine Smith, 1975.

Quotes Sharlot Hall's impression of Lees Ferry crossing from her diary of 1911.

Sloan, Richard E. *Memories of an Arizona Judge.* Stanford: Stanford University Press, 1932.

Snodgrass, Richard. *Prescott, Arizona: A Pictorial History.* Phoenix: Toney Pub., 1964.

Entirely photographs; many good nineteenth-century pictures.

Spaulding, R. "The Scenery of Arizona." *Science,* 6 (July 17, 1885), p. 44.

A trip from Flagstaff through Oak Creek Canyon, Beaver Creek Valley, and Fort Verde.

Those Early Days: Old Timers' Memories: Oak Creek, Sedona, and the Verde Valley. Sedona: Sedona Westerners, 1968.

Verde Valley Pioneers' Association. *Pioneer Stories of Arizona's Verde Valley.* Verde Valley, 1954.

Wagoner, Jay J. *Arizona Territory, 1863–1912, a Political History.* Tucson: University of Arizona Press, 1970.

Wagoner, Jay J. *Early Arizona: Prehistory to Civil War.* Tucson: University of Arizona Press, 1975.

Walker, Dale L. *Death Was the Black Horse: The Story of Rough Rider Bucky O'Neill.* Austin: Madrona Press, 1975.

Includes a good description of Prescott in the 1880s.

Wilder, Daniel W. *Annals of Kansas.* Topeka: Kansas Publishing House, 1975.

Wyllys, Rufus Kay. *Arizona: The History of a Frontier State.* Phoenix: Hobson & Herr, 1950.

Probably the best general history of Arizona.

Yavapai Cow Belles. *Echoes of the Past: Tales of Old Yavapai.* Prescott, 1955. 2 vols.

Yost, Nellie Snyder. *Medicine Lodge: The Story of a Kansas Frontier Town.* Chicago: Swallow Press, 1970.

Good background for Sharlot Hall's childhood in Barbour County, Kansas.

HISTORY AND GENERAL INFORMATION

Allen, J. S. "Yavapai Inferno." *Arizona Highways,* May 1941, pp. 30–31, 40.

Describes the Prescott fire of July 14, 1900.

Arizona (Terr.). Governor. *Annual Report to the Secretary of the Interior.* Prescott, Tucson, Phoenix, 1864–1909.

Arizona (Terr.). Territorial Historian. *Annual Report* by Sharlot M. Hall. Phoenix, 1909–1911.

Arizona Highways, 40 (Apr. 1964).

Entire issue is about Prescott.

Barnes, Will C. "The Black Canyon Stage." *Arizona Historical Review,* 6–7 (Apr. 1935), p. 49.

Describes the terrors of a stage trip from Prescott to Phoenix in 1892.

Barnett, Franklin. *Viola Jimula.* Prescott: Prescott Yavapai Indians, 1968.

Mrs. Jimula was Sharlot Hall's housekeeper in the 1930s.

Bingham, Edwin R. *Charles F. Lummis, Editor of the Southwest.* San Marino, Calif.: Huntington Library, 1955.

Burnside, Wesley M. *Maynard Dixon, Artist of the West.* Provo: Brigham Young University Press, 1974.

Dick, Everett. *The Sod-House Frontier, 1854–1890.* New York: Appleton-Century, 1937.

An excellent description of life in Kansas during the years the Hall family homesteaded there. Sharlot Hall annotated her own copy copiously.

Forrest, Earle R. *The Snake Dance of the Hopi Indians.* Los Angeles: Westernlore Press, 1961.

Gifford, Wava. *The Story of the Smoki People.* Prescott, 1974.

History of Arizona Territory Showing Its Resources and Advantages With Illustrations Descriptive of Its Scenery.... San Francisco: W. W. Elliott, 1884.

An interesting contemporary account of Arizona as the Halls found it in 1881.

Acknowledgments

I am grateful, first of all, to Lawrence Clark Powell, who suggested that I undertake this study and who has provided a sympathetic and interested ear for my findings as I have gone along. The University of Arizona granted me a sabbatical leave which allowed me time for necessary research and writing; the University of Arizona Foundation awarded me a travel grant which enabled me to visit the various libraries and archives in the Southwest where letters and documents pertinent to Sharlot Hall's life are to be found. Thanks are due the University of Arizona Press, and in particular my persistent and patient editor Kim Vivier, for sharpening the manuscript and for bringing about publication.

The biography could not have been written without the help of a number of knowledgeable and enthusiastic archivists and librarians. I spent several months of the fall of 1977 working with Sue Abbey and Carol Patrick at the Sharlot Hall Museum, Prescott. They made me welcome, providing not only access to Sharlot Hall's personal papers, but also a desk and space for my material. Glenna R. Schroeder, former archivist at the Southwest Museum, Los Angeles, kept in touch with me following my first brief visit to the Southwest Museum; she continued to search for material in the Museum's collection which might be germane to my study. As a result, I received much valuable information that I would not have found otherwise. Phyllis Ball, manuscripts librarian at the University of Arizona

Library, alerted me to uncatalogued resources in the Special Collections of the library. Without Margaret Bret-Harte's kindness in allowing me access to some of the special resources of the Arizona Historical Society, documentation of the last period of Sharlot Hall's life would have been seriously hampered. To each of these fine professionals I am particularly grateful.

I am also indebted to Jo Ann Troutman, University of Arizona Graduate Library School student assistant, and Patty Patrick, Graduate Library School secretary, who typed and proofread the manuscript; former Graduate Library School student assistant Carole Townsley-Johnson typed the footnotes.

In addition, the following individuals have provided much appreciated information and assistance: Blaise M. Gagliano, Archivist, Arizona State Library; Howard Levitt and Ralph Hinsberger, Alameda (California) Free Library; Mary Badgley, Librarian, *Albuquerque Journal;* Marcie Bagley, Librarian, *Phoenix Gazette;* Robert H. Becker, Bancroft Library, University of California, Berkeley; Katharine Bartlett, Librarian, Museum of Northern Arizona (Flagstaff); William H. Loos, Curator, Rare Book Room, Buffalo and Erie County (N.Y.) Public Library; Anne Caiger, Historical Manuscripts Librarian, University of California at Los Angeles Library; M. K. Swingle, Reference Librarian, California Historical Society; Lee Z. Johnson, Archivist, First Church of Christ, Scientist, Boston; Frank G. Dugan, Jr., Reference Librarian, Colgate University Library; Charles C. Colley, former Archivist and Field Collector, Arizona State University Library; Walter W. Wright, Dartmouth College Library; Pat Dawson, Reference, Cowles Library, Drake University; P. J. Santoro, General Electric Company Library, Schenectady, N. Y.; Valerie Franco, Huntington Library; Harold R. Jenkins, Director, Kansas City Public Library; Joseph Richardson, Reference Librarian, University of Kansas Libraries; Portia A. Allbert and Patricia A. Michaelis, Kansas State Historical Society Library; Mary S. Pratt, Principal Librarian, History Department, Los Angeles Public Library; Clodaugh M. Neiderheiser, University Archives, University of Minnesota Libraries; Alice E. Seeds, University of New Mexico Library; Joseph Stasko, New York Public Library; Margery D. Beeler, Reference Department, Schenectady County (N.Y.) Public Library; Lee Harris, Historical Librarian,

Ventura County (Calif.) Historical Society; Catherine S. Chadwick, Director, Ventura County Library Services Agency; Karel Yasko, Counselor for Fine Arts and Historic Preservation, General Services Administration, Washington, D.C.; John A. Peters and Josephine L. Harper, State Historical Society of Wisconsin; Leone Neegan, Reference Librarian, Yuma (Ariz.) City-County Library; Marian B. Stormont, Monday Club, Prescott; Mrs. Harry W. Nason, Historian, Arizona Federation of Women's Clubs; Mrs. A. J. Ochsner, Yuma Woman's Club; Claudette Simpson, *Prescott Courier;* James M. Deay, Colorado State University Library; John Irwin, Special Collections Librarian, Northern Arizona University Library; Ruth M. Christensen, Librarian, Southwest Museum, Los Angeles; Donald M. Powell, former head, Special Collections, University of Arizona Library; Fay Boblett; Wesley H. Burnside, University of Utah; Evelyn Carnapas; Platt Cline; C. Gregory Crampton, University of Utah; Carol Cunningham; H. L. Davisson; Richard H. Dillon; Constance Dixon; Maymie Duke; Sue Fain; Gail Gardner; Lorene (Mrs. Norman) Garrett; Frances Gillmor; Mrs. Russell J. Glass; John S. Goff; Dudley Gordon; Edith Hamblin; Hazel Hammonds; Viola (Mrs. Melvin) Hardy; Michael Harrison; Mary (Mrs. Sherman) Hazeltine; Dora Heap; Martha Hickey; Taylor T. Hicks, Sr.; Marian E. Jones; Ionne Ladd; Helen Lawler; Keith Lummis; Fred Metz; Eula (Mrs. Frank G.) Murphy; Morris Wing Payne; Allen Pendergraft; P. T. Reilly; Yale T. Richardson; Margaret Hays Rigden; Michael Roughton; Betty Ruffner; Marc Simmons; Eleanor Sloan; Meredith Snapp; Melvin Solve; Thelma C. Thomas; Betty Thomas Thompson, former Prescott Public Librarian; Mildred Vannorsdall, Chicago Public Library; Lucille (Mrs. Frank B.) Wallace; James J. Weston; Judith Wilder; Sally Munds Williams; Mary E. Wingerter; and Florence Yount.

MARGARET F. MAXWELL

Index